Fundamentals of Structured Program Design

Dan Robinson
Gwinnett Technical Institute

Prentice Hall

Upper Saddle River, New Jersey   Columbus, Ohio

Library of Congress Cataloging-in-Publication Data

Robinson, Dan.
    Fundamentals of structured program design / Dan Robinson.
       p.   cm.
    ISBN 0-13-927930-X
    1. Structured programming.   I. Title.
  QA76.6.R628   2000
  005.1'13—dc21

                                       99-19395
                                        CIP

Cover Photo: FPG International
Publisher: Charles E. Stewart, Jr.
Production Editor: Alexandrina Benedicto Wolf
Production Coordination: Custom Editorial Productions, Inc.
Cover Design Coordinator: Karrie Converse-Jones
Cover Designer: Linda Fares
Production Manager: Deidra M. Schwartz
Marketing Manager: Ben Leonard

This book was set in Times Roman by Custom Editorial Productions, Inc., and was printed and bound by The Banta Company. The cover was printed by The Banta Company.

© 2000 by Prentice-Hall, Inc.
Pearson Education
Upper Saddle River, New Jersey 07458

Notice to the Reader: All product names listed herein are trademarks and/or registered trademarks of their respective manufacturer.

The publisher and the author do not warrrant or guarantee any of the products and/or equipment described herein, nor has the publisher or the author made any independent analysis in connection with any of the products, equipment, or information used herein. The reader is directed to the manufacturer for any warranty or guarantee for any claim, loss, damages, costs, or expense arising out of or incurred by the reader in connection with the use or operation of the products or equipment.

The reader is expressly advised to adopt all safety precautions that might be indicated by the activities and experiments described herein. The reader assumes all risks in connection with such instructions.

Printed in the United States of America

10 9 8 7 6 5 4 3 2

ISBN   0-13-927930-X

Prentice-Hall International (UK) Limited, *London*
Prentice-Hall of Australia Pty. Limited, *Sydney*
Prentice-Hall Canada Inc., *Toronto*
Prentice-Hall Hispanoamericana, S. A., *Mexico*
Prentice-Hall of India Private Limited, *New Delhi*
Prentice-Hall of Japan, Inc., *Tokyo*
Prentice-Hall (Singapore) Pte. Ltd., *Singapore*
Editora Prentice-Hall do Brasil, Ltda., *Rio de Janeiro*

Preface

Fundamentals of Structured Program Design was written with several objectives in mind: to create a book that was easily understood by first-year college students with little or no programming background—a book based on real-life program examples with which students and teachers alike could identify; to keep the concepts of program design simple; and to present a structured approach that, if followed, would improve students' opportunities for success in school and in their new profession.

The textbook is replete with examples of meaningful programs that are reused and enhanced as new topics are introduced. To keep the concepts simple, the book emphasizes a building block approach to program design. These building blocks, which represent key functions that a program may be required to perform, are added to the program at predefined locations. Finally, while there may be several approaches that will produce a program that generates accurate results, experience has shown that techniques that work for one program may cause another program to fail. This text outlines an approach that can be used successfully for nearly all programs.

BOOK ORGANIZATION

This textbook is divided into four parts:

I. **Introduction:** The first two chapters introduce the concepts of information processing.

II. **Design Principles:** Chapters 3 through 7 introduce the primary design tools used throughout this textbook: program documentation, structure charts, flowcharts, and pseudo code.

III. **Basic Program Design Techniques:** Chapters 8 through 13 present the building blocks used in structured program design. Each chapter provides insight into a new topic or building block. These chapters also provide the information necessary to allow you to fully understand when the building block should be used and its logical placement within the program.

IV. **Advanced Program Design:** Chapters 14 through 17 introduce a variety of design considerations required for more complex programs. Some of these programs build upon the concepts learned in Part III, while others may deviate slightly from the standard program structure discussed in earlier chapters. Chapter 18 reviews the transition from the program design to a programming language.

These chapters have been organized and presented in a manner that minimizes transition time from one topic to the next. As you progress through the book, focus on each new topic and see how that building block fits into the existing program structure used in previous programs.

This approach emphasizes the concept that while each program you design may perform different tasks and accomplish different objectives, nearly every program will follow the same basic structure.

One technique used to minimize transition time and maximize your understanding of the topic is the frequent reuse of two sample programs throughout the book. As you work through the text, you will see that these two programs become increasingly complex with each chapter. As these programs become more complex, you will gain greater understanding of the topic by focusing on what has changed and what has remained the same from the previous versions of the same program.

FEATURES

Beginning with Part III, "Basic Program Design Techniques" (Chapter 8), topics are introduced using a program specification. The use of program specifications throughout the book will enhance your comprehension of each chapter by directly applying the topic to an actual program design. Sample programs that will maximize your understanding of the topic have been carefully selected for each chapter. Each chapter walks you through the entire program design process beginning with the assessment of the program specifications, through the development of the structure chart, and completing the design process with both flowcharts and pseudo code.

Each chapter offers multiple projects to test your comprehension of the current chapter, as well as retention of the concepts from previous chapters.

ACKNOWLEDGMENTS

I would like to express my appreciation to those who reviewed the manuscript and offered their thoughts and suggestions. The review team did a thorough job and I found their comments and feedback especially useful. I would like to thank Chia Han, University of Cincinnati; Juris Reinfelds, New Mexico State University; and Sue Conners, Purdue University-Calumet, for their participation in the review process. Many of their comments and suggestions have been incorporated into this book.

I would also like to thank the faculty of Gwinnett Technical Institute for all their help, assistance, and feedback during the period of field assessment. A special thanks to the hundreds of students at Gwinnett Technical Institute who suffered through the evolution of this book from the earliest version and working copies to the final edition.

Finally, I would like to thank my family for their support and patience during the writing of this book.

Dan W. Robinson

Contents

Part I

Introduction

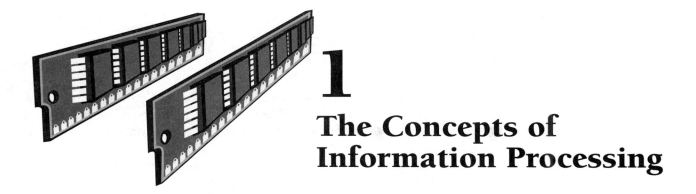

1

The Concepts of Information Processing

OBJECTIVES

- Understanding data and information.
- Understanding information processing.
- Understanding the data hierarchy.
- Understanding the role of computer programs.
- Understanding the three types of data.

INTRODUCTION **Data Versus Information**

Data

Let's start with the basics. What is data? Webster defines data as "facts used in reasoning or calculations." Let's take this definition and expand on it. Data is a collection of facts. In its raw form, data is relatively unusable. Let's consider the data in the following example to be factual. Although factual, we cannot understand it, nor can we use it effectively in its present form.

```
0142JOHN SMITH        4001350
0160PAUL JONES        3501150
0281MELINDA HARRISON  3901200
0339KAREN ROGERS      2801535
0455LLOYD KELLY       4001375
```

Information

We will define information as data that has been presented in a usable form. Webster defines information as "knowledge obtained from investigation, study, or instructions." If we combine these two ideas, we can infer that information has been obtained by applying a set of instructions to raw data. These instructions manipulate the data and present it to us in the form of information (that is, data made usable). For example, if we worked in a payroll department, the following information would be useful.

Empl Nmbr	Name	Hours Worked	Hourly Rate	Gross Pay	Taxes	Net Pay
0142	JOHN SMITH	40	13.50	540.00	81.00	459.00
0160	PAUL JONES	35	11.50	402.50	60.38	342.12

```
0281  MELINDA HARRISON  39     12.00  468.00  70.20  397.80
0339  KAREN ROGERS      28     15.35  429.80  64.47  365.33
0455  LLOYD KELLY       40     13.75  550.00  82.50  467.50
```

As you can see, the payroll information was obtained by putting some order and recognition into the data shown earlier. In this book we define *data* as raw facts. *Information* is data that has been transformed into a usable format.

As you recall, Webster says that information is obtained through investigation, study, or instructions. Likewise, we would need to perform a series of steps (or instructions) to produce the payroll information from the raw data. The process of transforming data into information is called *information processing*.

Information Processing

Information processing consists of step-by-step instructions that we provide to the computer instructing it to transform and manipulate data in order to provide the desired information. For example, now that you know what the data represents, you can look at the raw data and see that John Smith worked 40 hours and that his hourly rate is 13.50 (01350). (We will spend more time on interpreting data later in this chapter.)

While we, and the computer, can make sense of the data (that is, hours worked and rate of pay), we still need to provide the instructions to tell the computer how to compute gross pay (hours worked multiplied by the rate of pay). Furthermore, in this simplified example, we had to tell the computer that tax was computed as 15 percent of gross pay and that net pay was computed as gross pay minus taxes. Without these instructions, neither we nor the computer could produce the payroll information shown from the data presented.

Information processing has three components:

1. Input (data).
2. Processing (the set of instructions required to manipulate the data).
3. Output (information; the results of the processing).

UNDERSTANDING DATA

Since data is the starting point for the information processing cycle, let's develop a solid understanding of what data is and how it can be used.

Hierarchy of Data

Let's begin with the concept of an *entity*. An entity can be defined as a person, place, or thing. In information processing terms, entities are defined by *records*. Each record defines all relevant attributes and characteristics of an entity. For example, consider an employee in a company. Each employee has a record containing the attributes that fully define that employee to the company. What are some of the defining attributes? A short list of attributes might include the following:

- Employee number.
- Name (last and first).

- Gender (male or female).
- Date of birth.
- Date of hire.
- Department.

In information processing, these attributes are call *fields*. Each employee has one record with any number of fields used to define that employee. All records for all employees have the same fields. The data within each field may be different, but all records have the same fields. For example, each employee has a name, but all employees do not have the same name. They all have a date of birth, but they were probably not born on the same day. Exhibit 1–1 illustrates records and fields.

Exhibit 1–1
EXAMPLE OF RECORDS AND FIELD CONTENT

	Empl Nmbr	Name	Gndr	DOB	Hire Date	Dept	Hourly Rate
Record 1	0142	JOHN SMITH	M	081460	011688	013	01350
Record 2	0160	PAUL JONES	M	120150	020588	013	01150
Record 3	0281	MELINDA HARRISON	F	061866	081285	041	01200
Record 4	0339	KAREN ROGERS	F	100459	061590	005	01535

We have shown four records in Exhibit 1–1. In reality, this company has hundreds of employees. Each employee will have a record containing the same data fields and all of the records together make a *file*. Files are a collection of records describing similar entities. These four records, and hundreds like them, would make up the employee file.

Classes of Data

Data fields can be classified as numeric or alphanumeric.

Numeric Data

Numeric data is any field consisting exclusively of numbers. In the previous illustration of data, numeric fields could include employee number, department, hourly rate, and possibly date of birth and date of hire. Mathematical calculations (addition, subtraction, multiplication, and division) can be performed only on numeric data.

Alphanumeric Data

Alphanumeric data can contain numbers (0–9), letters (A–Z), and special characters (such as $, &, or *). In our data illustration, name and gender are alphanumeric fields. Although not shown, the employee's street address would be alphanumeric. Even the zip codes, although containing numeric data, could be classified as alphanumeric.

PROCESSING

We defined processing as the set of instructions required to manipulate the data and produce the required information. Computer programs are written to perform this task. Each program is designed to accept data using an input process to produce the desired information. For example, a payroll program will contain an instruction telling the computer how to compute gross pay. There will be another instruction for computing taxes, and yet another for net pay.

Types of Programs

There are countless types of computer programs that we interact with each day. Computer programs are used in retail transactions for credit card authentication and ATM transactions. Even the electronics of your automobile are controlled by computer programs. However, in an effort to keep this, and future chapters simple, we will focus almost exclusively on the types of programs used in a traditional business setting. Business applications include things such as payroll, accounts receivable, sales management, and inventory control. In this context, there are generally four types of computer programs.

1. *Reporting programs* produce hardcopy output. These reports may be printed on paper and sent to the client or they can be displayed on the workstation.
2. *Inquiry programs* provide the client information on the monitor or display terminal. The results of an inquiry generally relate to information about one entity.
3. *File creation programs* manipulate data and produce a file, normally for use in another program. For example, a payroll system may contain many programs but not all programs produce reports or paychecks. There may be one program that performs all of the calculations. This program may create a file containing all of the payroll data needed to print the paychecks. A second program reads this file and prints the checks.
4. *Update programs* are used to change data in some files. For example, an update program will be required to change an employee's department, hourly rate, or name in the employee file.

Types of Processing

Although there are only four basic types of programs, there are several types of processing that can occur within any of these programs. In fact, programs are typically built using one or more of the following processing strategies.

1. *Record selection:* In many cases, not all records from a file are necessary for processing. For example, if you need to produce a report showing all employees in department 013, you would use this strategy to select only those employees in that department for the report. (This will be covered in depth in Chapter 9.)
2. *Calculations:* The creation of derived data will normally occur within calculations. For example, gross pay is derived by multiplying hours worked by the employee's hourly rate. (Calculations are discussed in Chapter 8.)
3. *Accumulation:* Whenever totals are required for a report, the totals are accumulated. (Chapter 10 covers accumulations.)

4. *Control-break processing:* Control-breaks are the method by which subtotals are added to a report. (Control-breaks are discussed in Chapters 11 and 12.)

5. *Data validation:* Much of the data processed in an application is input from outside the system. For example, when payroll begins to run, someone needs to tell the computer how many hours each employee worked. The validation strategy is used to determine if the number of hours is correct and/or reasonable. This would prevent us from paying an employee for 200 hours of work in a single week. (Chapter 16 covers data validation.)

RELATIONSHIP OF DATA TO PROCESSING

By this time it should be clear that the processing step of the information processing cycle is used to manipulate data. But what is the relationship of data to the process?

Programs will read files for processing. When a program issues an instruction to read a file, the computer will return one record to the program The program will then process this record by dealing not with the record as a whole, but by referencing hourly rate, department number, name, and other fields separately.

Types of Data

Three types of data are used by the program: external, derived, and logical.

External Data

Data obtained from a file is considered *external data.* Refer back to the data discussed at the beginning of this chapter. In this simple payroll example, these records consisted of the following fields: employee number, name, hours worked, and hourly rate. For our simplified payroll example, these fields would be considered external data. This data was stored outside the program on a payroll file and obtained through a *read instruction.*

Derived Data

Data created by the program as a result of a calculation, normally based on external data, is called *derived data.* In our payroll example, we computed gross pay as the hourly rate multiplied by the hours worked. The employee's hourly rate and hours worked are external data fields because they were obtained from the payroll file. However, gross pay, taxes, and net pay were computed fields. Therefore, these fields are derived data because they were computed (derived) from external data.

Logical Data

Logical data will become more apparent as you progress through this book. For now, consider *logical data* as any data created by the program for use by the program. Logical data is typically used to control program logic flow and is normally not part of the output. Again, this will become clear as we go on.

Data Storage within the Program

All data being processed by the computer must be resident in the computer's memory. When the program obtains records for processing by reading a file, the record will be placed in memory. All derived data and logical data will likewise be stored in the computer's memory. Memory for a program is divided into three main sections. (See Exhibit 1–2.) The top portion of the diagram illustrates the *working area* of memory. This is where the program stores derived and logical data fields used by the program. The second section shown is *input area*. When the program reads a record from the file, the computer will put he record into this input area. The last section is the *output area*. When the program builds and writes the output, the output area contains the data.

Exhibit 1–2
MEMORY DIVIDED INTO THREE SECTIONS

Gross Pay	Taxes	Net Pay			
INPUT AREA					
OUTPUT AREA					

How the Computer Manages Data

Let's see how the computer manages memory by examining the processing for the first two records. The first two records look like this:

```
0142JOHN SMITH      4001350
0160PAUL JONES      3501150
```

Initially, the derived data fields (gross pay, taxes, and net pay) will be zero because we have not processed any records. The input area and output area are both empty. (See Exhibit 1–3a.) When the program reads the first record, the data is placed into the input area. (See Exhibit 1–3b.)

Exhibit 1–3a
CONTENT OF MEMORY WHEN PROGRAM BEGINS

Gross Pay	Taxes	Net Pay			
0	0	0			

Exhibit 1–3b
CONTENT OF MEMORY AFTER FIRST RECORD IS READ

Gross Pay	Taxes	Net Pay			
0	0	0			
0142JOHN SMITH 4001350					

Next, the program will calculate gross pay by multiplying hours worked (40) by the hourly rate (13.50). Taxes and net pay are also computed as described earlier. The result is shown in Exhibit 1–3c. At this point, the output can be built. The computer places the data to be printed into the output area and writes the report. (See Exhibit 1–3d.)

Exhibit 1–3c
CONTENT OF MEMORY AFTER CALCULATION OF DERIVED DATA

Gross Pay	Taxes	Net Pay			
540.00	81.00	459.00			
0142JOHN SMITH 4001350					

Exhibit 1–3d
CONTENT OF DATA AFTER OUTPUT AREA IS BUILT, BUT BEFORE OUTPUT IS WRITTEN

Gross Pay	Taxes	Net Pay			
540.00	81.00	459.00			
0142JOHN SMITH 4001350					
0142 JOHN SMITH 40 13.50 540.00 81.00 459.00					

After writing the results of the calculations to the output, the computer reads the next record and places it into the input area. (See Exhibit 1–3e.) At this point, it is important to notice and comprehend three distinct differences between Exhibits 1–3d and Exhibit 1–3e.

First, you will notice that the derived data did not change. Values for derived data, such as gross pay, taxes, and net pay, will not change until the program specifically instructs the computer to change them.

Second, notice that when the computer read the second record, Paul Jones, the first record was eliminated from the input area. After the computer reads a record, the contents of the previous record are no longer available. This is known as a *destructive read*. This destructive read concept plays an important role in program design.

Finally, notice that the data in the output area has also been deleted. Once the computer writes the output, the data is no longer available. This is known as a *destructive write*. Although this is also important, it is a less important factor than the destructive read in program design.

Exhibit 1–3e
CONTENT OF MEMORY AFTER FIRST OUTPUT IS WRITTEN AND SECOND INPUT RECORD READ

Gross Pay	Taxes	Net Pay			
540.00	81.00	459.00			
0160PAUL JONES 3501150					

As with the previous record, the program will compute gross pay, taxes, and net pay from the payroll data for Paul Jones. Exhibit 1–3f illustrates the results in memory.

Exhibit 1–3f
CONTENT OF MEMORY AFTER CALCULATION OF DERIVED DATA

Gross Pay	Taxes	Net Pay			
402.50	60.38	342.12			
0160PAUL JONES 3501150					

The last step of the program builds the output area and writes the output, as shown in Exhibit 1–3g.

Exhibit 1–3g
CONTENT OF MEMORY AFTER DATA IS BUILT, BUT BEFORE OUTPUT IS WRITTEN

Gross Pay	Taxes	Net Pay			
402.50	60.38	342.12			

0160PAUL JONES	3501150

0160 PAUL JONES   35   11.50 402.50 60.38 342.12

SUMMARY

Data is the raw material for the information process. *Information* is the output of the information process after the data has been made usable. *Information processing* is the process of transforming the data (raw material) into information (finished product). Information processing has three components: input, processing, and output.

For purposes of this text, the data hierarchy consists of three levels. One of these levels is the *record*. A record fully describes an *entity* to the computer. An entity can be a person, place, or thing. Records consist of *fields*. Each field represents one attribute or characteristic of the entity. Records defining similar entities are stored in *files*.

There are three basic types of data: *external*, *derived*, and *logical*. External data is stored on files and read into the program. Derived data is normally the result of a calculation. Logical data is created by the program and used within the program to control the program execution.

All data being processed by the computer must reside in memory at the time of execution. Memory is divided into three sections. These areas include the *working area,* where derived and logical data is stored; the *input area,* where data being read from a file is stored; and the *output area,* where data being written is stored.

REVIEW QUESTIONS

1. What is the difference between data and information?
2. What are the three steps of the information processing cycle?
3. Describe the hierarchy of data.
4. How does the program obtain external data for processing?
5. Where does derived data come from?

6. How is the computer's memory partitioned when the program is executing?

7. What is a computer program?

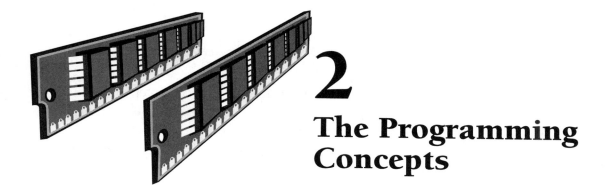

2
The Programming Concepts

OBJECTIVES

- Understanding the limitations of computers.
- Understanding fundamental concepts of programming.
- Understanding the definition of a program.

INTRODUCTION

Before progressing any further, let's take a moment to review some of the concepts you will be dealing with as you advance through this book. In this chapter, we will review some of the basic concepts of programming. You will be presented with the definition of a program, the limitations of computers, and some other basic concepts you will need to go forward.

UNDERSTANDING THE LIMITATIONS OF COMPUTERS

Depending on your experience using computers, you probably believe computers are extremely intelligent or possibly extremely ignorant. The computer has no intelligence of its own. Computers have no inherent intelligence—they are nothing more than plastic, silicone, metal, and glass. A computer "knows" only what we tell it, and can perform only the task(s) we instruct it to perform. Although computers have no real knowledge, they can *rapidly and efficiently* perform the instructions we provide. The typical desktop computers on the market today can process hudreds of millions of instructions per second.

Remember this key concept: While computers can quickly process the instructions we provide, they have no inherent intelligence.

FUNDAMENTALS OF PROGRAMMING

What Is a Program?

Let's take a moment to define a *computer program*. As we just learned, computers have no inherent intelligence. They can perform only the tasks they are instructed to perform. Computers get these instructions through computer programs. The following are some key points to understand about programs:

- Programs are a series of instructions for the computer.
- These instructions are complete, detailing all the steps the computer must perform in order to complete a task.
- These instructions must be written in a manner understood by the computer.

Categories of Programs

There are four major categories of computer programs. Each category requires different types of instructions and different methods of design and development. These four categories are the following:

1. *System software:* This includes software such as UNIX, Windows 95, Windows 98, and Norton Utilities. System software is the underlying software that actually runs the computer. This software allows the programs we write to interface with the computer devices, such as a printer or disk drives, without our knowledge of how the device actually works. The introduction of system software has made computer programming much easier. This textbook will not address system software design techniques.

2. *Office automation:* This includes software packages such as Microsoft Word, Excel, Lotus Notes, and other tools we can purchase to make the work around the office easier and more productive. Because office automation software requires a different process of development, we will not address this category of software.

3. *Games:* The one category with which we are most familiar is games. However, flight simulators and golf games are highly graphical and very reactionary; actions you take cause the computer to react differently. Design and development of games can be extremely complex, and will not be addressed here.

4. *Business applications:* The fourth category of software is business applications. Business applications are used to address specific business needs of a company. These applications include, but are not limited to, payroll, sales management, order processing, and inventory control. Business applications are the most easily understood of the four categories. In addition, most jobs in the market today are related to the development and maintenance of business software. This text will concentrate on the techniques for designing and developing programs for business applications.

Programming Concepts

Consider these two questions:

1. What is 2 + 2?
2. How many different (yet viable) routes could you take to go from your home to the nearest shopping mall?

Which of these questions most represents computer programming? You may answer "the first," because computers are math-related. But actually the second scenario is most like computer programming. Why? Math is an exact science. Two plus two is four. Yesterday, it was four. Today, it is four. And tomorrow it will still be four. Four is the only correct answer to the question. On the other hand, computer programming is not an exact science. The output you create must be correct, but the approach taken to achieve the correct answer can vary. As we progress, you will see that there are no firm rules dictating how everything must be done. You will learn certain structured concepts that work best, but you can deviate from these and still be correct. As long as the final output is correct, your program is correct. Just like the second question above, there are several routes you could take to get from your home to the mall. While some routes may be better than others (perhaps affected by time of day), any route that gets you there is correct.

Assumptions Made by Computers

Consider for a moment that you are a travel agent working in downtown Atlanta. A customer calls and asks you for the airfare to Chicago. Can you open a book (or computer terminal) and quote the rate? It is unlikely that you will find *one* rate. You will probably find several rates. For example, airlines have different rates for midday travel and the red-eye. The day of week can also affect the rate. Is the traveler going to stay over a weekend? These items and many, many others can affect the airfare.

Just as we cannot complete the exercise of pricing the airfare without all of the necessary information, the computer cannot complete its work until you provide all of the necessary data for processing. When designing a program, remember that computers make no assumptions. If you do not provide the necessary steps, the program cannot complete the work.

Self-Correction

Another flaw in the thinking of novice programmers is that a computer is smart enough to know when your program logic is wrong and that it will correct itself. Do not be trapped in this web of deceit. If your program is incorrect, the computer will not catch it. It will only execute the error(s) very quickly. Take the necessary time to review your logic and think about how it works.

SUMMARY

Throughout this textbook, we will deal with the design of computer programs for business applications. *Computer programs* are a set of instructions that tell the computer what to do and how to do it. Computers have no inherent intelligence; thus they must be provided every instruction necessary to perform a task. Computers make no assumptions, and in the design process you must recognize that no assumptions are made. Finally, it is important to remember that any program that performs the desired tasks correctly is a correct program. This textbook will present proven techniques for program design, but you must remember that these are not the only techniques that work.

Part II

Design Principles

3
Program Documentation

OBJECTIVES	<ul><li>Understanding the importance of good documentation.</li><li>Reading and understanding a program specification.</li><li>Understanding file layouts and file descriptions.</li><li>Reading and constructing a printer spacing chart.</li><li>Understanding and using the data dictionary.</li></ul>

INTRODUCTION

Business application systems contain programs designed to support a business function. Payroll, inventory control, general ledger, and billing are examples of business application systems. Each of these systems contain multiple application programs.

A major component contributing to the success or failure of an application is documentation. *Documentation,* in its many forms, fully describes the application to the developers, users, and future programmers who will be assigned to maintain and support the system. Imagine trying to work on your automobile without the appropriate repair manual to give you guidance. Try learning a new software package without the user manual. Would you contract builders if you thought they would construct the house from memory instead of a blueprint? Likewise, building a new program (or system) without the proper documentation is risky. Assuming responsibility for an undocumented application can be extremely frustrating. This chapter will outline the basic forms of documentation created during the design and development process. In future chapters, we will expand upon this topic and see how and where documentation fits into the development process.

PROGRAM SPECIFICATIONS

During the application design process, the analyst builds a model of the entire application. This model demonstrates in graphical form how the raw data is fed into the computer, what processing is required to transform the data into its final form, and what information is presented to the user. This transformation of data to information occurs in multiple programs throughout the application.

During the application design process, the analyst identifies all the programs required and decides what functions each program must perform. The analyst will decide how the report(s) will look, what files are necessary, and what rules must be invoked to build the desired results. The documentation describing each program is known as the *program specification*.

The program spec is not a step-by-step recipe for the programmer; rather it is an outline of the processing requirements. The specification provides the programmer with the business rules that must be followed in order to develop the correct output. The rules might include specific mathematical formulas, the handling of error conditions, or specifics on which records should be processed. Program specifications also include printer spacing charts and record layouts. Exhibit 3–1 is an example of an entire program specification used to develop a sales report.

In this book, file layouts will accompany all program specifications for problem sets and projects. Some of these program specifications will include a printer spacing chart, and others may require you to develop the printer spacing chart.

Exhibit 3–1 PROGRAM SPECIFICATION

Objective

To produce a Sales Report showing profitability by item. File will be sorted by:

Major: Sport code.

Intermediate: Equipment type.

Minor: Item number.

Processing Requirements

1. Read and print all records on the file.
2. Report the format shown on the printer spacing chart.
3. Use the following formulas:
   - Commissions Paid = Sales Amount * Commission Percent.
   - Total Cost = Quantity Sold * Purchase Cost.
   - Profit = Sales Amount – (Commissions Paid + Total Cost).
4. Provide control breaks and subtotals for Product Class and Product Category.
5. Provide report totals.
6. Report will be single-spaced.

SALES RECORD

01-02 SPORT CODE		SPRTCD
03-04 EQUIPMENT TYPE		ETYP
05-09 ITEM NUMBER		ITEM
10-24 ITEM DESCRIPTION		DESC
25-29 QUANTITY SOLD	(5.0)	QTY
30-38 SALES AMOUNT	(9.2)	SLSAMT

39-41 COMMISSION PERCENT (3.3)   CMPCT
42-48 PURCHASE COST   (7.2)   PRCHCST
49-60 Unused

Printer Spacing Chart

```
              111111111122222222223333333333444444444455555555556666666666777777777788888888889999999999 1111111111111111111111111111111
     123456789012345678901234567890123456789012345678901234567890123456789012345678901234567890123456789 0000000000111111111122222222223
                                                                                                          1234567890123456789012345678901234567890

RUN  MM/DD/YY   HH:MM                              ACME DISTRIBUTORS                                                            PAGE ZZZZ9
                                                    SALES REPORT

     SPORT      EQUIP     ITEM                      QUANTITY      SALES         COMMISSIONS      TOTAL
     CODE       TYPE      NMBR    ITEM DESCRIPTION     SOLD       AMOUNT           PAID          COST            PROFIT

      XX         XX      XXXXX    XXXXXXXXXXXXXXX    ZZ,ZZZ-    Z,ZZZ,ZZZ.99-   ZZZ,ZZZ.99-    ZZZ,ZZZ.99-    ZZZ,ZZZ.99-
      XX         XX      XXXXX    XXXXXXXXXXXXXXX    ZZ,ZZZ-    Z,ZZZ,ZZZ.99-   ZZZ,ZZZ.99-    ZZZ,ZZZ.99-    ZZZ,ZZZ.99-
      XX         XX      XXXXX    XXXXXXXXXXXXXXX    ZZ,ZZZ-    Z,ZZZ,ZZZ.99-   ZZZ,ZZZ.99-    ZZZ,ZZZ.99-    ZZZ,ZZZ.99-

                                  EQUIPMENT TYPE TOTAL         ZZ,ZZZ,ZZZ.99-  Z,ZZZ,ZZZ.99-  Z,ZZZ,ZZZ.99-  Z,ZZZ,ZZZ.99-

                                  SPORT CODE TOTAL             ZZ,ZZZ,ZZZ.99-  Z,ZZZ,ZZZ.99-  Z,ZZZ,ZZZ.99-  Z,ZZZ,ZZZ.99-

                                  REPORT TOTAL                 ZZ,ZZZ,ZZZ.99-  Z,ZZZ,ZZZ.99-  Z,ZZZ,ZZZ.99-  Z,ZZZ,ZZZ.99-
```

File Layouts

In Chapter 1, we discussed data hierarchy. Within this hierarchy, a file was defined as a collection of records. File layouts define how each record will be formatted. Each field on the record is shown, given a name, and defined as containing alphanumeric or numeric type data. If the field is numeric, the number of decimal positions will be indicated. Exhibits 3–2 and 3–3 illustrate these two basic formats.

The format illustrated in Exhibit 3–2 provides four basic pieces of information:

1. First, it tells you where in the record (what positions) you will find each field. From this information, you can compute the length of the field. *Field length* can be computed as [(ending position – starting position) + 1]. For example, look in Exhibit 3–2 for ITEM DESCRIPTION. The location of this field is shown as 10-24. This tells you that the field begins in position 10 of the record and ends in position 24. The entire length of the field is 15 bytes (characters). The length is calculated as (24 – 10) + 1.

2. The second piece of useful information is the *field name*. ITEM DESCRIPTION is the name of the field.

3. The third piece of information is the *data type*. This information tells you whether the field is numeric. If there is no indication, you can assume the field is alphanumeric. If the field is numeric, the record layout will also indicate how many positions are reserved for decimal places. For example, the field QUANTITY SOLD shows a data type of 5.0. This means that the field is five (5) positions in length with no decimals. SALES AMOUNT is defined as 9.2. This indicates that the entire field is nine (9) positions in length, with the last two reserved for decimal places (i.e., cents). The highest number that can be stored in this field is 9999999.99 with seven (7) positions to the left of the decimal and two (2) positions to the right. You will notice that the entire length of SALES AMOUNT is nine positions, from 30 through 38. Decimal points are not placed in data stored in files. Decimal places are defined in file descriptions, but the computer does not store the decimal point. Remember, numeric fields must contain numeric values, which are numbers ranging from 0–9. A decimal point is not a numeric value; therefore, it is not stored with the data. Computer programs utilize a concept known as an *assumed decimal*. That is, in the record description, you indicate where the decimal should be placed, and the computer will assume it is there for all records.

4. Finally, the fourth piece of information provided is the *programming name* of the field. This gives us the name of the field we should use within the program. The programming name for the DESCRIPTION field is DESC.

Exhibit 3–3 shows an alternate method of file layout. The field name is specified in the top line of the layout. The starting and ending positions of each field are specified below the name. The format of the field is specified at the bottom. If no field format is given, you can assume the field is alphanumeric.

Most of today's data modeling software will produce a file layout similar to Exhibit 3–2. Since the layout in Exhibit 3–2 is more commonly used, we will use it whenever possible.

Exhibit 3–2
RECORD LAYOUT
VERSION 1
FILE LAYOUT

SALES RECORD

01-02 SPORT CODE		SPRTCD
03-04 EQUIPMENT TYPE		ETYP
05-09 ITEM NUMBER		ITEM
10-24 ITEM DESCRIPTION		DESC
25-29 QUANTITY SOLD	(5.0)	QTY
30-38 SALES AMOUNT	(9.2)	SLSAMT
39-41 COMMISSION PERCENT	(3.3)	CMPCT
42-48 PURCHASE COST	(7.2)	PRCHCST
49-60 Unused		

Exhibit 3–3
RECORD LAYOUT
VERSION 2

Sport Code	Equipment Type	Item Number	Item Descr.	Qty	Sales Amount	Comm. Pct.	Purch. Cost	Unused
1-2	3-4	5-9	10-24	25-29	30-38	39-41	42-48	49-60
				5.0	9.2	3.3	7.2	

Printer Spacing Charts

Reading the Printer Spacing Chart

The printer spacing chart provides the programmer with an example of how the report will look when completed. The printer spacing chart shows the title of the report, fields to be printed, length of each field, how each field will be titled on the report, whether the report is single- or double-spaced, and how totals will be displayed. Refer to the printer spacing chart that accompanies the program specification in Exhibit 3–1.

At the top of the printer spacing chart you will find three rows of numbers. Read vertically, these numbers represent the location on the report where the fields will be printed. Printer fonts and paper orientation can be altered in such away as to print from 80 to 200 characters on a print line. The standard is 132 characters per line.

Fields specified with an X represent alphanumeric data. SPORT CODE, for example, will be a two (2) position, alphanumeric field. The Z represents numeric data that will be zero suppressed. *Zero suppression* means that leading zeros will not be printed. Normally, all numeric fields will be printed using zero suppression. Notice that the QUANTITY SOLD field is defined as ZZ,ZZZ-. This indicates that leading zeros are to be suppressed, a comma will be inserted separating the thousands, and the hyphen printed if the number is negative. Other fields, such as COMMISSIONS PAID, TOTAL COST, and PROFIT will also have the decimal point inserted into the number.

Building the Printer Spacing Chart

In Chapter 2, we discussed the concepts behind program design. The first step of program design is defining the desired output. The printer spacing chart is the communication vehicle between the analyst and the report user for approval of the output. The report user can review the printer spacing chart and decide if the proposed report will meet the requirements.

Developing the printer spacing chart requires thought, planning, and knowledge of how the report will be used. You must consider what data will be presented on the report. You must plan for an easy-to-read, user-friendly report. The information must be well organized and neatly spaced to make it easy to use and easy to understand. Finally, you must know how the report will be used in order to develop the format that will be most useful. There are eight basic steps to follow when designing a report and developing the printer spacing chart:

1. Identify the information to be presented.
2. Determine the placement of the information on the page.
3. Determine the headings that will be used to title the information.
4. Determine the display format for fields.
5. Determine the amount of print positions required for each record on the report.
6. Determine the number of blank spaces to be inserted between fields.
7. Determine how subtotals and report totals will be shown.
8. Complete the spacing chart with company-standard title lines.

Identify the Information to be Presented

From either interviews with the user, or from the program specifications, you should have a sense of the information that must be presented on the report. Make a list of the data you need to print. This is where knowledge of how the report will be used is very helpful. Knowing the purpose of the report will significantly enhance your ability to determine what data is important and what data is not relevant to the report.

Determine the Placement of Information on the Page

Whenever possible, the order in which the fields are listed, from left to right, must follow a logical progression of the data. Two rules govern this process. The first rule is *sort order,* or the sequential order of the data in the file. The major sort field should be the left-most field, followed by the intermediate sort field(s), followed by the minor field. In the printer spacing chart shown in Exhibit 3–1, the major sort field is sport code; the intermediate field is the equipment type; and the minor sort field is item number. Sort order is identified in the program specification.

The second rule you must follow is related to *data dependence* and *logical grouping.* Normally, all descriptive data should precede volume information, such as dollars and/or quantity. Within these groupings you should look at dependence of data, and order the fields with dependent data to the right of the information upon which it is dependent. For example, TOTAL SALES is the product of multiplying QUANTITY and PRICE. Therefore, we can say that TOTAL SALES is dependent on QUANTITY and PRICE and should follow these two fields. Likewise, COMMISSIONS PAID is dependent on TOTAL SALES, and therefore follows it. If there is no dependence, the left-most field of a group should be the field of greater importance or greater use.

Determine the Headings that Will Be Used to Title the Information

Once you have listed the fields and determined the placement of the data, you should assign titles to the fields. These titles will show in the headers above the data fields on the report. These headings should be descriptive but not verbose. Abbreviations are encouraged, as long as they are meaningful. For example, DIV could be used for DIVISION and DEPT can be used for DEPARTMENT.

An abbreviation of D for both DEPARTMENT and DIVISION would be unwise.

Determine Display Format for Fields

After you have identified each field that will be printed, you should decide how this data will be displayed. While alphanumeric data can be printed directly as is, most numeric data should be displayed in a readable format. This means incorporating decimal points and commas. Decide if dollar signs ($) are appropriate on the report. Also, if this field can be a negative number, indicate that with the appropriate negative indicator. This is normally done by placing a minus sign (–) behind the number. Depending on the report, you may wish to place the minus sign in front of the number. In some reports, such as financial statements, negative numbers are enclosed in parentheses. For example, a negative 100 might be shown as (100).

Determine the Number of Print Positions Required for Each Line on the Report

After deciding the heading names that will be printed above each field of the report, determine how many print positions will be required for each column. This is done by determining which will require more spaces to print: the heading name or the data. The greater of the two will be used to define the total number of print positions required for the report. Exhibit 3–4 illustrates the process of determining how many print positions are required for the report defined in the program specification. After determining how many print positions are required for each column in the print line, add them together to arrive at the total number of print positions required for each line of print.

Determine Number of Blank Spaces to Be Inserted Between Fields

In order to create a readable report, the data must be spaced evenly and neatly across the page. You do not want to scatter small amounts of data across an entire print line; nor do you want to print the data tightly together, making the fields hard to decipher. To make the report easy to use, evenly space the fields and create equal margins on both sides of the report. To accomplish this, first determine how many print positions will be required to insert spaces between the fields. When possible, you should use from three

(3) to eight (8) positions between fields. Less than three places between fields places data too tightly together, and more than eight spreads the data further apart than necessary. In our example, we used four blank spaces between each field. Determine the total number of blank spaces required. Add this number to the total number of print positions required to obtain the number of used positions on the print line. Subtract this number from 132 to determine the number of spaces remaining for the left and right margins of the report. Divide this by two (2) to arrive at the margin width for each side of the report. Exhibit 3–5 completes this worksheet.

Determine if Subtotals and Report Totals Will Be Shown

If subtotals and report totals are to be included on the report, these should be shown at this time. Indicate the label you wish to give the totals, and add them to the total fields of the report layout by placing them under the columns being totaled.

Complete the Spacing Chart with Company-standard Title Lines

Finalize the printer spacing chart as shown in Exhibit 3–1.

Exhibit 3–4
DETERMINING COLUMN WIDTH

Report Field	Display Format	Data Size	Column Title	Heading Size	Required Positions
Sport Code	X	2	SPORT CODE	5	5
Equipment Type	X	2	EQUIP TYPE	5	5
Item Number	X	5	ITEM NMBR	4	5
Item Description	X	15	ITEM DESCRIPTION	16	16
Quantity	ZZ,ZZZ-	7	QUANTITY SOLD	8	8
Sales Amount	Z,ZZZ,ZZZ.99-	13	SALES AMOUNT	6	13

Commissions Paid	ZZZ,ZZZ.99-	11	COMMISSIONS PAID	11	11
Cost	ZZZ,ZZZ.99-	11	TOTAL COST	10	11
Profit	ZZZ,ZZZ.99-	11	PROFIT	6	11

			Total Print Positions		85

Exhibit 3–5
DETERMINING FINAL REPORT SPACING

Total Print Positions	85
Spaces Between Fields	32

Total Positions Used	117
Total report width	132
Total positions used	117

Available for margins	15
Margin size	8

Mapping the Data Using the Printer Spacing Chart

Before proceeding with program design, we must understand the information to be printed. To do so, we must have a full understanding of the output fields and the source of data to be printed. In Chapter 1, we learned the difference between external data and derived data. In the mapping process, we identify each data field and whether the source is external or derived.

The first step of the mapping process is to identify all output data fields. Using the mapping form, simply list the fields as they appear, left to right, on the report. Exhibit 3–6 illustrates the results of this step.

The second mapping step is to define what input data can be moved directly to the report. As the programmer, you will map the information on the report to a field on the input file. Exhibit 3–7 illustrates the mapping between the input fields and the report. Notice that the source is shown as the programming name of the field.

The next step of the design process is to identify derived data. Earlier, we defined derived data as data created by the program, normally as the result of a calculation. According to the specifications in Exhibit 3–1, three fields are computed. Exhibit 3–8 expands on Exhibit 3–7, by illustrating the derived data to be included on the report and the formulas used to compute the fields.

Finally, determine which fields, if any, will be totaled and shown on the report. Determine if any derived data, such as averages or record counts, will be included in the totals. Exhibit 3–9 illustrates the results of this process.

Exhibit 3–6
IDENTIFYING OUTPUT FIELDS

Output Field	Source	Derived Computation	Totals
Sport Code			
Equipment Type			
Item Number			
Item Description			
Quantity Sold			
Sales Amount			
Commissions Paid			
Cost			
Profit			

Exhibit 3–7
MAPPING DATA TO REPORT

Output Field	Source	Derived Computation	Totals
Sport Code	SPRTCD		
Equipment Type	ETYP		
Item Number	ITEM		
Item Description	DESC		
Quantity Sold	QTY		
Sales Amount	SLSAMT		
Commissions Paid			
Cost			
Profit			

Exhibit 3–8
EXPANDING WITH DERIVED DATA

Output Field	Source	Derived Computation	Totals
Sport Code	SPRTCD		
Equipment Type	ETYP		
Item Number	ITEM		
Item Description	DESC		
Quantity Sold	QTY		
Sales Amount	SLSAMT		
Commissions Paid	Derived	SLSAMT * CMPCT	
Cost	Derived	QTY * PRCHCST	
Profit	Derived	SLSAMT – (Commissions Paid + Cost)	

Exhibit 3–9
INDICATING SUBTOTALS AND TOTALS

Output Field	Source	Derived Computation	Totals
Sport Code	SPRTCD		
Equipment Type	ETYP		
Item Number	ITEM		
Item Description	DESC		
Quantity Sold	QTY		
Sales Amount	SLSAMT		X
Commissions Paid	Derived	SLSAMT * CMPCT = CMPD	X
Cost	Derived	QTY * PRCHCST = (NAME FIELD)	X
Profit	Derived	SLSAMT – (Commissions Paid + Cost)	X

DATA DICTIONARY

The *data dictionary* provides a wealth of information on the data used in the application. The record layout discussed earlier gives you an idea of a record format, field lengths, and whether the field is numeric or alphanumeric. The data dictionary expands on this and provides you with additional information about each field. The data dictionary can provide a definition of each field, valid values, edit rules, and other useful information. Appendix A of this book contains the data dictionary for the application referenced throughout this book. Do not hesitate to use this data dictionary if you have any questions about the data when working on projects in this book. Exhibit 3–10 contains a portion of the data dictionary related to the file used to create the report depicted in this chapter.

Exhibit 3–10 DATA DICTIONARY

Sales File

This file contains total year-to-date sales data by item.

Field:	Sport Code	Name: SPRTCD
	Class:	Numeric
	Size:	2
	Description:	This code defines the primary sport in which the product is used. Valid values are defined in the sport code description file.

Field:	Equipment Type	Name: ETYP
	Class:	Numeric
	Size:	2
	Description:	Equipment type is a code that defines the type of equipment. Types of equipment include shoes, rackets, and balls. Valid values are defined in the equipment type description file.

Field:	Item Number	Name: ITEM
	Class:	Alphanumeric
	Size:	5
	Description:	This field contains the item number of the product sold.

Field:	Item Description	Name: DESC
	Class:	Alphanumeric
	Size:	15
	Description:	This field contains the description of the item.

Field:	Quantity Sold	Name: QTY
	Class:	Numeric
	Size:	5.0
	Description:	Total units of the item sold for the year. This quantity may be negative if returns were greater than sales.

SUMMARY

In this chapter, we learned the importance of good *documentation.* We learned to read and understand the *program specification.* We know that the program specification contains an outline of processing required by the program, required formulas for calculating derived data, the record layouts for the files being processed, and the required output. In many cases, the program specification will include a *printer spacing chart* depicting the desired report. In other cases, the specification may contain only the required data, and the developer will be required to define the appearance of the report. For those cases where the programmer will be defining the report, you have learned the eight steps in developing an easy-to-use report. You also learned in this chapter the first real step in program design: understanding the output and mapping the input data to the output report. Finally, you learned that the data dictionary provides essential information about the data used in the application.

REVIEW QUESTIONS

1. What is the purpose of the program specification?
2. What information is contained in the record layout?
3. What is the purpose of the printer spacing chart?
4. What is the objective of mapping data to the report?
5. When mapping the data to the report, how do you know what formula to use for derived computations?

PROJECT

Objective

Develop a report that will provide product managers and the purchasing department with a list of products that need to be ordered.

Business Overview

Acme Distributors maintains current item and inventory data in the item master file. Current inventory levels are kept in a QUANTITY ON HAND field (IM-QOH). As products are sold, this field is adjusted to accurately reflect current inventory.

The item master file also has a field named ORDER POINT (IM-ORDPT). This field represents the point at which the product is reordered. Whenever a product's QUANTITY ON HAND (IM-QOH) drops below the ORDER POINT for that product, this program must identify the item to order and print the report shown on the printer spacing chart. When ordering an item, Acme orders a fixed quantity of each item. This quantity is contained in the field IM-ORD-QTY.

1. Select and print from the item master file any item where the quantity on hand has dropped below the order point.

2. The following formulas will be required:
   - Extended Cost = Order Quantity * Purchase Cost.
   - Sales Tax = Extended Cost * 5%.
   - Total Cost = Extended Cost + Sales Tax.
3. The report will be single-spaced.

ITEM MASTER

01-05	ITEM NUMBER	IM-ITEM
06-20	DESCRIPTION	IM-DESC
21-22	SPORT CODE	IM-SPRTCD
23-24	EQUIPMENT TYPE	IM-ETYP
25-27	COMMISSION PERCENT (3.3)	IM-PCT
28-33	VENDOR	IM-VNDR
34-40	PURCHASE COST (7.2)	IM-COST
41-47	RETAIL PRICE (7.2)	IM-PRICE
48-52	QUANTITY ON HAND (5.0)	IM-QOH
53-57	ORDER POINT (5.0)	IM-ORDPT
58-62	ORDER QUANTITY (5.0)	IM-ORD-QTY
63-70	Unused	

Printer Spacing Chart

```
                                                                    1111111111111111111111111111111111
          111111111122222222223333333333444444444455555555556666666666777777777788888888889999999999000000000011111111112222222222
 123456789012345678901234567890123456789012345678901234567890123456789012345678901234567890123456789012345678901234567890123456789

DATE RUN:  MM/DD/YY                            ACME DISTRIBUTORS                                     PAGE ZZZZ9
TIME RUN:  HH:MM                          PRODUCT REPLENISHMENT REPORT


                  ITEM                       ORDER    PURCHASE      EXTENDED      SALES      TOTAL
          VENDOR  NUMBER  DESCRIPTION          QTY      COST          COST         TAX       COST

          XXXXXX  XXXXX   XXXXXXXXXXXXXXX    ZZ,ZZZ   Z,ZZZ.99    ZZZ,ZZZ.99   Z,ZZZ.99   ZZZ,ZZZ.99
          XXXXXX  XXXXX   XXXXXXXXXXXXXXX    ZZ,ZZZ   Z,ZZZ.99    ZZZ,ZZZ.99   Z,ZZZ.99   ZZZ,ZZZ.99
          XXXXXX  XXXXX   XXXXXXXXXXXXXXX    ZZ,ZZZ   Z,ZZZ.99    ZZZ,ZZZ.99   Z,ZZZ.99   ZZZ,ZZZ.99
          XXXXXX  XXXXX   XXXXXXXXXXXXXXX    ZZ,ZZZ   Z,ZZZ.99    ZZZ,ZZZ.99   Z,ZZZ.99   ZZZ,ZZZ.99
          XXXXXX  XXXXX   XXXXXXXXXXXXXXX    ZZ,ZZZ   Z,ZZZ.99    ZZZ,ZZZ.99   Z,ZZZ.99   ZZZ,ZZZ.99
          XXXXXX  XXXXX   XXXXXXXXXXXXXXX    ZZ,ZZZ   Z,ZZZ.99    ZZZ,ZZZ.99   Z,ZZZ.99   ZZZ,ZZZ.99
          XXXXXX  XXXXX   XXXXXXXXXXXXXXX    ZZ,ZZZ   Z,ZZZ.99    ZZZ,ZZZ.99   Z,ZZZ.99   ZZZ,ZZZ.99
          XXXXXX  XXXXX   XXXXXXXXXXXXXXX    ZZ,ZZZ   Z,ZZZ.99    ZZZ,ZZZ.99   Z,ZZZ.99   ZZZ,ZZZ.99
```

ASSIGNMENT

1. Complete the mapping between the input file and output report layout.
2. Identify all derived data fields and the appropriate calculations.

Note: Do not lose sight of the mapping objective. The purpose of mapping is to identify the output information required and the source for that information. The program specification provides more information than is needed to perform this first step of program design. Do not get caught in the "I can't see the forest for the trees" pitfall. Focus only on the mapping process.

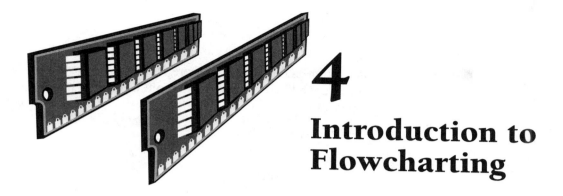

4

Introduction to Flowcharting

OBJECTIVES

- Recognizing the basic flowchart symbols.
- Understanding the use of each flowchart symbol.
- Understanding structured flowcharting.

INTRODUCTION

A *flowchart* is a graphical representation of a program. The flowchart serves as the program's blueprint. This blueprint details the instructions that need to be executed and the sequence in which to execute them. In this chapter, we will cover the basic symbols used when flowcharting and discuss common program structures.

FLOWCHART SYMBOLS

Terminal

The *terminal symbol* represents the beginning or end of a procedure or program. All flowcharts and procedures within a flowchart will have a terminal at the start and at the end. Terminals beginning a procedure will contain the name of the procedure. Terminal ending a procedure should contain the word EXIT, indicating that the procedure exits at this point.

Examples:

CALCULATE   EXIT

Process

The *process symbol* represents a processing task within the program. Any data manipulation, computation, or movement of data within the program must be illustrated using a process symbol.

Examples:

GRSPAY = HRSWRK * RATE   MOVE DATA TO OUTPUT

Decision

A *decision* represents a point in the program where the logic flow will follow one of two paths depending on a given situation. Decisions will be discussed later in this chapter.

Example:

Predefined Process

A *predefined process* indicates that the instructions to be executed are located elsewhere in the program. This is normally used when the designer/developer wishes to keep the code simple by separating a portion of it. Another reason to use a predefined process is when the same instructions are required in two or more places in the program. The procedure containing these instructions can be defined once and referenced via the predefined process at each location where the instructions are needed.

Example:

Predefined processes can also be used to represent the execution of a subprogram. A *subprogram* contains a set of instructions that may be required by several programs. Instead of embedding the logic into every program, the logic may reside in a subprogram and be called. An example would be logic required to convert a Gregorian date (05/28/1999) to a Julian date (1999137).

Input-Output Process

This symbol is used to indicate that some input or output operation is being performed. The purpose of a program is to transform data into information, thereby making the data more valuable to the user. Data is brought into the program through some form of input operation. *Input operations* include reading files and interacting with the user in an online environment. Once the data has been processed, the program will output the information via an *output operation*. Output operations include writing files, writing reports, and displaying information to a user in an interactive environment.

Examples:

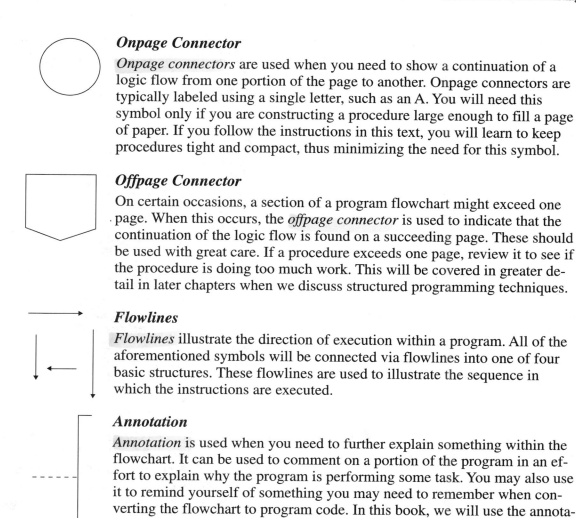

Onpage Connector

Onpage connectors are used when you need to show a continuation of a logic flow from one portion of the page to another. Onpage connectors are typically labeled using a single letter, such as an A. You will need this symbol only if you are constructing a procedure large enough to fill a page of paper. If you follow the instructions in this text, you will learn to keep procedures tight and compact, thus minimizing the need for this symbol.

Offpage Connector

On certain occasions, a section of a program flowchart might exceed one page. When this occurs, the *offpage connector* is used to indicate that the continuation of the logic flow is found on a succeeding page. These should be used with great care. If a procedure exceeds one page, review it to see if the procedure is doing too much work. This will be covered in greater detail in later chapters when we discuss structured programming techniques.

Flowlines

Flowlines illustrate the direction of execution within a program. All of the aforementioned symbols will be connected via flowlines into one of four basic structures. These flowlines are used to illustrate the sequence in which the instructions are executed.

Annotation

Annotation is used when you need to further explain something within the flowchart. It can be used to comment on a portion of the program in an effort to explain why the program is performing some task. You may also use it to remind yourself of something you may need to remember when converting the flowchart to program code. In this book, we will use the annotation symbol as a reminder of actions we need to take in initializing our program for execution. This will be discussed in more detail in later chapters.

BASIC STRUCTURES

Knowing the purpose of the symbols is only the beginning of flowcharting. Now let's look at how these symbols are employed. There are four basic flowcharting structures:

1. Sequence.
2. Decision.
3. Do While.
4. Do Until.

Sequence Structure

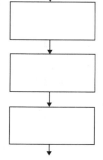

The most basic structure is the *sequence structure.* The sequence indicates a sequence of instructions to be executed, and illustrates the order in which these instructions will be performed. In the illustration to the left, the program will always perform instructions in the first process symbol, followed by instructions indicated in the second process symbol, followed by the third. Although this example uses only the process symbol, the sequence structure can have any combination of processes, predefined processes, and input-output processes.

Examples:

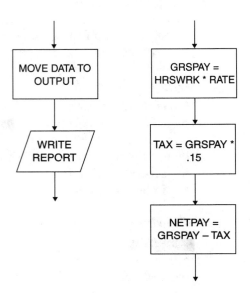

Decision Structure

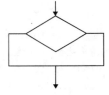

The *decision structure* is used to dictate a change in logical path depending on some condition. The condition is stated in a form that can be answered with a YES/NO or TRUE/FALSE. A condition such as "How many hours did an employee work" would be an invalid decision structure because it cannot be answered YES or NO. However, the condition "Did the employee work more than 40 hours" would be valid. All decision structures have one entry point at the top, and two paths where the logic will flow. One path (either side) is used to show the logic executed if the condition is TRUE; the other path depicts the logic executed when the condition is FALSE. Finally, logic paths of the decision structure rejoin to form a single exit point.

Example:

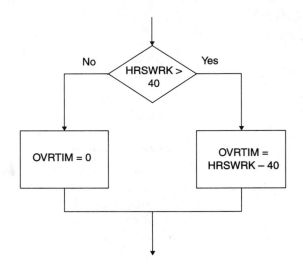

Do While

The *Do While structure,* shown at the left, illustrates code that will be repeatedly executed while a given condition exists. In a Do While structure, the condition is checked before the intended process is executed. Depending on the results of the condition, the process may be bypassed. The process will continue to be executed while the condition continues to exist. Do While structures will be covered in greater detail in Chapter 13.

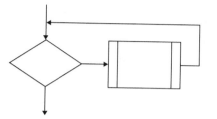

Do Until

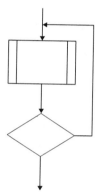

The *Do Until structure* is similar to the Do While in that the program will repeatedly execute one or more instruction until a condition exists. The main difference between the Do Until and the Do While is that the Do Until will execute the instructions one time before checking the condition. As you recall, the Do While checks the condition first. With the Do Until, the process will always be performed at least one time. The Do Until structure is illustrated at the left.

SUMMARY

In this chapter, we learned the basic symbols used to define a flowchart. We also covered the four flowchart structures that will be employed throughout this book. This chapter is the starting point for flowcharting. Chapter 5 will continue this thought process by introducing the fundamental structured programming techniques. We will also construct our first program flowchart in Chapter 5.

REVIEW QUESTIONS

1. What is the purpose of the terminal symbol?
2. What is the difference between a process and a predefined process?
3. How does a decision structure work?
4. When would you use a sequence structure?
5. What are the purposes of the flowlines?
6. Explain the basic difference between the Do While structure and the Do Until structure.

PROJECT

Using the flowchart on the next page, compute the final results for each of the four variables (fields). For each problem, start with the values provided for each variable.

	Starting Values				**Ending Values**			
	A	B	C	X	A	B	C	X
Ex.	8	5	3	0	7	10	3	3
1.	7	3	10	0	___	___	___	___
2.	5	8	8	0	___	___	___	___
3.	4	0	2	0	___	___	___	___
4.	3	1	3	0	___	___	___	___
5.	5	9	1	0	___	___	___	___
6.	4	6	3	0	___	___	___	___
7.	5	5	0	0	___	___	___	___
8.	7	2	9	0	___	___	___	___
9.	1	3	2	0	___	___	___	___
10.	0	0	0	0	___	___	___	___

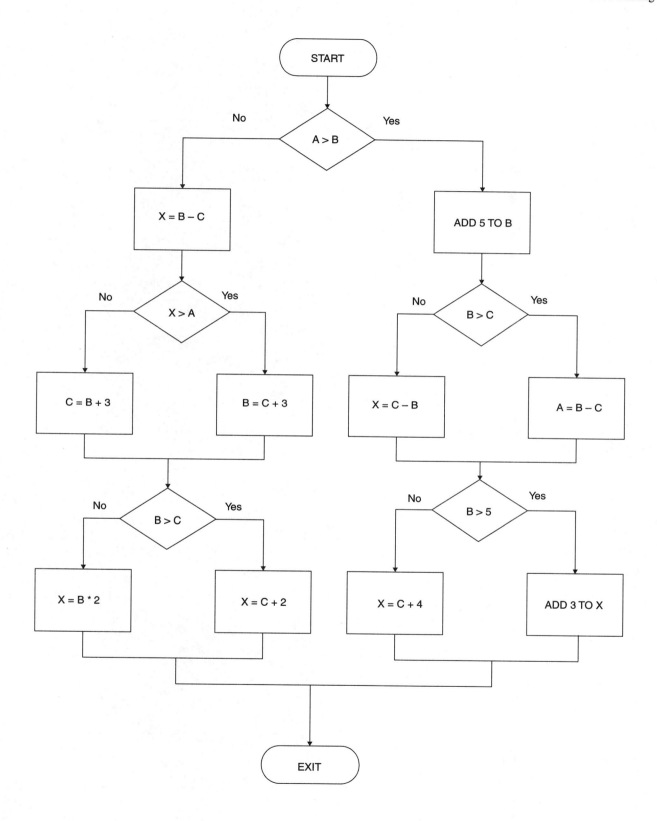

5
Structured Programming

OBJECTIVES

- Understanding the fundamentals of structured programming.
- Matching the flowchart symbols to program tasks.
- Reading and understanding a program flowchart.
- Learning to assemble flowchart symbols into a complete program flowchart.

INTRODUCTION

As we learned in the previous chapter, the flowchart is a graphical representation of a program. Structured programs are composed of building blocks called *procedures*. These building blocks are assembled in the order required to achieve the program objectives.

STRUCTURED PROGRAMMING TECHNIQUES

There are three fundamental objectives to be achieved with every program designed and written:

1. Making the program work correctly.
2. Creating a program that is easily understood by another programmer.
3. Creating a program that is easily maintained.

Developing programs that are well organized and properly structured increase the chances that you will succeed in all three objectives with relative ease. Structured programs are composed of procedures, or building blocks. Each procedure serves a specific purpose and should be easily understood. To better understand this concept, let's take a look at the organization of a computer program.

Program Organization

Figure 5–1 illustrates the flowchart for the MAINLINE routine of a program. Programs for business applications generally consist of three key

41

procedures, with each procedure serving a very important function of the program:

1. INITIALIZATION.
2. PROCESS.
3. END-OF-JOB.

Initialization

All programs need to execute a set of instructions in preparation for the work to be done. These instructions are executed one time, and one time only, in the INITIALIZATION procedure. Exhibit 5–1 contains some of the tasks that INITIALIZATION might perform in any given program. All programs will have an INITIALIZATION procedure and, as the name implies, its purpose is to execute the initialization tasks required by the program.

Process

All programs are written to serve some purpose, whether it is to write a report, update a file, or create an extract file for future use. The PROCESS procedure of the program contains all the instructions necessary for the program to accomplish the tasks intended.

Using the MAINLINE flowchart in Figure 5–1 as an example, PROCESS will continue to be executed while END-FLAG is not ON. (*Do While END-FLAG not ON.*) We will discuss END-FLAG shortly. For now, it

Figure 5–1
Mainline

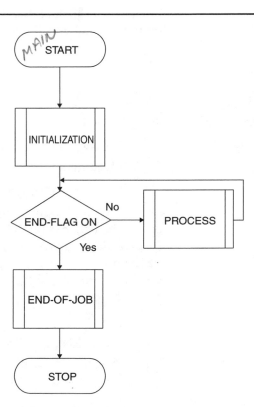

is important to understand the purpose of PROCESS. Again, PROCESS performs whatever tasks the program is intended to do. Exhibit 5–1 contains a list of tasks PROCESS might perform in any given program. These tasks will be covered in detail in later chapters.

End-of-Job

All programs will perform a set of tasks when PROCESS has been completed. END-OF-JOB serves this purpose. END-OF-JOB (or EOJ) performs any and all tasks that are performed one time, and one time only, at the end of program execution. Exhibit 5–1 contains a list of tasks associated with EOJ.

End-Flag

In Chapter 1, we discussed the different types of data and their sources. One of the data types we reviewed was logical data, which is data created by the program for internal use within the program. One example of a logical data field is a status flag. A *status flag* is a field that can be turned on or off in one procedure of the program. Later in the execution, another procedure of the program can then interrogate the status of the flag (hence, the name status flag) and, using a decision, direct the logic flow in either of two directions. END-FLAG is an example of a status flag. One of the steps within INITIALIZE will set END-FLAG off. In MAINLINE, Figure 5–1, we will loop through PROCESS (using a DoWhile structure) *while* the status of END-FLAG is off. We will turn END-FLAG on when we encounter some condition that should result in stopping the program. Normally, you will turn END-FLAG on when you have no more records to process. Figure 5–2 contains an entire program that we will review later in the chapter. At that time, we will discover where and how END-FLAG is turned on.

Exhibit 5–1
TASK LIST FOR EACH SECTION OF THE PROGRAM

INITIALIZATION	PROCESS	END-OF-JOB
Initialize	Record selection	Major control-break
Open files	Control-break	Final calculations
Process special files	Calculate	Print final totals
Read input file ⟍ LAST	Accumulate	Close files
	Write	
	Read ⟍ LAST	

Rules of Structured Programming

Earlier in this chapter, we mentioned that a program is composed of procedures, which act as building blocks during program construction. INITIALIZATION, PROCESS, and EOJ are examples of procedures.

There are three rules to be followed when designing procedures:

1. *Each procedure performs one task and one task only.* A procedure may consist of many instructions, but all of the instructions within any given procedure work to accomplish a single objective. As shown in Exhibit 5-1, INITIALIZATION can have many instructions, but all are related to accomplishing the INITIALIZATION tasks of the program. Likewise for PROCESS and EOJ. If, during the steps of program design, you discover that you have designed a procedure performing two or more unrelated tasks, you should split the module into two or more procedures.

2. *Each procedure has only one exit and one entrance.* Each procedure you design will have only one entry point and one exit point. As we review the program depicted in Exhibit 5–2, notice that all procedures shown have a single entrance and a single exit.

3. *Each procedure does what the name implies.* A good program designer will label each procedure by the task it performs. For example, INITIALIZATION will initialize the program for execution. PROCESS performs the processing required to accomplish the task. Later you will see modules such as READ and WRITE doing what their names imply. If you design a procedure that is not doing what the name implies, you have either misnamed the procedure or you have included instructions that are not appropriate for that procedure.

Some will argue that a program does not have be structured in order to work correctly. They are correct. However, although you can design an unstructured program that will work, you also increase the risk of designing one that will not perform correctly. And, when problems do arise, it is much more difficult to find an error in an unstructured program than in one that has been properly designed and structured. If you adhere to the techniques and principles outlined in this book, your chances of success will increase. If you choose to ignore these concepts and principles, you may still design a correct program, but you will also increase the risk of failing.

EXAMPLE PROGRAM

Figure 5–2 illustrates a simple but effective program. This program reads a file and creates a report. The layout of the input file is shown in Exhibit 5–2, and the report produced is shown in Exhibit 5-3. Let's take a close look at the program, see what it is doing, and review the flowchart that defines that program.

Exhibit 5–2
INPUT FILE

ITEM MASTER

01-05 ITEM NUMBER		IM-ITEM
06-20 DESCRIPTION		IM-DESC
21-22 SPORT CODE		IM-SPPTCD
23-24 EQUIPMENT TYPE		IM-ETYP
25-27 COMMISSION PERCENT	(3.3)	IM-PCT
28-34 PURCHASE COST	(7.2)	IM-COST
35-41 RETAIL PRICE	(7.2)	IM-PRICE
42-50 Unused		

Exhibit 5–3
PRINTER SPACING CHART FOR OUTPUT

```
                            1111111111222222222233333333334444444444555555555566666666667777777777888888888899999999990000000000111111111111111111111111111111
                  1234567890123456789012345678901234567890123456789012345678901234567890123456789012345678901234567890123456789012345678901234567890

           ITEM                         SPORT    EQUIP    PURCHASE      LIST      COMM
           NUMBER    DESCRIPTION        CODE     TYPE     COST          PRICE     PCT

           XXXXX     XXXXXXXXXXXXXX     XX       XX       ZZ,ZZZ.99     ZZ,ZZZ.99    .999
           XXXXX     XXXXXXXXXXXXXX     XX       XX       ZZ,ZZZ.99     ZZ,ZZZ.99    .999
           XXXXX     XXXXXXXXXXXXXX     XX       XX       ZZ,ZZZ.99     ZZ,ZZZ.99    .999
           XXXXX     XXXXXXXXXXXXXX     XX       XX       ZZ,ZZZ.99     ZZ,ZZZ.99    .999
```

Referring to Figure 5–2 notice first the standard MAINLINE logic routine. (This MAINLINE looks exactly like the one shown in Figure 5–1.) In all cases within this text, MAINLINE will always be structured in this

Figure 5–2
Example program

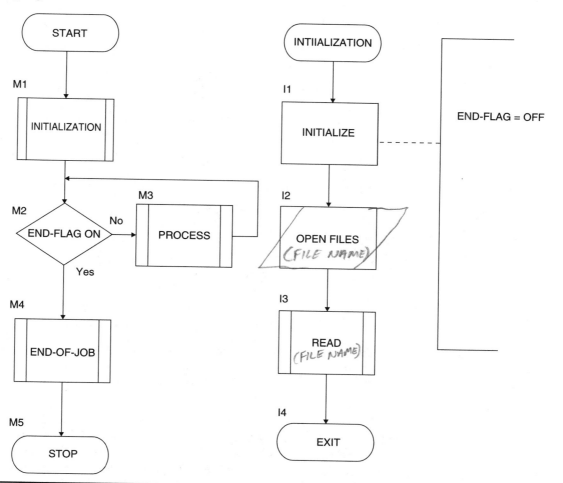

(continued on next page)

Figure 5–2
(continued)

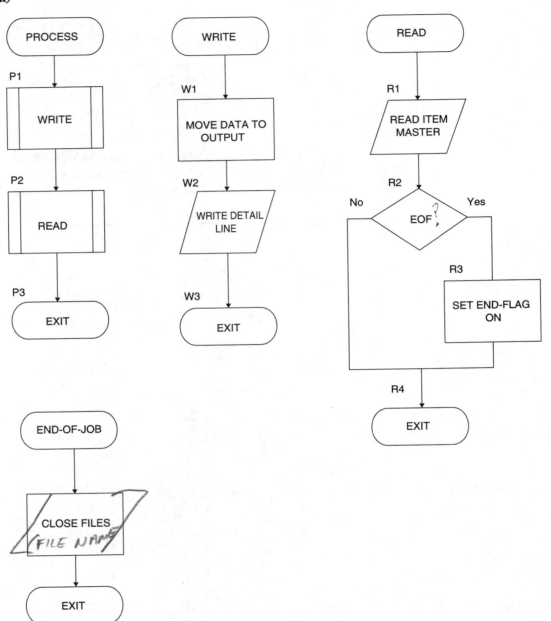

manner. Logic for the program begins at the MAINLINE terminal labeled START. The first symbol encountered is designated M1 (MAINLINE / Step 1). This is a predefined process that will perform the procedure INITIALIZATION. At this time, the program jumps to the procedure called INITIALIZATION. When INITIALIZATION is complete, the program will return to the point the predefined process was invoked. The program flows as follows:

1. **M1** Perform the predefined process INITIALIZATION. The program jumps to the procedure labeled INITIALIZATION and begins to execute.

2. **I1** Initialize logical and derived data fields within the program. In this program we will initialize END-FLAG to OFF, meaning we have not yet reached the end of the input file. As we progress through the chapters of this book, we will discover a number of items that we initialize at this time.

3. **I2** Open files. All files must be opened by the program. This is a reminder to us that we must open all the files at this time.

4. **I3** Perform the predefined process labeled READ. The last task we always do in INITIALIZATION is read the first record of the file being processed.

5. **R1** Control is passed to the READ procedure from the predefined process at I3. Here it issues an input-output instruction to read the input file. This retrieves the next record in the file. In this case, the next record is the first record.

6. **R2** After every READ, we must check to see if the file being read has reached its end, meaning there are no more records to process. When the file is at its end, this decision will branch to the TRUE direction. Let's assume at this time the file was not at its end. We take the FALSE logic path from the decision, so R3 will not be executed at this time.

7. **R4** This is where the READ procedure is exited. At this time, the program will return to the point where READ was called. As you remember, READ was called from I3.

8. **I4** After the program returns to I3, it moves to the next instruction, which is I4. I4 is the exit for the INITIALIZATION procedure. The program will now exit INITIALIZATION and return to the point where it was called. INITIALIZATION is always called from MAINLINE; in this case, M1.

9. **M2** In MAINLINE, we check to see if END-FLAG has been turned ON. Since it has not, we proceed to M3. Notice that the combination of M2 and M3 form a *Do-While loop. While* END-FLAG is OFF, we will *do* PROCESS.

10. **M3** Perform the predefined process labeled PROCESS. The program will now pass control to the PROCESS procedure.

11. **P1** The first step of PROCESS is to perform the predefined process labeled WRITE. The program will now jump to the WRITE procedure.

12. **W1** The first step of WRITE is to move data from the input record to the output area.

13. **W2** Write the report line.

14. W3 Exit WRITE and return to P1, the predefined process symbol that called WRITE.

15. P2 Perform READ to obtain the next record on the file. READ is always the last step of PROCESS.

16. R1 Read the next record from the file.

17. R2 Check to see if the file is at its end. Assume again that it is not at its end, so we follow the FALSE logic path.

18. R4 Exit READ and return to P2.

19. P3 P3 is the exit for PROCESS. At this time we exit PROCESS and return to M3.

We have completed our first execution of PROCESS. So far we have read the first record of the file (from INITIALIZATION), written the first record to the report (from WRITE), and read the second record on the input file. Now let's continue.

20. M2 The Do While loop returns to the decision (M2) to see if END-FLAG has been turned ON. Since is has not, the program again proceeds to M3.

Steps 10 through 20 will continue to be executed just as they were above until an end-of-file condition occurs on the input file. When this occurs, the program behavior will change. Let's pick up the program as we enter PROCESS with the final record.

21. P1 We have just entered PROCESS for the last record. Our first step is to perform the predefined process labeled WRITE. As before, the program will transfer control to the WRITE procedure.

22. W1 Here we will move data from the input record to the output area.

23. W2 Write the report line.

24. W3 Exit WRITE and return to P1, the predefined process symbol that we have named WRITE.

25. P2 Perform READ to obtain the next record on the file.

26. R1 Read the next record from the file.

27. R2 Check to see if the file is at its end. At this time, there are no more records on the file, so we follow the TRUE logic path.

28. R3 We execute R3 for the first and only time in this program. Since there are no more records on the input file, we will turn END-FLAG ON.

29. R4 We exit from READ and return control to P2. Remember, P2 is where we were positioned when we called READ.

30. P3 We exit PROCESS and return to M3.

31. M2 Again, after exiting process, we loop back to M2 to check the status of END-FLAG. Since we turned END-FLAG ON, this condition is now true and we proceed to M4, END-OF-JOB. Setting END-FLAG ON stopped the Do While loop that kept PROCESS executing.

32. M4   Perform the predefined process, END-OF-JOB.

33. E1   Close all files used during the process. Any file opened during INITIALIZATION will be closed here.

34. E2   Exit END-OF-JOB. In later chapters, we will learn other tasks performed during the END-OF-JOB procedure.

35. M5   After exiting END-OF-JOB, the program returns to the point where it was called and continues to the next instruction. In this case, the next instruction is the terminal STOP. This indicates that the program is done.

SUMMARY

In this chapter, we were introduced to the MAINLINE routine and how this routine passes control to the procedures of the program. We learned that programs contain the procedures INITIALIZATION, PROCESS, and END-OF-JOB. These procedures perform specific tasks in every program. We learned to read a flowchart and understand how to follow the logic path of the program. We also learned that there are three objectives when developing a program: making a program work correctly; creating a program that is easily understood by others; and creating a program that is easily maintained. While there is still more to learn, understanding the concepts presented here and using them as the foundation for program design will increase your chances of successfully meeting the three objectives.

REVIEW QUESTIONS

1. What are the three primary, or key, procedures of a program?
2. What is the purpose of the INITIALIZATION procedure?
3. What is the purpose of the PROCESS prodecure?
4. What is the purpose of the END-OF-JOB procedure?
5. How many times is the INITIALIZATION procedure executed when the program is processed? How about PROCESS? END-OF-JOB?
6. Explain how the predefined process works.
7. What is the purpose of END-FLAG? How does END-FLAG get turned off? How does END-FLAG get turned on?
8. END-FLAG is an example of a logical data field. What is the purpose of a logical data field?

6
Pseudo Code

OBJECTIVES

- Understanding the techniques of pseudo coding in program design.
- Gaining familiarity with coding constructs.
- Reading existing pseudo code.

INTRODUCTION

Pseudo coding is another method of program design. It can be used in place of flowcharting or as the next step after the flowchart has been developed. *Pseudo coding* is abbreviated program code with specific constructs used to outline the program logic in written form. A *construct* is the pseudo code's structural equivalent to flowchart structures. Each action defined in pseudo code has a specific construct that must be used. Once pseudo coding is complete, writing the actual program code can be straightforward. Pseudo code allows you to preview a written version of the program before the actual programming takes place.

PSEUDO CODE CONSTRUCTS

Basic Pseudo Code Constructs

There are four basic pseudo code constructs:

- IF-THEN-ELSE: Used to alter the flow of processing based on a decision. This is the pseudo code equivalent to the decision structure in flowcharting. The IF-THEN construct can be designed without the ELSE if no alternate action is required from the decision.
- READ: Used to define processing required to read a file and what action is taken when the end-of-file is reached.
- DOWHILE and DOUNTIL: Used to perform looping processes. These are the pseudo code equivalent to the Do While and Do Until flowchart structure.

These constructs are used to organize the code and standardize the method of pseudo code development. All constructs terminate with an END-x statement, where x represents the construct being written. For example, the READ construct will terminate with END-READ and IF-THEN-ELSE will terminate with END-IF.

As you practice pseudo coding, pay attention to the indentation in the lines of code. The code that you will be writing will be indented within the construct. This indentation is highly recommended to maintain readability and to assist in the structuring of the program.

Pseudo Code Verbs

A *verb* is an action command. While verbs are not constructs, they do conform to specific coding rules. Some common verbs are the following:

- DO xxx: Execute or perform the procedure represented by xxx. This is the pseudo code equivalent to the internal predefined process.
- SET: Set a working field to a value. SET constructs can be used to set a field to a specific value or they can be used in conjunction with a mathematical formula.
- WRITE: Write the output file or report.
- OPEN: Open files for processing.
- CLOSE: Close files when processing is complete.

The IF-THEN-ELSE Construct

When making decisions within the program, you must state a condition that can be answered yes/no or true/false. When developing code for that decision, you will use an IF statement. The condition is worded such that IF a condition is true, THEN perform some action; ELSE perform a different action.

The construct for the IF-THEN-ELSE condition is as follows:

```
IF condition THEN
      statement(s)
    ELSE
      statements(s)
END-IF
```

For example, suppose we needed to determine the number of overtime hours worked by an employee. The standard work week is 40 hours. Hours worked in excess of 40 are considered overtime. If the employee has not worked more than 40 hours, overtime hours equals 0.

```
IF hours-worked > 40 THEN
      SET overtime-hours = hours-worked - 40
    ELSE
      SET overtime-hours = 0
END-IF
```

The READ Construct

The format for the READ construct is as follows:

```
READ filename
  .
  .
  END-READ
```

The READ construct is often combined with the IF-THEN-ELSE construct to handle the end-of-file condition. As you recall, when we reach end-of-file, we set END-FLAG on. If we have not reached end-of-file, we take no further action. Although this is technically an IF-THEN-ELSE condition, we have no alternate action.

The final READ construct is as follows:

```
READ payroll file
     IF end-of-file THEN
          SET end-flag on
     END-IF
END-READ
```

The DOWHILE and DOUNTIL Constructs

Like their flowchart counterparts, these constructs are used when defining a loop. MAINLINE is the common looping routine used in all programs. Using MAINLINE as our example, the DOWHILE construct is as follows:

```
DOWHILE end-flag off
    DO process
END-DOWHILE
```

The DOUNTIL construct for this same logic is as follows:

```
DOUNTIL end-flag on
    DO process
END-DOUNTIL
```

DESIGNING THE COMPLETE PROGRAM IN PSEUDO CODE

To illustrate a program design using pseudo code, let's recall the program we flowcharted in Chapter 5.

Developing the Pseudo Code

As we develop the pseudo code for this program, you may want to refer to Chapter 5, Figure 5–2, which illustrates the flowchart for this program. As you will discover, the pseudo code for this program follows the same structure as the flowchart. The only difference between these two methods of program design is that the flowchart is graphical in nature and the pseudo code is written in abbreviated program code.

MAINLINE

As with any program, the first step of detailed program design is MAINLINE. MAINLINE for this program is as follows:

```
mainline:
     DO initialization
     DOWHILE end-flag off
         DO process
     END-DOWHILE
     DO end-of-job
     STOP
```

Notice that the first line of the program is *mainline:*. In pseudo coding the procedure name is the first item of the procedure, replacing the terminal symbol of the flowchart. All procedure names end with a colon (:).

INITIALIZATION

The INITIALIZATION procedure will accomplish three tasks: initialize any variables, open files, and execute the read procedure to obtain the first input record. The pseudo code for INITIALIZATION is as follows:

```
initialization:
        INITIALIZE flags:      end-flag = off
        OPEN files
        DO read-file
```

As you see in the INITIALIZATION procedure, all verbs are uppercase. Field names and procedures are lowercase.

PROCESS

The PROCESS procedure for this program will perform two tasks: write and read. Pseudo code for this procedure is as follows:

```
process:
        DO write
        DO read-file
```

Notice that this is exactly the same as the PROCESS procedure in the flowchart in Figure 5–2 in Chapter 5. The DO procedure verb is used in pseudo coding just as the internal predefined process is used in the flowchart.

WRITE

The WRITE procedure does not vary in structure or processing requirements from the WRITE procedure in Chapter 5. We will then move the appropriate data to the output and print the report. The pseudo code for the WRITE procedure is as follows:

```
write:
        MOVE data to output
        WRITE output report
```

READ

In INITIALIZATION and PROCESS we have the DO verb reference a procedure called READ-FILE. The pseudo code for this procedure follows the READ construct:

```
read-file:
        READ item master file
            IF end-of-file THEN
                    SET end-flag on
            END-IF
        END-READ
```

END-OF-JOB

Finally we have the EOJ procedure. For this program, we need only close our files. Pseudo code for this procedure is as follows:

```
end-of-job:
        CLOSE files
```

Putting It All Together

Exhibit 6–1 contains the pseudo code for this entire program. You will find that this code exactly follows the flowchart from Chapter 5, Figure 5–2. When developing pseudo code you are freer to expand on thoughts and ideas. In most cases, you know in advance the programming language you will be using to code the program, so the pseudo code you develop can better reflect the final program than a flowchart might. Take advantage of this freedom by adding useful information to the pseudo code.

Exhibit 6–1
PSEUDO CODE FOR SAMPLE PROGRAM

```
mainline:
        DO initialization
        DOWHILE end-flag off
            DO process
        END-DOWHILE
        DO end-of-job
        STOP
initialization:
        INITIALIZE flags:     end-flag = off
        OPEN files
        DO read-file
process:
        DO write
        DO read-file
write:
        MOVE data to output
        WRITE output report
read-file:
        READ item master file
            IF end-of-file THEN
                    SET end-flag on
            END-IF
        END-READ
end-of-job:
        CLOSE files
```

SUMMARY

Pseudo code is abbreviated program code that can be adapted to almost any programming language. Pseudo coding follows the rules of structured programming, plus a few additional rules regarding specific constructs. The coding rules of pseudo code are similar to the structures of flowcharting.

Examples of constructs include IF-THEN-ELSE and DOWHILE. Pseudo coding also employs verbs as the action commands. Examples of verbs are MOVE, SET, and DO.

REVIEW QUESTIONS

1. What is a construct?
2. What is a verb?
3. What is an advantage of pseudo coding over flowcharting?

7
Structure Charts

OBJECTIVES

- Understanding structured program organization.
- Understanding the cohesion within program procedures.
- Understanding coupling between program procedures.
- Understanding a procedure's span of control.
- Understanding the control and process levels of the structure chart.
- Transitioning from the structure chart to the flowchart.

INTRODUCTION

In Chapter 5, we learned the importance of a structured program. A structured program will have fewer design flaws and will be easier to debug (eliminate errors). A structured program is easier for someone else to read and understand, and consequently is easier to maintain. In this chapter, we will learn how structured programs are planned, organized, and designed. Specifically, we will study the role of the program structure chart and its importance in the design process.

What Is a Structure Chart?

A *structure chart* is a graphical representation of the program's organization. Flowcharts, such as the one we constructed in Chapter 5, illustrate how the program will create the desired output. However, before you begin flowcharting the program and defining how the program will work, it is imperative that you know what the program must do.

Program specifications provide an overview of the major objectives and functionality for the program we will be designing. However, specifications alone are not enough to begin the detailed design process (i.e., flowcharting). Without careful consideration of the functionality the program must perform and in what order this processing must occur, developing a flowchart can be extremely risky and subject to error. We will use the structure chart to identify what tasks must be performed by the program and the sequential order in which these tasks must be performed. A structure chart shows what tasks the program must perform, while the flowchart shows how the program will perform these tasks. Development of the structure chart must precede development of the flowchart. After all, if you do not know what you are going to do, you cannot effectively decide how to do it.

Understanding the Structure Chart

Exhibit 7–1 lists and defines the types of functionality that might be required in a program. These functions are segregated into the three main procedures of the program: INITIALIZATION, PROCESS, and END-OF-JOB. They are shown in the order in which they are typically performed within these procedures. Structure charts are used to show which of these functions are required by the program and to illustrate the sequence in which these functions must be performed. Figure 7–1 contains the structure chart for the program we flowcharted in Chapter 5.

Let's take a closer look at the program's structure chart shown in Figure 7–1 and gain a better understanding of what it is telling us. You will notice that this structure chart has three tiers or levels. The first and second levels of the structure chart are known as the *control levels.* The lowest level is called the *process level.* We will concentrate on the process level when we transition from the structure chart to the flowchart.

The first level of the structure chart shows the name of the program, REPORT.

The second tier shows the MAINLINE components of the program. Remember, the structure chart illustrates the program's organization. Since the program will contain the three basic procedures (INITIALIZATION, PROCESS, and END-OF-JOB) we need to show these in the chart. And since these are the key procedures of the program, we show them on the second tier. You will notice that the decision symbol for END-FLAG is not shown on the structure chart. This is because the decision symbol illustrates how the program will determine if it should continue with PROCESS, or proceed to END-OF-JOB. The structure chart does not address how the program will work.

The third tier contains the processes that must be performed within each of the three main procedures of the program. Let's look at the INITIALIZATION procedure. What functions will INITIALIZATION perform? It must initialize (more on this in later chapters), open files, and read the first record. You will notice that these tasks are displayed in the structure chart in the same order in which they are listed in Exhibit 7–1 (only we excluded the tasks related to processing special files, since this was not needed in this program). This structure chart shows no decisions, no I/O symbols, and no predefined process symbols, because these flowchart symbols show how the program will perform the required tasks. Remember, we are not concerned with how at this point.

Now let's look at PROCESS. When you ask the question, "What is the purpose of this program?", the answer is, "Write a record to a report." Therefore, PROCESS will consist of only two procedures: (1) to write the report, and (2) to read the next record. Do not concern yourself with moving data to the output before writing, or checking for end-of-file when reading. These are considerations only when deciding how the program will perform these tasks. Again, we are concentrating on what PROCESS needs to do, not how. Again, referring to Exhibit 7–1, you will notice that we excluded a number of tasks that this program does not require. You will also see that the two tasks we did select, WRITE and READ, are depicted in the structure chart in the same order in which they are listed in Exhibit 7–1.

Finally, let's look at END-OF-JOB. In this case, all we need to do is close files. In later chapters we will discover several more tasks that are put in END-OF-JOB.

Exhibit 7–1
PROGRAM
FUNCTIONALITY
CHECKLIST

INITIALIZATION

Initialize: Set all program-created variables to their beginning values. Program variables include logical data (such as END-FLAG), counters, derived data not yet computed, and arrays (to be discussed later).

Open Files: Open all files required by the program.

Process Special Files: Programs that will process special files, such as a parameter file or a file that will be loaded to an array, will generally process these files in the INITIALIZATION section of the program.

Read Input File: Always read the first record of your input file in INITIALIZATION, and always make the READ the last item in the section.

PROCESS

Record Selection: In some programs, we will choose to process only those records that meet certain criteria. When designing an extract program, you must decide when to use a record and when that record should be bypassed. This determination is normally the first item in PROCESS. We will discuss this further in Chapter 9.

Control-Break: Control-break is a method of breaking a report into manageable segments, often with subtotals. In Chapters 11 and 12 we will learn about control-break. You will see that control-break logic will fit into PROCESS at this point.

Calculate: If any derived data is be computed for the record being processed, it is computed at this point.

Accumulate: If any totals are to be computed, then the accumulation of these totals will take place after calculate. Accumulation computes totals that span multiple records.

Write: Write any output by the program. This output may be a line on a report or a record written to an output file.

Read Input File: PROCESS must always read the next record on the input file, and this READ is always the last thing done.

END-OF-JOB

Major Break Routine: We will discuss this in Chapter 11.

Final Calculations: Some programs may require us to perform some calculations that cannot be performed until we have reached the end of our data. When we have such a requirement, these calculations are performed in EOJ.

Print Final Totals: Print any and all final totals required by the program.

Close Files: Close all files opened by the program.

TRANSITION TO THE FLOWCHART

You cannot efficiently design your program if you allow yourself to consider the entire program at once. Instead, you must focus on each individual component of the program. Concentrate on how you will accomplish each of the processes identified in the structure chart.

Using the structure chart in Figure 7–1, let's take a look at how the transition to the flowchart is performed. To keep the transition simple, focus only on the procedure you are flowcharting and do not allow yourself to become overwhelmed with the entire program.

Build MAINLINE

Always begin your program with MAINLINE. Using a terminal symbol as the entry point, label the mainline routine with the program name, REPORT. Next, complete MAINLINE with the three sections. When performing the transition from the structure chart to the flowchart, you must consider how your program will do the work. The MAINLINE routine must have a decision to determine whether to perform PROCESS or proceed to END-OF-JOB. During this transition, you must add any and all step-by-step instructions and decisions required to show how the program will work. Figure 7–2 shows the relationship between the first two tiers of the structure chart and the flowchart.

Build INITIALIZATION

Next, we flowchart INITIALIZATION. Look at the structure chart in Figure 7–1 to determine what this procedure needs to accomplish. INITIALIZATION will

Figure 7–1
Structure chart for program flowcharted in Chapter 5

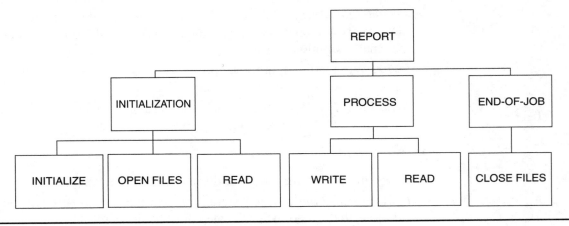

Figure 7–2
Transition from structure
chart to flowchart
(MAINLINE)

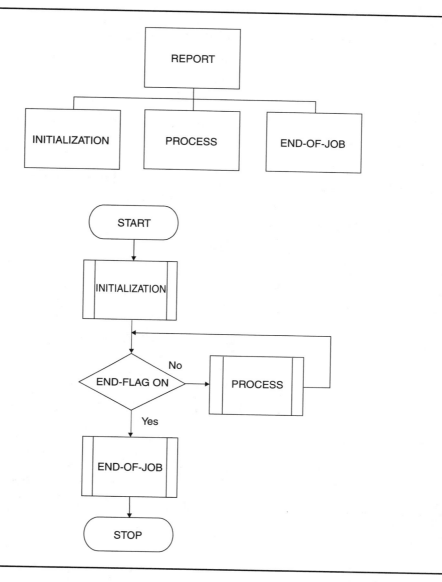

initialize, open files, and read the first record. Since the program will read records as part of INITIALIZATION and PROCESS, we will define a READ procedure, and refer to it using a predefined process. Figure 7–3 illustrates the relationship between the structure chart and the flowchart for INITIALIZATION.

Build PROCESS

In this program, PROCESS performs two functions. It will write a line on the report and read the next record on the file. Although WRITE is performed in only one place and is fairly simple, we will define a procedure called WRITE and refer to it using a predefined process symbol. The relationship between the structure chart and the flowchart for PROCESS is shown in Figure 7–4.

Figure 7–3
Transition from structure chart to flowchart (INTIALIZATION)

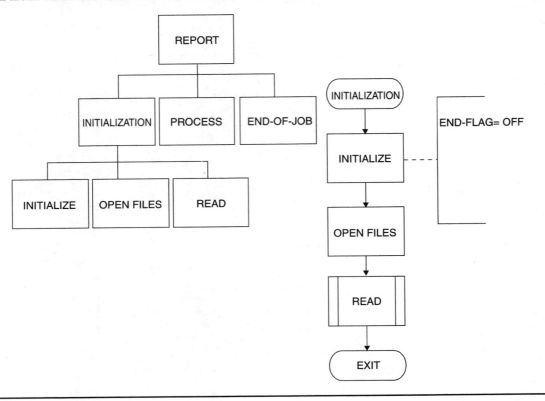

Figure 7–4
Transition from structure chart to flowchart (PROCESS)

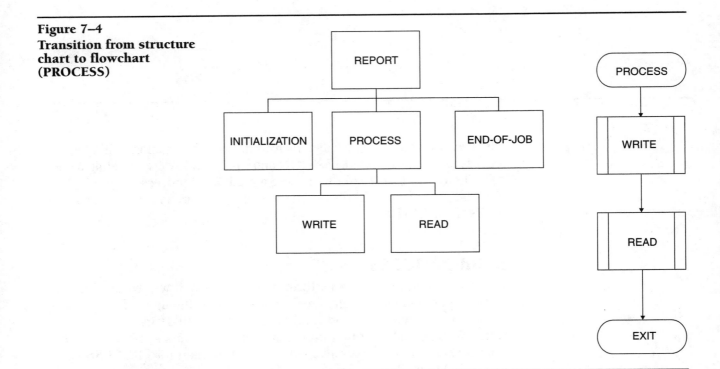

WRITE and READ Procedures

Next we will flowchart the WRITE and READ procedures. Figure 7–5 illustrates this part of the flowchart. Notice the consistency among the required processes shown on the structure chart, the procedures identified within the predefined process symbols of the flowchart, and the procedure names themselves as identified by the terminals.

Figure 7–5
Transition from structure chart to flowchart (expanding PROCESS)

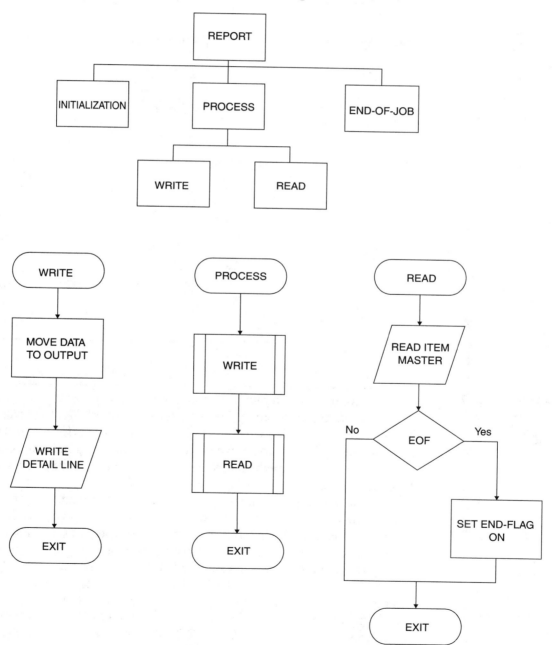

Build END-OF-JOB

Finally, we flowchart EOJ with the single process required by this program. Figure 7–6 illustrates this section of the flowchart. In future chapters, we will see this part of the program expanded and doing much more work.

Figure 7–6
Transition from structure chart to flowchart (END-OF-JOB)

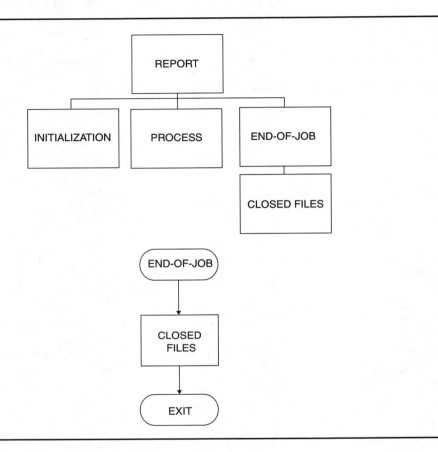

BUILDING THE STRUCTURE CHART

Now that we have a better understanding of the structure chart, let's build a second structure chart from the specifications in Exhibit 7–2. (See page 67.) We begin by determining what tasks the program must perform in order to create the desired report. After we decide what processing must be accomplished and the order in which this processing must occur, we can construct the structure chart.

The first step of program design is to complete the mapping process outlined in Chapter 3. Using the program specifications shown in Exhibit 7–2, we map the data as illustrated in Figure 7–7. As you can see, we have identified three derived data fields that must be calculated in this program.

With this complete map in mind, let's take a moment to review Exhibit 7–1 again. This provides us with the list of processes we may need and the sequence in which these processes are normally performed.

As with all programs, this program will contain the three fundamental procedures: INITIALIZATION, PROCESS, and END-OF-JOB. Let's see what processing tasks these three sections will perform.

Figure 7–7
Results of data mapping for example program

Output Field	Source	Derived Computation	Totals
SPORT CODE	SPRTCD		
EQUIPMENT TYPE	ETYP		
ITEM NMBR	ITMNBR		
ITEM DESCRIPTION	DESC		
QTY SOLD	QTY		
SALES AMOUNT	SLSAMT		
COMMISSIONS PAID	Derived	SLSAMT * CMPCT	
TOTAL COST	Derived	QTY * PRCHCST	
PROFIT	Derived	SLSAMT – (COMM-PD + COST)	

INITIALIZATION

INITIALIZATION will perform the following tasks:

- INITIALIZE variables.
- OPEN FILES.
- READ the first record.

PROCESS

Referring to the program specification and the results of the mapping step, we see that we must compute the value for three fields. These fields are Commissions Paid, Total Cost, and Profit.

Computations and formulas provided in the program specification define how derived data is computed. When building the structure chart, we need only concern ourselves with what we need to accomplish, not how to accomplish it. Let's look at the task list for PROCESS as defined in Exhibit 7–1, and determine what processing we might need for this program.

We do not require record selection because all records will be processed. Control breaks are also not required by this project. We do have three fields that we must compute, so CALCULATE will be required. We have no to-tals to accumulate, so we can omit the accumulation step. We do need to WRITE the report, and we always conclude PROCESS with READ.

After reviewing the potential tasks, we have determined that PROCESS will perform the following functions:

- CALCULATE derived data.
- WRITE a print line.
- READ another record.

Decomposing Procedures

Some procedures of a program are straightforward and require no additional design information (for example, INITIALIZE and OPEN FILES). Other procedures, such as WRITE and READ, remain consistent from one pro-gram to another. Further details of these procedures are not necessary. How-ever, calculating derived data is not self-defining. Calculations can change from program to program and we have discovered that the sequence in which derived data must be calculated can be critical. In reviewing the for-mulas provided you will see that Commissions Paid is a product of mul-tiplying Sales Amount and Commission Percent. Both of these fields are contained in the input record. Likewise, Total Cost is calculated by mul-tiplying Quantity Sold and Purchase Cost, both of which are in the input record. However, you will see that the formula for Profit uses both Commissions Paid and Total Cost. Therefore, before we can compute Profit, we must compute Commissions Paid and Total Cost. We have now identified three tasks and the relative order in which these tasks must be completed. Therefore, we will decompose the CALCULATE process into more finite processes:

CALCULATE
- Calculate Commissions Paid.
- Calculate Total Cost.
- Calculate Profit.

When finished, PROCESS will contain the following tasks:

CALCULATE
- Commissions Paid.
- Total Cost.
- Profit.

WRITE
READ

END-OF-JOB

Finally, EOJ has not changed since the first example. In this program, EOJ simply closes the files.

Figure 7–8
Structure chart for example program

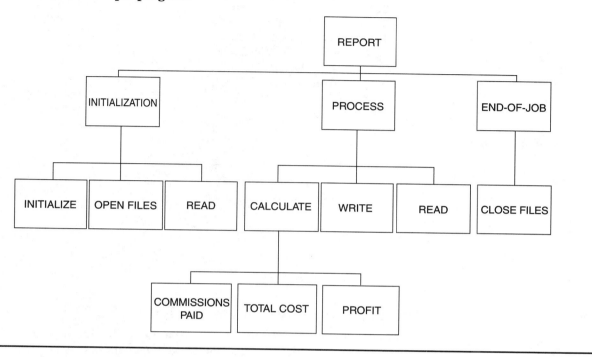

Completed Structure Chart

The final structure chart for this program is shown in Figure 7–8. As you can see, the structure chart shows only the tasks the program must perform and the sequence in which these tasks are to be performed. No formulas are shown, no decisions are shown, and there is no implied logical path.

Exhibit 7–2
**PROGRAM
SPECIFICATION FOR
EXAMPLE PROGRAM**

Objective

Produce a report that will list, for each item, the quantity sold and the profit earned on the sales.

Processing Requirements

1. For each record, calculate the following:
   - Commissions Paid = Sales Amount * Commission Percent.
   - Total Cost = Quantity Sold * Purchase Cost.
   - Profit = Sales Amount – (Commissions Paid + Total Cost).

2. Write the report showing all of the information shown on the printer spacing chart.

3. Single-space the report.

SALES RECORD

01-02	SPORT CODE		SPRTCD
03-04	EQUIPMENT TYPE		ETYP
05-09	ITEM NUMBER		ITMNBR
10-24	ITEM DESCRIPTION		DESC
25-29	QUANTITY SOLD	(5.0)	QTY
30-38	SALES AMOUNT	(9.2)	SLSAMT
39-41	COMMISSION PERCENT	(3.3)	CMPCT
42-48	PURCHASE COST	(7.2)	PRCHCST
49-60	Unused		

Printer Spacing Chart

```
                                                                                   1111111111111111111111111111111111
          11111111112222222222333333333344444444445555555555666666666677777777778888888888999999999900000000001111111111222222222333
 12345678901234567890123456789012345678901234567890123456789012345678901234567890123456789012345678901234567890123456789012345678901234567890

RUN  MM/DD/YY  HH:MM                          ACME DISTRIBUTORS                                            PAGE ZZZZ9
                                               SALES REPORT

     SPORT    EQUIP    ITEM                         QUANTITY      SALES         COMMISSIONS     TOTAL
     CODE     TYPE     NMBR    ITEM DESCRIPTION      SOLD         AMOUNT        PAID            COST        PROFIT
      XX       XX      XXXXX   XXXXXXXXXXXXXXX        ZZ,ZZZ-      Z,ZZZ,ZZZ.99-  ZZZ,ZZZ.99-   ZZZ,ZZZ.99-  ZZZ,ZZZ.99-
      XX       XX      XXXXX   XXXXXXXXXXXXXXX        ZZ,ZZZ-      Z,ZZZ,ZZZ.99-  ZZZ,ZZZ.99-   ZZZ,ZZZ.99-  ZZZ,ZZZ.99-
      XX       XX      XXXXX   XXXXXXXXXXXXXXX        ZZ,ZZZ-      Z,ZZZ,ZZZ.99-  ZZZ,ZZZ.99-   ZZZ,ZZZ.99-  ZZZ,ZZZ.99-
```

Completing the Program Design

We will develop the flowchart for this program in Chapter 8. Also in Chapter 8, we will learn how derived data and logical data are managed within the program. We will also introduce page headings and control page overflow.

Before proceeding with the transition to the flowchart, we need to first review the structure chart for adherence to the basic structure design philosophy. There are three important concepts that we use to test compliance to the principles of structure design:

Span of Control

Span of control is defined as the family of processes that fall under a control level procedure. INITIALIZATION, PROCESS, END-OF-JOB, and even CALCULATE are considered to be at the control level because each of these have been decomposed to a lower level. Processes within these procedures define the function's span of control.

Cohesion

If designed properly, you will find that all tasks within a procedure relate directly to the objective of that procedure. *Cohesion* refers to the level in which these tasks bind together. For example, in a CALCULATE procedure, all tasks should relate specifically to calculating derived data. A WRITE process should never appear in CALCULATE because it would not directly support the objective of the CALCULATION procedure. It is important to remember that in structured programming *procedures will perform one task, and one task only*. Review your structure chart to ensure that no procedure is performing tasks unrelated to its purpose. This becomes very important as our program designs continue to grow and become more complex.

Coupling

Coupling refers to the connection or communication between tasks or procedures of a program. One example of coupling between procedures is the communication between READ and MAINLINE by way of END-FLAG. Likewise, data coupling can occur between tasks. For example, in the structure chart we just completed, Commissions Paid and Total Cost are both passed to the process that computes Profit. Understanding the coupling concept can help to ensure that processes are being performed in the correct sequence.

SUMMARY

In this chapter we learned how to organize our thoughts and build the structure chart for a program. The structure chart illustrates program organization, required processes of the program, and shows the sequence in which the processes must be performed. We also learned the basic fundamentals of structured program design and how we can evaluate the quality of the design by ensuring that functions and processes adhere to cohesion and coupling. We also learned how to make the transition from the structure chart to the flowchart.

REVIEW QUESTIONS

1. What is the purpose of a structure chart?
2. How do you use the structure chart when flowcharting?
3. What is cohesion?
4. What is coupling?
5. What is meant by span of control?
6. Are formulas required for calculations shown in the structure chart?
7. Why would you decompose CALCULATE into more finite processes, but not decompose READ?
8. Why is it important to maintain consistency in procedure names between the structure chart and the flowchart?

PROJECT 1

Objective

This program will provide a report showing customer sales of current year and prior year.

This program will be preceded by another program that builds the file containing year to date sales by month. The file will contain sales only for current year and prior year through the most recently completed month. Therefore, total year to date sales for current and prior years can be computed by adding all twelve months together, regardless of time of year.

Processing Requirements

1. Process all records on the file.

2. Use the following formulas:
- Prior Year Sales = the sum of the sales for all twelve months of the prior year.
- Current Year Sales = the sum of the sales for all twelve months of the current year.
- Sales Increase = Current Year Sales − Prior Year Sales.
- Percent Increase = (Sales Increase / Prior Year Sales) * 100.

3. Print the report as shown on the printer spacing chart.

4. The report will be single-spaced.

Assignment

1. Start by mapping the output report. Identify all source data, including derived data and the formula for computing the derived data.

2. Build the structure chart for this program.

CUSTOMER SALES FILE

01-02	REGION		CS-RGN
03-06	CUSTOMER NUMBER		CS-CUST
07-31	CUSTOMER NAME		CS-NAME
32-33	SPORT CODE		CS-SPRTCD
34-35	EQUIPMENT TYPE		CS-ETYP
36-43	CURRENT YEAR JANUARY	(8.2)	CS-CYJAN
44-51	CURRENT YEAR FEBRUARY	(8 2)	CS-CYFEB
52-59	CURRENT YEAR MARCH	(8.2)	CS-CYMAR
60-67	CURRENT YEAR APRIL	(8.2)	CS-CYAPR
68-75	CURRENT YEAR MAY	(8.2)	CS-CYMAY
76-83	CURRENT YEAR JUNE	(8.2)	CS-CYJUN
84-91	CURRENT YEAR JULY	(8.2)	CS-CYJUL
92-99	CURRENT YEAR AUGUST	(8.2)	CS-CYAUG
100-107	CURRENT YEAR SEPTEMBER	(8.2)	CS-CYSEP
108-115	CURRENT YEAR OCTOBER	(8.2)	CS-CYOCT
116-123	CURRENT YEAR NOVEMBER	(8.2)	CS-CYNOV
124-131	CURRENT YEAR DECEMBER	(8.2)	CS-CYDEC
132-139	PRIOR YEAR JANUARY	(8.2)	CS-PYJAN
140-147	PRIOR YEAR FEBRUARY	(8.2)	CS-PYFEB
148-155	PRIOR YEAR MARCH	(8.2)	CS-PYMAR
156-163	PRIOR YEAR APRIL	(8.2)	CS-PYAPR
164-171	PRIOR YEAR MAY	(8.2)	CS-PYMAY
172-179	PRIOR YEAR JUNE	(8.2)	CS-PYJUN
180-187	PRIOR YEAR JULY	(8.2)	CS-PYJUL
188-195	PRIOR YEAR AUGUST	(8.2)	CS-PYAUG
196-203	PRIOR YEAR SEPTEMBER	(8.2)	CS-PYSEP
204-211	PRIOR YEAR OCTOBER	(8.2)	CS-PYOCT
212-219	PRIOR YEAR NOVEMBER	(8.2)	CS-PYNOV
220-227	PRIOR YEAR DECEMBER	(8.2)	CS-PYDEC
228-250	Unused		

Printer Spacing Chart

```
                                                                                              11111111111111111111111111111111
          111111111122222222223333333333444444444455555555556666666666777777777788888888889999999999000000000011111111112222222222
          1234567890123456789012345678901234556789012345678901234567890123456789012345678901234567890123456789012345678901234567890123456789

RUN MM/DD/YY                               ACME DISTRIBUTORS                                                        PAGE ZZZZ9
TIME HH:MM                               CUSTOMER SALES REPORT


                                  SPORT   EQUIP      CURR YEAR       PRIOR YEAR        SALES        PERCENT
REGION   CUSTOMER   CUSTOMER NAME  CODE   CLASS        SALES           SALES         INCREASE       INCREASE

  XX      XXXXX     XXXXXXXXXXXXXXXXXXXXXXXXXXX   XX     XX     Z,ZZZ,ZZZ.99-    Z,ZZZ,ZZZ.99-    ZZZ,ZZZ.99-     ZZZZ.9-
  XX      XXXXX     XXXXXXXXXXXXXXXXXXXXXXXXXXX   XX     XX     Z,ZZZ,ZZZ.99-    Z,ZZZ,ZZZ.99-    ZZZ,ZZZ.99-     ZZZZ.9-
  XX      XXXXX     XXXXXXXXXXXXXXXXXXXXXXXXXXX   XX     XX     Z,ZZZ,ZZZ.99-    Z,ZZZ,ZZZ.99-    ZZZ,ZZZ.99-     ZZZZ.9-
```

PROJECT 2

Objective

This program will produce a report providing the relative profit of the product sold by Acme Distributors.

Processing Requirements

1. Process all records on the item master file.

2. Produce a report containing the following information:
   - Item number.
   - Item description.
   - Retail price.
   - Purchase cost.
   - Commission percent.
   - Commission paid.
   - Profit.
   - Profit margin.

3. Use the following formulas:
   - Commission Paid = Retail Price * Commission Percent.
   - Profit = Price – (Purchase Cost + Commission Paid).
   - Profit Margin = (Profit / Retail Price) * 100.

4. The report will be single spaced.

Assignment

1. Create the printer spacing chart for this report.

2. Map the output data to the source data, including derived data and the formula for computing the derived data.

3. Build the structure chart for this program.

ITEM MASTER

01-05	ITEM NUMBER		IM-ITEM
06-20	DESCRIPTION		IM-DESC
21-22	SPORT CODE		IM-SPRTCD
23-24	EQUIPMENT TYPE		IM-ETYP
25-27	COMMISSION PERCENT	(3.3)	IM-PCT

```
28-33  VENDOR                        IM-VNDR
34-40  PURCHASE COST        (7.2)    IM-COST
41-47  RETAIL PRICE         (7.2)    IM-PRICE
48-52  QUANTITY ON HAND     (5.0)    IM-QOH
53-57  ORDER POINT          (5.0)    IM-ORDPT
58-62  ORDER QUANTITY       (5.0)    IM-ORD-QTY
63-70  Unused
```

Part III

Basic Program Design Techniques

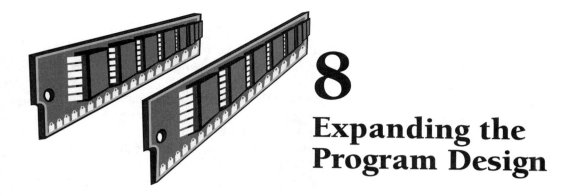

8
Expanding the Program Design

OBJECTIVES

- Understanding the process of page break and page overflow.
- Understanding the creation of derived data.
- Understanding how and when derived data is calculated within the program.

INTRODUCTION

Most of the programs you will be developing in your career will be far more complicated than the one we completed in Chapter 5. Chapter 7 hinted at the first enhancement, when we added the calculation requirements to the structure chart. This is only the beginning of the program expansions we will be addressing over the next several chapters.

In this chapter, we will cover two topics. The first is the steps required to print report titles and page headings at the top of each page of the report. The second topic will be how and where calculations, such as those added to the structure chart in Chapter 7, are included in the flowchart.

For starters, take a look at the program specifications in Exhibit 8–1. (See page 78.) You will notice that these specifications are the same as those in Chapter 7. In this chapter, we will complete the program we designed in the previous chapter.

PAGE BREAKS AND HEADERS

If you look at reports printed on a computer, you will notice two very important features. First, all pages have the report name and column headings at the top. Second, the information on each report stops before the end of the page, and will never print over the paper's perforation. How is this accomplished?

Before laser printers, standard computer paper used by computer printers was 16 inches wide and 11 inches long. The printers would print six lines per inch. This allowed the printer to print as many as 66 lines on a single page. The printer was already adjusted to print the first line one inch from the top of each page. This one-inch margin at the top of the report eliminated 6 possible print lines, and left 60 remaining. We would also leave a one-inch margin at the bottom of the page. This reduced the available print space by another 6 lines, leaving us with a maximum of 54 lines for printing.

Today, most of our printing is performed on laser printers that print on a standard $8^1/2''$ by $11''$ sheet of paper. Using a standard font, you will find that these laser printers are scaled so that they still print a maximum of 66 lines per page, and still provide a margin at the top eliminating 6 print lines. Likewise we will still keep a margin at the bottom of the page equal to 6 print lines. Therefore, under normal conditions, you do not need to be aware of the type of printer you will be using.

Now let's look at the printer spacing chart defined by the program specifications in Exhibit 8–1. Assuming that the first line of the title will be printed on the first available print line, there are a total of 6 lines reserved for the headers, including the blank line preceding the first detail line. This leaves 48 available print lines for the detailed section of the report. We now know that we can print no more than 48 detail lines, without encroaching on the bottom margin of the report.

Now that we know how many lines we can put on a page, let's discuss how we can control the number of lines we print and how we put the headers at the top.

Page Overflow

As we print each detail line, we will need to count the number of lines we have printed on that page. Once we have printed the 48 lines available, we must perform a routine that will print the headers for the next page. To do this, we will create a logical data variable called LINE-CNT that we use to count the number of lines printed to a page. Each time a line is printed, we will increment LINE-CNT by 1. When LINE-CNT is 48, we will have printed the maximum number of detail lines on that page.

Printing Headers

We will define a procedure within our programs to print the report headers. Let's look at what this procedure must do. Look at the upper right-hand corner printer spacing chart in Exhibit 8–1. You will notice that the page number is displayed. How do we keep track of the page number? We create the logical variable PAGE-CNT, which we will increment by 1 each time the headers are printed.

After we print the headers, we will need to set LINE-CNT to 0. This is required to properly count the next page. Remember, we printed our headers because LINE-CNT was 48. If we do not set LINE-CNT to 0, it will continue to hold the value 48.

The WRITE Procedure

Figure 8–1 contains the new WRITE procedure, flowchart, and pseudo code. We will use this version of WRITE for the remainder of this book. You will notice that WRITE now performs a procedure called HDR-RTN. HDR-RTN will likewise remain constant for the remainder of this book.

Figure 8–1
**Standard WRITE and
HEADER-ROUTINE/
(HDR-RTN) for reporting
programs**

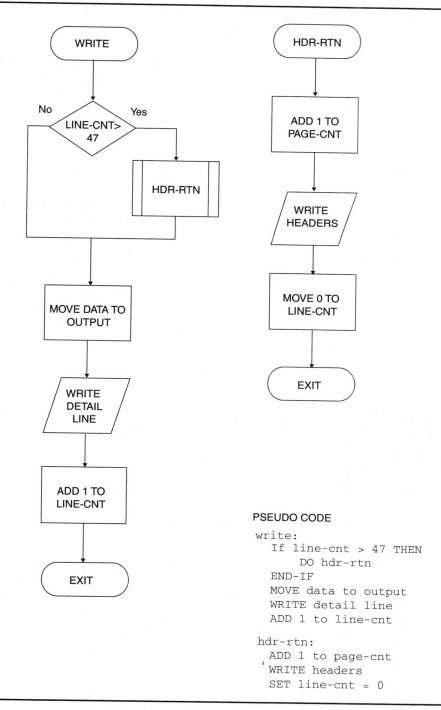

PSEUDO CODE

```
write:
    If line-cnt > 47 THEN
        DO hdr-rtn
    END-IF
    MOVE data to output
    WRITE detail line
    ADD 1 to line-cnt

hdr-rtn:
    ADD 1 to page-cnt
    WRITE headers
    SET line-cnt = 0
```

   The first step of WRITE will determine if it is time to print headers. This is done by determining if LINE-CNT has exceeded 47 (indicating that we have printed 48 lines). It is safer to check for LINE-CNT > 47, than LINE-CNT = 48. Although it will make no difference in this program, it will in programs we design in later chapters. Therefore, it is best to get into the habit of always checking for "greater than" when determining page over-flow.

If LINE-CNT has not exceeded 47. we print the report detail line. If LINE-CNT has exceeded 47, we perform HDR-RTN (header routine) prior to printing the detail line. Let's look at HDR-RTN. First, it increments PAGE-CNT by 1. We then print the headers. Finally, we set LINE-CNT to 0.

Printing Headers on the First Page

With the exception of the first page, we have successfully determined how to print the headers on each page. In order to ensure printing the headers on the first page, we need to initialize LINE-CNT to some number greater than 47. This will allow us to print the headers without making any changes to the program. Always initialize LINE-CNT to 99 in the INITIALIZATION section of your program. This will ensure that the first time we perform WRITE, we recognize the need to print the headers (if LINE-CNT is 99, then the condition LINE-CNT > 47 will be YES). Although setting LINE-CNT to any value greater than 47 will work in this program, other programs could be 48, or 49, or some other value. Initializing LINE-CNT to 99 will always work. It is a good idea to get into the habit of doing what always works.

Exhibit 8–1
**PROGRAM
SPECIFICATION FOR
EXAMPLE PROGRAM**

Objective

Produce a report that will list, for each item, the quantity sold and the profit earned on the sales.

Processing Requirements

1. Process all records on the file.
2. For each record read, calculate the following:
   - Commissions Paid = Sales Amount * Commissions Percent.
   - Total Cost = Quantity Sold * Purchase Cost.
   - Profit = Sales Amount – (Commissions Paid + Total Cost).
3. Write the report showing all of the information shown on the printer spacing chart.
4. Single-space the report.

SALES RECORD

01-02	SPORT CODE		SPRTCD
03-04	EQUIPMENT TYPE		ETYP
05-09	ITEM NUMBER		ITEM
10-24	ITEM DESCRIPTION		DESC
25-29	QUANTITY SOLD	(5.0)	QTY
30-38	SALES AMOUNT	(9.2)	SLSAMT
39-41	COMMISSION PERCENT	(3.3)	CMPCT
42-48	PURCHASE COST	(7.2)	PRCHCST
49-60	Unused		

Printer Spacing Chart

```
             1111111111222222222233333333334444444444555555555566666666667777777777888888888899999999990000000000111111111111111111111111111111
    1234567890123456789012345678901234567890123456789012345678901234567890123456789012345678901234567890123456789012345678901234567890

RUN  MM/DD/YY   HH:MM                                    ACME DISTRIBUTORS                                              PAGE ZZZZ9
                                                          SALES REPORT

     SPORT     EQUIP     ITEM                        QUANTITY       SALES           COMMISSIONS       TOTAL
     CODE      TYPE      NMBR    ITEM DESCRIPTION       SOLD        AMOUNT            PAID            COST          PROFIT

      XX        XX      XXXXX   XXXXXXXXXXXXXXX       ZZ,ZZZ-     Z,ZZZ,ZZZ.99-    ZZZ,ZZZ.99-     ZZZ,ZZZ.99-   ZZZ,ZZZ.99-
      XX        XX      XXXXX   XXXXXXXXXXXXXXX       ZZ,ZZZ-     Z,ZZZ,ZZZ.99-    ZZZ,ZZZ.99-     ZZZ,ZZZ.99-   ZZZ,ZZZ.99-
      XX        XX      XXXXX   XXXXXXXXXXXXXXX       ZZ,ZZZ-     Z,ZZZ,ZZZ.99-    ZZZ,ZZZ.99-     ZZZ,ZZZ.99-   ZZZ,ZZZ.99-
```

CREATION OF DERIVED DATA

Before continuing, let's review the specifications for the program we are going to use as the sample for this discussion. Exhibit 8-1 contains the program specifications. Figure 8–2 contains the structure chart. This is the same structure chart built in Chapter 7.

After reviewing the specifications (Exhibit 8–1), the data map (Figure 7–7 in Chapter 7), and the structure chart (Figure 8–2), we see that there are three pieces of information that are required on the report, but not provided in the input data. This information is Commissions Paid, Total Cost, and Profit. As we discussed in Chapter 1, fields such as Commissions Paid, Total Cost, and Profit are called derived data, because they are derived from a calculation using available data.

We illustrate a computation of derived data by using a process symbol along with the formula required to perform the calculation. As we look at the structure chart, we see that the computations are performed in the

Figure 8–2
Structure chart for example program

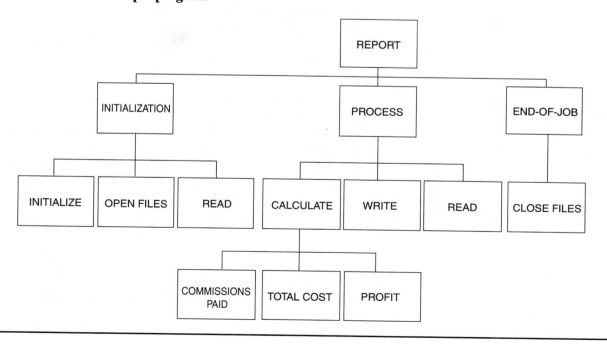

Figure 8–3
CALCULATE procedure
for sample program

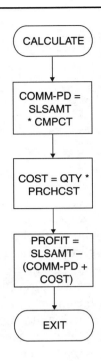

PSEUDO CODE

```
calculate:
  SET comm-pd = slsamt * cmpct
  SET cost = qty * prchcst
  SET profit = slsamt -(comm-pd + cost)
```

CALCULATE procedure. Since we are calculating three fields, we will use a sequence structure consisting of three processes within the procedure CALCULATE. Figure 8–3 shows how CALCULATE will look.

CHANGES TO THE FLOWCHART

Now that we have isolated and discussed how headers are printed and how derived data is computed, let's insert these new components into the flowchart. Back in Chapter 5, we constructed a very similar flowchart. The only differences were that these two components were not included. (Refer to Figure 5–2 in Chapter 5.) You will notice that Figure 8–4 will look very similar to Figure 5–2 in Chapter 5, with the exception that CALCULATE is included, and WRITE is expanded.

Notice also the change to PROCESS. The structure chart in Figure 8–2 defines PROCESS as performing CALCULATE, WRITE, and READ. Therefore, when flowcharting PROCESS, we must now incorporate all of these steps. And of course, CALCULATE must precede WRITE. This is because we must calculate any data required for the output before we can write the output.

Figure 8–4
Complete flowchart for example program

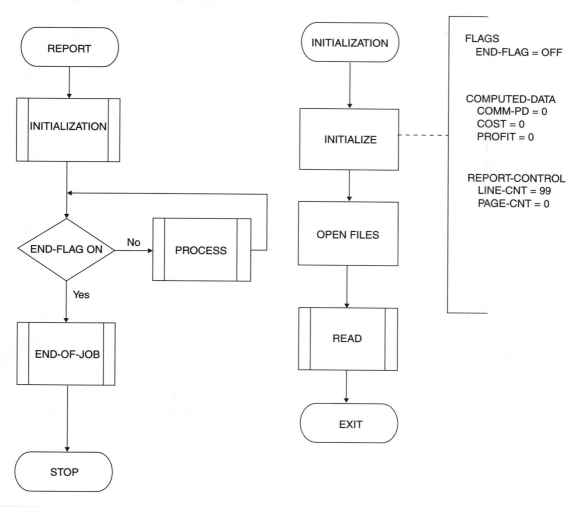

(continued on the next page)

Figure 8–4
(*continued*)

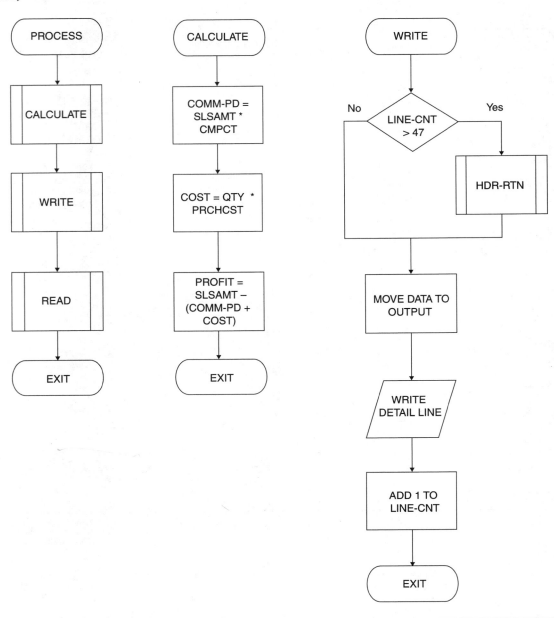

Figure 8–4
(continued)

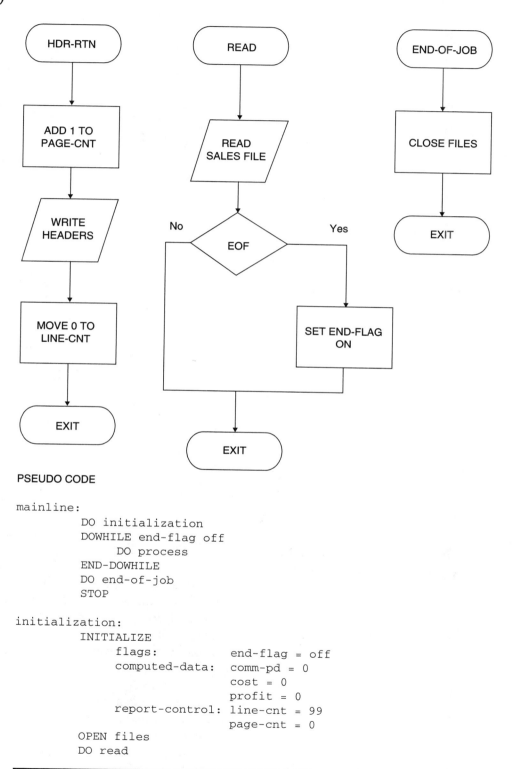

PSEUDO CODE

```
mainline:
        DO initialization
        DOWHILE end-flag off
            DO process
        END-DOWHILE
        DO end-of-job
        STOP

initialization:
        INITIALIZE
            flags:          end-flag = off
            computed-data:  comm-pd = 0
                            cost = 0
                            profit = 0
            report-control: line-cnt = 99
                            page-cnt = 0
        OPEN files
        DO read
```

(continued on the next page)

Figure 8–4
(*continued*)

```
process:
        DO calculate
        DO write
        DO read

calculate:
        LET comm-pd = slsamt * cmpct
        LET cost = qty * prchcst
        LET profit = slsamt - (slsamt + cost)

write:
        IF line-cnt > 47 THEN
            DO hdr-rtn
        END-IF
        MOVE data to output
        WRITE detail line
        ADD 1 to line-cnt

hdr-rtn:
        ADD 1 to page-cnt
        WRITE headers
        LET line-cnt = 0

read:
        READ sales file
            IF end-of-file THEN
                SET end-flag on
            END-IF
        END-READ

end-of-job:
        CLOSE files
```

RECOGNIZING COMMONALITY

As you look at the program presented in Chapter 5, and the flowchart in Figure 8–4, you should notice a number of similarities. In fact, as mentioned earlier, the only difference is the inclusion of the logic to print the report headers and the computation of the derived data. The fact that the remainder of the program is unchanged is not a coincidence.

While every program you write will most likely create an output result different than your previous program, it is important to understand and recognize the similarities between all data processing programs. All programs read input. All programs process that input. And finally, all programs will produce some form of output, whether it is a report or a file.

In an effort to make program design and development as easy as possible, it will behoove you to recognize commonality between all programs. To use an old adage, "Do not reinvent the wheel." Look for parts of programs that will remain constant from program to program and simply copy the logic. Trying to make every program unique and special requires tremendous effort with no benefit. Look for commonality. And whenever possible, copy the flowchart from one program to another, For example, until further notice, assume that all READ procedures will be alike. You will read a file, and if the file is at end, you will set END-FLAG to ON. Likewise, when preparing a report, the WRITE procedure will always be as shown in this chapter. And remember, MAINLINE never changes.

Within PROCESS, look for a common thread in the sequence of events, and follow that sequence whenever possible. You will find that nearly all programs can conform to the template described in Exhibit 7–1 of Chapter 7. Do not hesitate to refer back to this when designing programs. Some programs may require that you customize these procedures; however, this will be rare. Recognize this, and keep your programs consistent. You will reduce your chance of errors. You will better understand what you are doing if you do it consistently and you will be able to design and develop programs more rapidly.

SUMMARY

The maximum number of print lines that are allowed on a single page is 66. Allowing for the top and bottom margins on the page reduces the allowable print lines to 54. Subtracting the number of lines required for the title and header lines from 54 gives us the maximum number of detail lines we can put on one page. We use LINE-CNT to count the number of lines we have printed on a page, and when LINE-CNT reaches the maximum number of detail lines possible, we invoke the header routine to print the headers on the next page. The CALCULATE procedure is used to calculate derived data. The CALCULATE procedure always precedes WRITE. Finally, we learned to recognize the commonality in our programs. While every program we write may perform different functions and produce different reports than the previous program, it is important to realize that nearly all programs are structured the same. Understanding this commonality between programs, and making the decision not to reinvent the wheel with every program you design, will enable you to design and develop programs more rapidly and with fewer errors.

REVIEW QUESTIONS

1. What is the purpose of LINE-CNT?
2. We have learned that most fields are initialized to zero, so why is LINE-CNT initialized to 99?
3. How do you compute the number of print lines that can be printed on a page?
4. Why is the CALCULATE procedure executed before the WRITE procedure?
5. How do you know what sequence calculations should be performed?

PROJECT 1

Objective

This program will provide sales management for Acme Distributors a report showing customer sales of current year and prior year by customer and product line information.

This program will be preceded by another program that builds the file containing year-to-date sales by month. The file will contain sales only for current and prior years through the most recently completed month. Therefore, total year-to-date sales for current and prior years can be computed by adding all twelve months together, regardless of time of year.

Processing Requirements

1. Process all records on the file.
2. Use the following formulas:
   - Prior Year Sales = the sum of the sales for all twelve months of the prior year.
   - Current Year Sales = the sum of the sales for all twelve months of the current year.
   - Sales Increase = Current Year Sales – Prior Year Sales.
   - Percent of increase = (Sales Increase / Prior Year Sales) * 100.
3. Print the report as shown on the printer spacing chart.
4. Report will be single-spaced.

Assignment

1. You should have performed the mapping process, and built the structure chart for this program following Chapter 7. This assignment is to develop the flowchart or pseudo code for this program.

CUSTOMER SALES RECORD

01-02	REGION		CS-RGN
02-06	CUSTOMER NUMBER		CS-CUST
07-31	CUSTOMER NAME		CS-NAME
32-33	SPORT CODE		CS-SPRTCD
34-35	EQUIPMENT TYPE		CS-ETYP
36-43	CURRENT YEAR JANUARY	(8.2)	CS-CYJAN
44-51	CURRENT YEAR FEBRUARY	(8.2)	CS-CYFEB
52-59	CURRENT YEAR MARCH	(8.2)	CS-CYMAR
60-67	CURRENT YEAR APRIL	(8.2)	CS-CYAPR
68-75	CURRENT YEAR MAY	(8.2)	CS-CYMAY
76-83	CURRENT YEAR JUNE	(8.2)	CS-CYJUN
84-91	CURRENT YEAR JULY	(8.2)	CS-CYJUL
92-99	CURRENT YEAR AUGUST	(8.2)	CS-CYAUG
100-107	CURRENT YEAR SEPTEMBER	(8.2)	CS-CYSEP
108-115	CURRENT YEAR OCTOBER	(8.2)	CS-CYOCT
116-123	CURRENT YEAR NOVEMBER	(8.2)	CS-CYNOV
124-131	CURRENT YEAR DECEMBER	(8.2)	CS-CYDEC
132-139	PRIOR YEAR JANUARY	(8.2)	CS-PYJAN
140-147	PRIOR YEAR FEBRUARY	(8.2)	CS-PYFEB
148-155	PRIOR YEAR MARCH	(8.2)	CS-PYMAR

156-163	PRIOR YEAR APRIL	(8.2)	CS-PYAPR
164-171	PRIOR YEAR MAY	(8.2)	CS-PYMAY
172-179	PRIOR YEAR JUNE	(8.2)	CS-PYJUN
180-187	PRIOR YEAR JULY	(8.2)	CS-PYJUL
188-195	PRIOR YEAR AUGUST	(8.2)	CS-PYAUG
196-203	PRIOR YEAR SEPTEMBER	(8.2)	CS-PYSEP
204-211	PRIOR YEAR OCTOBER	(8.2)	CS-PYOCT
212-219	PRIOR YEAR NOVEMBER	(8.2)	CS-PYNOV
220-227	PRIOR YEAR DECEMBER	(8.2)	CS-PYDEC
228-250	Unused		

Printer Spacing Chart

```
          11111111112222222222333333333344444444445555555555666666666677777777778888888888999999999900000000001111111111111111111111111111
 1234567890123456789012345678901234567890123455678901234567890123456789012345678901234567890123456789012345678901234567890123456789

RUN MM/DD/YY
TIME HH:MM                                        ACME DISTRIBUTORS
                                              CUSTOMER SALES REPORT                                                      PAGE ZZZZ9


REGION   CUSTOMER   CUSTOMER NAME              SPORT    EQUIP    CURR YEAR        PRIOR YEAR        SALES         PERCENT
                                               CODE     TYPE     SALES            SALES            INCREASE      INCREASE
  XX      XXXXX     XXXXXXXXXXXXXXXXXXXXXXXXX    XX       XX    Z,ZZZ,ZZZ.99-    Z,ZZZ,ZZZ.99-    ZZZ,ZZZ.99-    ZZZZ.9-
  XX      XXXXX     XXXXXXXXXXXXXXXXXXXXXXXXX    XX       XX    Z,ZZZ,ZZZ.99-    Z,ZZZ,ZZZ.99-    ZZZ,ZZZ.99-    ZZZZ.9-
  XX      XXXXX     XXXXXXXXXXXXXXXXXXXXXXXXX    XX       XX    Z,ZZZ,ZZZ.99-    Z,ZZZ,ZZZ.99-    ZZZ,ZZZ.99-    ZZZZ.9-
```

PROJECT 2

Objective

This program will produce a report providing the relative profit of product sold by Acme Distributors.

Processing Requirements

1. Process all records on the item master file.
2. Produce a report containing the following information:
   - Item number.
   - Item description.
   - Retail price.
   - Purchase cost.
   - Commission percent.
   - Commission paid.
   - Profit.
   - Profit margin.
3. Use the following formulas:
   - Commission paid = Retail Price * Commission Percent.
   - Profit = Price – (Purchase Cost + Commission Paid).
   - Profit margin = (Profit / Price) * 100.
4. The report will be single-spaced.

Assignment

1. You should have created the printer spacing chart, performed the mapping process, and built the structure chart for this program

following Chapter 7. This assignment is to develop the flowchart or pseudo code for this program.

ITEM MASTER

01-05	ITEM NUMBER		IM-ITEM
06-20	DESCRIPTION		IM-DESC
21-22	SPORT CODE		IM-SPRTCD
23-24	EQUIPMENT TYPE		IM-ETYP
25-27	COMMISSION PERCENT	(3.3)	IM-PCT
28-33	VENDOR		IM-VNDR
34-40	PURCHASE COST	(7.2)	IM-COST
41-47	RETAIL PRICE	(7.2)	IM-PRICE
48-52	QUANTITY ON HAND	(5.0)	IM-QOH
53-57	ORDER POINT	(5.0)	IM-ORDPT
58-62	ORDER QUANTITY	(5.0)	IM-ORD-QTY
63-70	Unused		

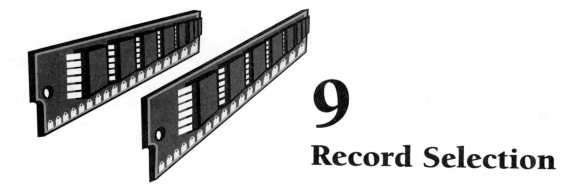

9
Record Selection

OBJECTIVES

- Understanding the record selection process.
- Understanding the structure of a selection program.
- Understanding AND decisions and OR decisions.
- Understanding the parameter file's role in the selection program.

INTRODUCTION

Many of the reports you will design will contain only a subset of the records on a file. Programs producing these reports will read the entire file and decide which records should be printed and which should not be printed. Such programs employ the *record selection technique.* These programs read the entire file and process only records that conform to specific selection criteria. In this chapter, we will review the selection process. We will see how the program is structured and how the selection logic is incorporated into the program.

THE SELECTION PROCESS

Record selection is the technique used to determine which records on a file should be processed by the program. Selection logic will be added to the program and each record will be tested against this selection criteria. All records satisfying the criteria will be processed. Those records that do not satisfy the selection criteria will not be processed.

In most cases, the selection process will be the first task performed in the PROCESS procedure. This is to ensure that we either select or reject the record prior to performing any other processing on that record.

Let's take a look at a simple reporting program where only selected records will be printed. Exhibit 9–1 contains the program specification for this example. Take a moment to review the program specification. As always, we will begin the design process by building the structure chart. After completing the structure chart, we will flowchart the appropriate procedures and see how the selection process fits into the programming structures we have already learned.

Exhibit 9–1
PROGRAM SPECIFICATIONS FOR EXAMPLE RECORD SELECTION PROGRAM

Objective

The Marketing department will begin a campaign to sell a new product. This product will most likely be sold in department stores. In order to support the Marketing department in this effort, they have requested that we produce a report showing all department store customers on the customer file.

Processing Requirements

1. Read the customer file.
2. Select and print all department stores.
3. Department stores will have a customer type of DS.
4. Print report shown on the printer spacing chart.

CUSTOMER MASTER RECORD

01-05	CUSTOMER NUMBER	CUST NO
06-30	CUSTOMER NAME	NAME
31-50	STREET ADDRESS	ADDR
51-65	CITY	CITY
66-67	STATE	ST
68-72	ZIP CODE	ZIP
73-74	CUSTOMER TYPE	CTYPE
75-76	REGION	RGN
77-78	AREA	AREA
79-83	HEADQUARTER ID	HQ
84-91	LAST PURCHASE (YYYYMMDD)	LSTPRCH
92-100	Unused	

Printer Spacing Chart

```
                                                                           1111111111111111111111111111111111
         1111111111222222222233333333334444444444555555555566666666667777777777888888888899999999990000000000111111111122222222
123456789012345678901234567890123456789012345678901234567890123456789012345678901234567890123456789012345678901234567890123456789

RUN  MM/DD/YY  HH:MM                       ACME DISTRIBUTORS                                          PAGE ZZZZ9
                                        TARGET CUSTOMER REPORT

         CUSTOMER
         NUMBER   NAME                      STREET ADDRESS        CITY             STATE  ZIP    REGION

          XXXXX   XXXXXXXXXXXXXXXXXXXXXXXXX  XXXXXXXXXXXXXXXXXXX   XXXXXXXXXXXXXX    XX    XXXXX    XX
          XXXXX   XXXXXXXXXXXXXXXXXXXXXXXXX  XXXXXXXXXXXXXXXXXXX   XXXXXXXXXXXXXX    XX    XXXXX    XX
          XXXXX   XXXXXXXXXXXXXXXXXXXXXXXXX  XXXXXXXXXXXXXXXXXXX   XXXXXXXXXXXXXX    XX    XXXXX    XX
```

Structure Chart Considerations

How do we determine if a record selection is required? Two elements of the program specification will lead you to this conclusion. Items (2) and (3) of the program specification indicate that we will have to select the records where the customer type is department store (DS). In general, if a program specification does not indicate specific records to be processed, then the program should process all records.

Refer back to Exhibit 7–1, in Chapter 7. This exhibit provided us a list of the tasks performed in each of the three key procedures of the program.

Within PROCESS, you will see that SELECT is the first task to be performed. When we are designing a program that will select specific records for processing, we will normally place the SELECT procedure as the first task of PROCESS.

Based on the specifications, we must first determine what functionality is required for this program. Let's take a look at Figure 7–1 and determine which functions are appropriate.

INITIALIZATION

> *Initialize*: Always required.
>
> *Open Files*: Always required.
>
> *Process Special Files*: Not required in this program.
>
> *Read Input File*: Always required as last step in INITIALIZATION.

PROCESS

> *Record Selection*: This will be required.
>
> *Control-Break*: Not required for this program.
>
> *Calculate*: Not required in this program.
>
> *Accumulate*: Not required in this program.
>
> *Write*: This is required to write the report.
>
> *Read*: Always required as the last step in PROCESS.

END-OF-JOB

> *Major Control-Break*: Not required in this program.
>
> *Final Calculations*: Not required in this program.
>
> *Print Final Total*: Not required in this program.
>
> *Close Files*: Always required.

From the above analysis we can now build the structure chart. Based upon the standard processing sequence, we will build the structure chart containing the required tasks. Figure 9–1 illustrates the completed structure chart.

Notice again, the structure chart shows only *what* functions this program will need to perform and the order in which these functions must be performed. There is no indication as to *how* the selection process will be accomplished.

Designing the SELECT Procedure

Now that we have determined what the program must do, let's see how we accomplish it. In this section, we will learn the structured approach to the selection procedure. This structure will work for almost all selection procedures. You would be wise to use this structure whenever designing a program that will be selecting specific records. This will allow you to maintain consistency across all of your programs.

Figure 9–1
Structure chart for example program

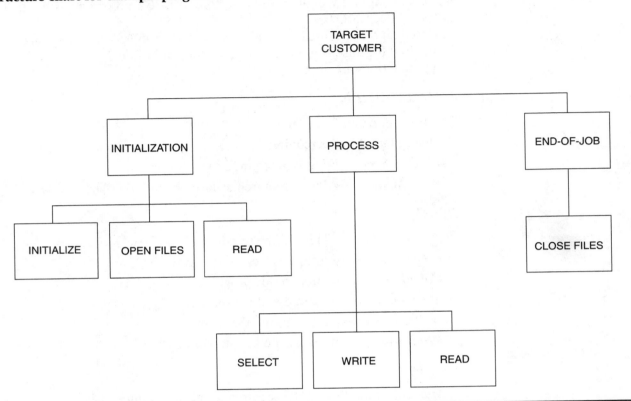

Figures 9–2a and 9–2b illustrate the logic for the PROCESS and the SELECT procedures for this program. Figure 9–2c contains the pseudo code for the same procedures. Let's take a close look at the key features.

SELECT-FLAG

The first difference between this version of PROCESS (Figure 9–2a) and previous versions of PROCESS is that we now have a decision within the PROCESS procedure. After we perform SELECT, we check the status of SELECT-FLAG. If SELECT-FLAG is ON, we will perform WRITE. If SELECT-FLAG is OFF, we bypass WRITE.

SELECT-FLAG is a logical data element, similar to END-FLAG. SELECT-FLAG will be used to determine if the record we are processing has been selected by the SELECT procedure. If SELECT-FLAG is ON, the program will know that the SELECT procedure determined that this record should be written to the report. If SELECT-FLAG is OFF, then PROCESS will know the record we are currently processing did not meet the selection criteria.

Figure 9–2
(a) PROCESS procedure
with SELECT, (b) SELECT
procedure, and (c) pseudo
code examples of
PROCESS and SELECT

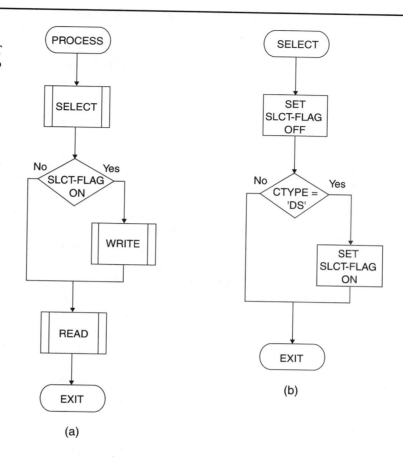

(a)

(b)

PSEUDO CODE

```
process:
        DO select
        IF slct-flag = on THEN
                    DO write
        END-IF
        DO read
select:
        LET slct-flag = off
        IF ctype = 'DS' THEN
                    LET slct-flag = on
        END-IF
```

(c)

In nearly all selection programs you will design, all but two procedures within PROCESS will be dependent on the status of SELECT-FLAG. SELECT and READ will not be dependent on SELECT-FLAG. SELECT is not dependent because it sets SELECT-FLAG. READ is never dependent on SELECT-FLAG because regardless of whether the current record has been selected for further processing, we must always read the next record. When applying Exhibit 7–1 to a selection program, CONTROL-BREAK, CALCULATE, ACCUMULATE, and WRITE will almost always be within the SELECT-FLAG's decision structure, along the "yes" path.

The SELECT Procedure

The sole purpose of the SELECT procedure is to determine if processing of the current record should continue, or if further processing should be bypassed and the next record read.

The first step of the SELECT procedure will set SELECT-FLAG off. This must *always* be the first step. SELECT will turn SELECT-FLAG on once it has been determined that the record should be processed. If SELECT determines that the record does not meet the selection criteria, SELECT-FLAG will not be turned on.

Remember, SELECT-FLAG is a logical data field. Therefore, the value of SELECT-FLAG will remain the same until the program specifically changes the values. SELECT-FLAG will never automatically change value. A good design habit to acquire is to always turn the flag off at the beginning of SELECT, and then turn it on again when you have determined that the record being processed meets the selection criteria.

Refer to Figure 9–2b and examine the standard approach for the SELECT procedure. Again, the first step is to turn SELECT-FLAG off. The next step is to perform whatever decisions are necessary to determine if the record being processed should be selected. In this case, we are testing to see if the customer type, CTYPE, is DS (the value that indicates that the customer is a department store). If the condition statement is true (CTYPE = 'DS') then we will set SELECT-FLAG ON. If the condition statement is false (CTYPE not = 'DS') then we exit SELECT without turning SELECT-FLAG on.

The PROCESS Procedure

After returning to PROCESS from SELECT, we test SELECT-FLAG. If SELECT-FLAG is on, then we know that the customer type is DS, and we write this customer to the report. If SELECT-FLAG is off, then we know that the customer is not a department store, and we bypass the WRITE procedure.

Other Procedures of the Program

Other procedures of the program remain unchanged. WRITE will continue to look identical to the WRITE procedure shown in Chapter 8. READ and END-OF-JOB remain unchanged. The only difference will be in INITIALIZATION. We must show SELECT-FLAG in the INITIALIZE annotation, and it will be initialized to OFF.

STRUCTURING COMPLEX SELECTION LOGIC

The previous example was very simple in that only one selection criteria was used (customer type of DS). Let's take a look at how we flowchart more complex selection logic involving multiple conditions. To do this, we will explore the AND and OR conditions.

AND Logic

AND logic requires that all selection criteria joined by the AND must be true in order to select the record. For example, suppose Marketing had wanted to restrict the above report to all department stores in region 01. This would require AND logic. We would want to select customers that are department stores AND in region 01. If the customer did not satisfy both criteria, we would not want the record. The logic flow to support this AND condition is shown in Figure 9–3.

Figure 9–3
Example of AND logic

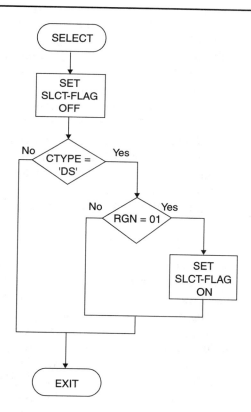

```
PSEUDO CODE

select:
  LET slct-flag = off
  IF ctype = 'DS' THEN
      IF rgn = 01 THEN
             LET slct-flag = on
        END-IF
  END-IF
```

OR Logic

OR logic requires that conditions in only one leg of the decision structure need to be present in order to select the record. For example, suppose that Marketing had wanted all customers that were department stores or sporting goods stores to be reported. This would reflect an OR condition. We would want the customer if they were a department store (customer type DS) OR a sporting good store (customer type SG). Figure 9–4 illustrates a simple OR condition.

Understanding the Difference between ANDs and ORs

It is common for inexperienced program designers to misuse AND and OR logic. As you read program specifications, take the time to analyze the requirements and decide if the selection logic requires an AND or an OR condition. *Specifications can be misleading if you do not think them through carefully.* For example, suppose Marketing had requested that the report show all customers coded as department stores and sporting good stores. Would this be an AND or an OR condition? Many would say AND because the instructions clearly state "department stores and sporting good stores." However, how many customers would be both department stores and sporting goods stores? Remember, department stores are identified with customer type of DS. Sporting goods stores are identified with customer type of SG. No customer can have a customer type of DS and SG. Therefore, this cannot be an AND condition. If you specified it as an AND, no records would be selected because a customer cannot satisfy both requirements. It is very important to give careful consideration to the program specifications before taking them at face value.

Combining ANDs and ORs

In most cases, selection logic becomes even more complex, by combining ANDs and ORs to determine if a record should be processed.

Let's look at the situation where Marketing has requested the report to contain department stores and sporting goods stores. They also want to limit the report to regions 02 and 03. Let's examine this request and see exactly what they are asking for. After we have determined their exact request, we can then design the program. First we know that a customer cannot be a department store (DS) *and* a sporting goods store (SG); therefore, this must be an OR condition. Likewise, a customer cannot be in both regions 02 and 03. After some analysis, we have determined that we should select department stores or sporting goods stores that are in either regions 02 or 03. In short, our logic will look something like this:

```
Customer type 'DS' or 'SG'
       and
    Region 02 or 03
```

Figure 9–5 illustrates this SELECT.

Figure 9–4
Example of OR logic

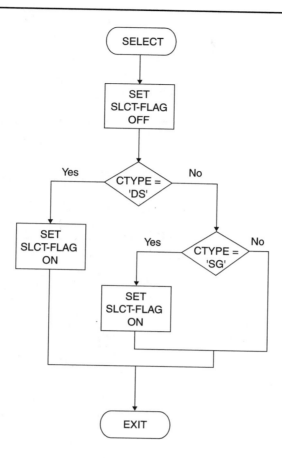

PSEUDO CODE

```
select:
    LET slct-flag = off
    IF ctype = 'DS' THEN
        LET slct-flag = on
      ELSE
        IF ctype = 'SG' THEN
            LET slct-flag = on
        END-IF
    END-IF
```

Figure 9–5
Example combining AND logic with OR logic

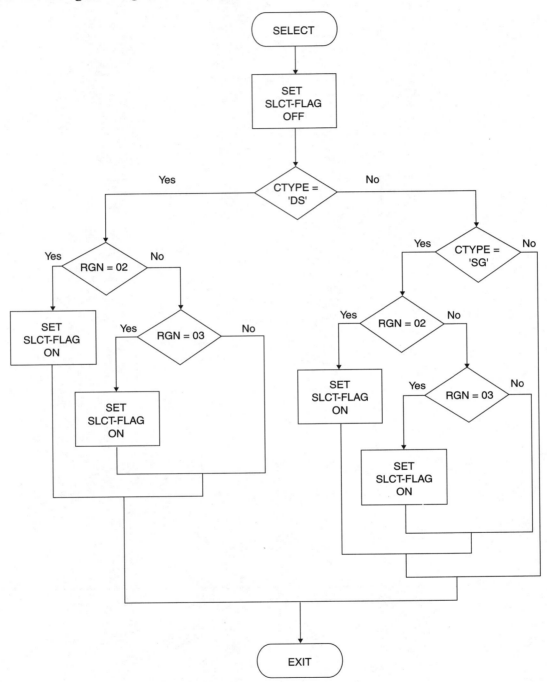

Figure 9–5
(continued)

PSEUDO CODE

```
select:
                LET slct-flag = off
                IF ctype = 'DS' THEN
                    IF rgn = 02   THEN
                                LET slct-flag = on
                        ELSE
                                IF rgn = 03 THEN
                                        LET slct-flag = on
                                END-IF
                    END-IF
                 ELSE
                    IF ctype = 'SG' THEN
                        IF rgn = 02 THEN
                                LET slct-flag = on
                            ELSE
                                IF rgn = 03 THEN
                                        LET slct-flag = on
                                END-IF
                        END-IF
                    END-IF
                END-IF
```

Simplified version:

```
    select:
                LET slct-flag = off
                IF ctype = 'DS' THEN
                    IF rgn = 02 or 03 THEN
                                LET slct-flag = on
                    END-IF
                 ELSE
                    IF ctype = 'SG' THEN
                        IF rgn = 02 or 03 THEN
                                LET slct-flag = on
                        END-IF
                    END-IF
                END-IF
```

More simplified version:

```
    select:
                LET slct-flag = off
                IF ctype = ('DS' or 'SG') THEN
                    IF rgn = (02 or 03) THEN
                                LET slct-flag = on
                    END-IF
                END-IF
```

PARAMETER FILE PROCESSING

Purpose of Parameter Files

In most cases, we do not want to design a selection program to select the same records each time the program executed. For example, suppose Marketing were to return to us a few weeks later and request another set of targeted customers. There is a very good chance than the selection criteria for choosing potential customers for this second report will be different than the selection criteria for the first report. If the selection criteria changed, we would either be required to change the program or write a new one.

In reality, such programs are normally designed and written so that the selection criteria can change without changing the program. This is done by adding a parameter file to the program.

In information processing terminology, *parameter files* are files that provide the program guidelines for execution. In this case, we will use a parameter file to provide the program with the selection criteria.

Parameter files will be read once. The selection process will then test a field in the input record (such as the customer type) with the value in the parameter data.

Let's take a look at how a program with a parameter file is structured and how the flowchart will appear. Refer to Exhibit 9–2 for the program specifications we will use for this sample program.

Exhibit 9–2
SPECIFICATION FOR EXAMPLE RECORD SELECTION PROGRAM WITH A PARAMETER FILE

Objective

This program will supply the Marketing department with key customers when new products are introduced. The program will be written so that the selection criteria will be supplied from the parameter file. Marketing will supply the requested customer type and region each time the program is processed.

Processing Requirements

1. Read the parameter file to obtain the selection criteria.
2. Read the customer master file and select the customers whose customer type and region match the criteria supplied on the parameter file.
3. Print report shown in the printer spacing chart.

CUSTOMER MASTER RECORD

01-05	CUSTOMER NUMBER	CUST NO
06-30	CUSTOMER NAME	NAME
31-50	STREET ADDRESS	ADDR
51-65	CITY	CITY
66-67	STATE	ST
68-72	ZIP CODE	ZIP
73-74	CUSTOMER TYPE	CTYPE
75-76	REGION	RGN
77-78	AREA	AREA
79-83	HEADQUARTER ID	HQ
84-91	LAST PURCHASE (YYYYMMDD)	LSTPRCH
92-100	Unused	

PARAMETER FILE

01-02 CUSTOMER TYPE   PARM-TYPE
03-04 REGION NUMBER   PARM-RGN

Printer Spacing Chart

```
          1111111111222222222233333333334444444444555555555566666666667777777777888888888899999999990000000000111111111111111111111111111111
          1234567890123456789012345678901234567890123456789012345678901234567890123456789012345678901234567890123456789012345678901234567890123456789

RUN  MM/DD/YY   HH:MM                          ACME DISTRIBUTORS                                                          PAGE ZZZZ9
                                               TARGET CUSTOMER REPORT

         CUSTOMER
         NUMBER   NAME                   STREET ADDRESS          CITY               STATE   ZIP     REGION

          XXXXX   XXXXXXXXXXXXXXXXXXXXXX  XXXXXXXXXXXXXXXXXX  XXXXXXXXXXXXXX    XX    XXXXX     XX
          XXXXX   XXXXXXXXXXXXXXXXXXXXXX  XXXXXXXXXXXXXXXXXX  XXXXXXXXXXXXXX    XX    XXXXX     XX
          XXXXX   XXXXXXXXXXXXXXXXXXXXXX  XXXXXXXXXXXXXXXXXX  XXXXXXXXXXXXXX    XX    XXXXX     XX
```

Structure Chart Changes

The first step in designing programs with a parameter file is understanding when parameter files are required. Referring back to the program specifications in Exhibit 9–2, three items tell us that a parameter file is required. First, look at the second sentence of the Objectives paragraph. This clearly states that selection criteria will be supplied by a parameter file. Next, look for a parameter file layout. The parameter file layout follows the layout of the customer master tile. Finally, point two of the processing requirements defines the selection criteria as any record where the customer type and region match that supplied by the parameter file. Not all program specifications will be as clear, but you will learn to identify key items such as these when designing programs.

Parameter files fall into the category of "special files." When we refer back to Exhibit 7–1, in Chapter 7, we see that "process special files" will be the third step of INITIALIZATION. This step will read the parameter file so that the program can obtain the values to be used in the selection process.

The structure chart for this program is shown in Figure 9–6. Notice that the only change in the structure of the program is the step to read the parameter file in INITIALIZATION. As always, do not be concerned at this time with how the selection logic will work. When organizing the program and building the structure chart, our only consideration should be what we have to accomplish. In this case, we know that we must read a parameter file in INITIALIZATION. Moreover, PROCESS has not changed in its purpose. PROCESS will still select, write, and read. The flowchart for SELECT will undergo some minor changes, but the flowchart illustrates how we will do the record selection. Remember, when building the structure chart, do not consider how something will be accomplished.

Transition to the Flowchart

Now that we know what the program must do, let's see how we will accomplish the work. While we will review the major components of this program separately, Figures 9–8 through 9–11 contain the entire program. MAINLINE, which never changes, is shown in Figure 9–7.

Figure 9–6
Structure chart for example program

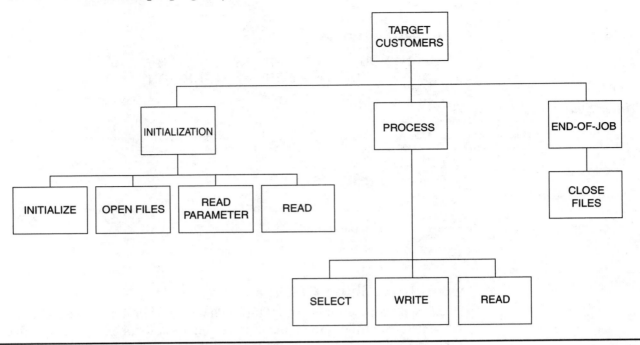

Figure 9–7
MAINLINE for example program

```
PSEUDO CODE

mainline:
    DO initialization
    DOWHILE end-flag off
      DO process
    END-DOWHILE
    DO end-of-job
    STOP
```

INITIALIZATION

Figure 9–8 illustrates the INITIALIZATION procedure for this program. Notice that we have added an Input-Output process to represent the read of the parameter file. This is done only one time, because only one parameter record will be read into the program.

PROCESS

Figure 9–9 illustrates PROCESS. As you can see, nothing has changed from our first look at PROCESS for a selection program. This reinforces

Figure 9–8
INITIALIZATION procedure for example program

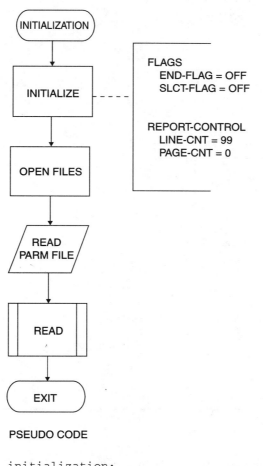

PSEUDO CODE

```
initialization:
     INITIALIZE    flag:  end-flag = off
                          slct-flag = off

                   report control:  line-cnt = 99
                                    page-cnt = 0

     OPEN files
     READ parameter file
     DO read
```

Figure 9–9
PROCESS procedure for example program

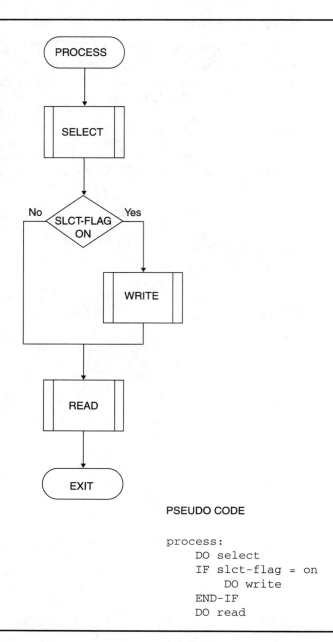

PSEUDO CODE

```
process:
    DO select
    IF slct-flag = on
        DO write
    END-IF
    DO read
```

the concept that while this program will select records differently than the selection program we designed earlier in this chapter, all selection programs can still be designed in the same manner.

SELECT

Figure 9–10 contains the selection logic. Notice in this program the customer type CTYPE is not compared to DS or SG. In this case, CTYPE is compared to the value of PARM-TYPE. PARM-TYPE is the field in the

Figure 9–10
SELECT procedure
for example program
referencing parameter
fields

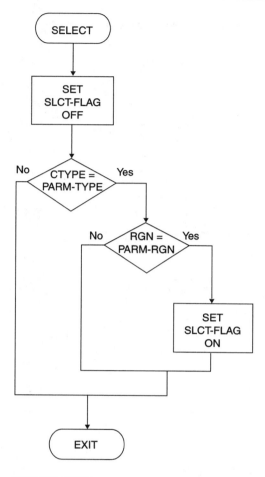

PSEUDO CODE

```
select:
    LET slct-flag = off
    IF ctype = parm-type THEN
        IF rgn = parm-rgn    THEN
            LET slct-flag = on
        END-IF
    END-IF
```

parameter file that contains the customer type that Marketing wants reported. Likewise, the customer region, RGN, is compared to PARM-RGN.
Records satisfying both arguments of the selection criteria will be selected.

WRITE/READ/EOJ

Figure 9–11 contains the remainder of the program. Notice that none of these
procedures have changed from earlier programs. Again, this reinforces the
fact that most aspects will remain consistent from one program to another.

Figure 9–11
WRITE, HDR-RTN, READ and EOJ procedures for example program

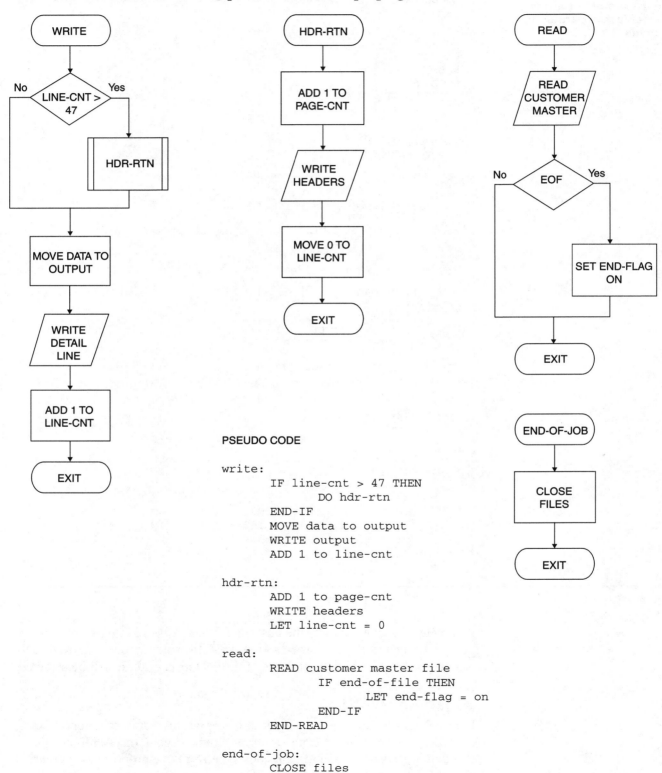

PSEUDO CODE

```
write:
      IF line-cnt > 47 THEN
            DO hdr-rtn
      END-IF
      MOVE data to output
      WRITE output
      ADD 1 to line-cnt

hdr-rtn:
      ADD 1 to page-cnt
      WRITE headers
      LET line-cnt = 0

read:
      READ customer master file
            IF end-of-file THEN
                  LET end-flag = on
            END-IF
      END-READ

end-of-job:
      CLOSE files
```

SUMMARY

The selection process is used when only a subset of the entire file is required for processing. Records are tested against the selection criteria, and only records that are selected will be processed. Records not selected will bypass the processing steps. SELECT-FLAG is used by the SELECT procedure to identify whether the record is selected.

Parameters may be included in selection programs so that the selection criteria can change without causing the program to be changed. Parameter files are read once, in INITIALIZATION. The data obtained from the parameter file can be used in the record selection logic.

REVIEW QUESTIONS

1. What is the purpose of the SELECT procedure?
2. What is the purpose of SELECT-FLAG?
3. Why is SELECT-FLAG turned off at the beginning of SELECT?
4. Why should SELECT always be the first procedure in PROCESS?
5. What are parameter files?
6. Why are parameter files read in INITIALIZATION and not in PROCESS?
7. Does the WRITE procedure change in a SELECTION program? If so, how?
8. By now you have seen two versions of the PROCESS procedure. You have seen PROCESS without SELECT, and another version with SELECT. What is the difference between the two versions?

EXERCISE

A local company wants to target specific students of your school for a special promotion. The targeted students are male, enrolled in the computer science program, and live within 5 miles of the school. For this example, assume that zip codes 30044, 30045, and 30046 are the target zip codes.

Develop the flowchart or pseudo code for the PROCESS and SELECT procedures based on the following criteria:

Select male students who live in the area and are enrolled in the computer science program.

- Local students live in zip codes 30044, 30045, and 30046.
- Males are identified with a gender code of M.
- Computer science students are identified with a program code of CS.

Hint: Decisions do not always need to be made in the order specified in the instructions.

Use the following field names: ZIP for the student's zip code.

GNDR-CD for the student's gender code.

PGM-CD for the student's program code.

PROJECT

Objective

Throughout the year, Acme Distributors must prepare for the beginning of each sporting season. In the winter, Acme prepares for baseball and soccer so that they have adequate inventory in the spring. In the summer, Acme stocks football and hockey equipment in preparation for the fall season.

Acme needs a program that can be requested by the sales manager for each sport (i.e., baseball, football, tennis, etc.) to identify what products need to be purchased in order to prepare for their upcoming season. The sport code to be reported will be provided via a parameter file.

Acme Distributors maintains current merchandise inventory levels using the Quantity On Hand field (IM-QOH) on the item master file. As products are sold, this field is adjusted by the quantity sold. For that reason we can assume IM-QOH will always reflect an accurate current inventory.

The item master file also has a field named Order Point (IM-ORDPT). Whenever inventory level (IM-QOH) drops below the Order Point, it is time to order this item. This program must identify and report those items that must be ordered. Acme orders a predetermined quantity of the item whenever it is ordered. This quantity is contained in the field IM-ORD-QTY.

Processing Requirements

1. Read the sport code parameter file to obtain the sport code that is to be selected and printed.

2. Read the item master file and select all items that have the requested sport code and where the inventory level has dropped below the order point.

3. The following formulas will be required:
   - Extended Cost = Order Quantity * Purchase Cost.
   - Sales Tax = Extended Cost * 5%.
   - Total Cost = Extended Cost + Sales Tax.

ITEM MASTER RECORD

01-05	ITEM NUMBER		IM-ITEM
06-20	DESCRIPTION		IM-DESC
21-22	SPORT CODE		IM-SPRTCD
23-24	EQUIPMENT TYPE		IM-ETYP
25-27	COMMISSION PERCENT	(3.3)	IM-PCT
28-33	VENDOR		IM-VNDR
34-40	PURCHASE COST	(7.2)	IM-COST
41-47	RETAIL PRICE	(7.2)	IM-PRICE
48-52	QUANTITY ON HAND	(5.0)	IM-QOH
53-57	ORDER POINT	(5.0)	IM-ORDPT
58-62	ORDER QUANTITY	(5.0)	IM-ORD-QTY
63-70	Unused		

SPORT CODE PARAMETER RECORD

01-02	SPORT CODE	PARM-SPRTCD

Printer Spacing Chart

```
                                                                                      1111111111111111111111111111111
        11111111112222222222333333333344444444445555555555666666666677777777778888888888999999999900000000001111111111122222222222
123456789012345678901234567890123456789012345678901234567890123456789012345678901234567890123456789012345678901234567789

DATE RUN:  MM/DD/YY                             ACME DISTRIBUTORS                                        PAGE ZZZZ9
TIME RUN:  HH:MM                          PRODUCT REPLENISHMENT REPORT

              ITEM                    ORDER     PURCHASE      EXTENDED      SALES        TOTAL·
     VENDOR  NUMBER   DESCRIPTION      QTY        COST          COST         TAX         COST
     XXXXXX  XXXXX   XXXXXXXXXXXXXX   ZZ,ZZZ     Z,ZZZ.99     ZZZ,ZZZ.99   Z,ZZZ.99    ZZZ,ZZZ.99
     XXXXXX  XXXXX   XXXXXXXXXXXXXX   ZZ,ZZZ     Z,ZZZ.99     ZZZ,ZZZ.99   Z,ZZZ.99    ZZZ,ZZZ.99
     XXXXXX  XXXXX   XXXXXXXXXXXXXX   ZZ,ZZZ     Z,ZZZ.99     ZZZ,ZZZ.99   Z,ZZZ.99    ZZZ,ZZZ.99
     XXXXXX  XXXXX   XXXXXXXXXXXXXX   ZZ,ZZZ     Z,ZZZ.99     ZZZ,ZZZ.99   Z,ZZZ.99    ZZZ,ZZZ.99
```

Assignment

1. Perform the mapping process.
2. Build the structure chart for this program.
3. Flowchart or pseudo code the entire program.

10
Accumulations and Report Totals

OBJECTIVES

- Understanding how accumulations work.
- Understanding how report totals are printed.

INTRODUCTION

Most reports printing numeric data, such as dollar amount or quantities, will be required to print totals at the end of the report. *Report totals* show the total of the report detail. In this chapter, we will learn how totals are calculated, where in the program these instructions must take place, and how and where these totals are printed.

WHAT IS ACCUMULATION?

In Chapter 8, we discussed the calculation of derived data. We learned that the calculation step of a program is required whenever derived data is to be computed for each record read. In most cases, the derived data calculated at the record level is printed as part of the detail line of the report. Refer back to commissions paid, total cost, and profit data in the program we designed in Chapter 8.

Let's continue enhancing the program we designed in Chapter 8. Exhibit 10–1 contains the program specifications we will use in this chapter. You will find that this program will be the same as the one we designed in Chapter 8, except that now we have included report totals for sales amount, commissions paid, total cost, and profit. Creation of totals for a report requires that we *accumulate* the totals and then print the totals when the report is finished.

Exhibit 10–1
PROGRAM SPECIFICATION FOR EXAMPLE PROGRAM WITH REPORT TOTALS

Objective

Produce a report that will list, for each item, the quantity sold and the profit earned on the sales.

Processing Requirements

1. For each record read, calculate the following:
   - Commissions Paid = Sales Amount * Commissions Percent.
   - Total Cost = Quantity Sold * Purchase Cost.
   - Profit = Sales Amount – (Commissions Paid + Total Cost).

2. Write the report showing all of the information shown on the printer spacing chart.

3. Provide report totals at the end of the report.

4. Single-space the report.

SALES RECORD

01-02	SPORT CODE	SPRTCD
03-04	EQUIPMENT TYPE	ETYP
05-09	ITEM NUMBER	ITEM
10-24	ITEM DESCRIPTION	DESC
25-29	QUANTITY SOLD (5.0)	QTY
30-38	SALES AMOUNT (9.2)	SLSAMT
39-41	COMMISSION PERCENT (3.3)	CMPCT
42-48	PURCHASE COST (7.2)	PRCHCST
49-60	Unused	

Printer Spacing Chart

```
                                                                                          1111111111111111111111111111111
                  1111111111222222222233333333334444444444555555555566666666667777777777888888888899999999990000000000111111111222222222
          123456789012345678901234567890123456789012345678901234567890123456789012345678901234567890123456789012345678901234567890123456789

RUN  MM/DD/YY  HH:MM                          ACME DISTRIBUTORS                                              PAGE ZZZZ9
                                               SALES REPORT

     SPORT    EQUIP    ITEM                    QUANTITY      SALES        COMMISSIONS     TOTAL
     CODE     TYPE     NMBR    ITEM DESCRIPTION  SOLD       AMOUNT          PAID          COST        PROFIT

      XX       XX     XXXXX   XXXXXXXXXXXXXXX   ZZ,ZZZ-   Z,ZZZ,ZZZ.99-   ZZZ,ZZZ.99-   ZZZ,ZZZ.99-   ZZZ,ZZZ.99-
      XX       XX     XXXXX   XXXXXXXXXXXXXXX   ZZ,ZZZ-   Z,ZZZ,ZZZ.99-   ZZZ,ZZZ.99-   ZZZ,ZZZ.99-   ZZZ,ZZZ.99-
      XX       XX     XXXXX   XXXXXXXXXXXXXXX   ZZ,ZZZ-   Z,ZZZ,ZZZ.99-   ZZZ,ZZZ.99-   ZZZ,ZZZ.99-   ZZZ,ZZZ.99-

                             REPORT TOTALS       ZZ,ZZZ,ZZZ.99-  Z,ZZZ,ZZZ.99-  Z,ZZZ,ZZZ.99-  Z,ZZZ,ZZZ.99-
```

Overview of the Process

How Are Report Totals Accumulated?

By dictionary definition, accumulation means to "increase . . . by addition." For example, in order to obtain a report total for sales amount, we will need to add the sales amount of each record to a derived data field dedicated to *accumulating* the sales total.

Since accumulation appears to be something that must occur with each record processed, it stands to reason that the procedure that performs the accumulation will be contained within the span of control for PROCESS. The definition of accumulation tells us this is done through addition. Therefore, in order to obtain the report total for sales amount, we simply add the sales amount for each record to the field designated for the sales total.

How Are the Report Totals Printed?

Report totals are printed similar to the way the detail lines of a report are printed. The key to printing totals, however, is not *how*, but *when*. Since report totals should reflect the totals for all records processed by the program, it would not make sense to print the totals in PROCESS. Report totals are printed once, after we have completed processing all records on the file. Therefore, printing of totals must be located in the END-OF-JOB section of the program.

How Does the Program Structure Change to Accommodate Report Totals?

First, let's look at how we determine if we need to accumulate totals on a report. A quick review of the program specifications in Exhibit 10–1 will reveal two elements that lead us to know that we need totals. First, statement three of the processing requirements states that we need to provide report totals at the end of the report. Printer spacing chart gives us the other clue whether accumulation is required. Notice that "report totals" is the last line of the report. This indicates that we are to print totals for the report.

When performing the mapping process for this program, we must indicate that totals are required and which fields will be totaled. According to the printer spacing chart, we will print totals for Sales Amount, Commissions Paid, Total Cost, and Profit. The results of the mapping step are shown in Exhibit 10–2, with the shaded area indicating the portion that defines which fields are to be totaled.

Now let's take a look at each of the three sections of the program, and see what changes are required to support the development and printing of report totals. To determine the appropriate changes, it is important to remember the tasks that each section of the program can perform, and the relative order of these tasks. Refer back to Exhibit 7–1 in Chapter 7 for a complete task list.

Exhibit 10–2
RESULTS OF THE MAPPING FOR PROGRAM SPECIFICATIONS IN EXHIBIT 10–1

Output Field	Source	Derived Computation	Totals
Sport Code	SPRTCD		
Equipment Type	ETYP		
Item Number	ITEM		
Item Description	DESC		
Quantity Sold	QTY		
Sales Amount	SLSAMT		X
Commissions Paid	Derived	SLSAMT * CMPCT	X
Cost	Derived	QTY * PRCHCST	X
Profit	Derived	SLSAMT – (Commissions Paid + Cost)	X

INITIALIZATION

In reviewing the potential task list for the INITIALIZATION section of the program, we find the following tasks that may be performed: initialize, open files, process special files, and read. Accumulation requires no special files. Accumulation requires additional derived data fields that we will use to obtain the totals, but we need no additional files. Therefore, except for noting the additional derived fields required for our totals (within the initialize annotation), there are no changes to INITIALIZATION from previous programs. INITIALIZATION will perform the following tasks:

- Initialize.
- Open files.
- Read.

PROCESS

Our next step is to review the potential task list and determine which functions are appropriate for this program. Again, we are never concerned with how we perform any of the functions. The first step of designing a program is to understand what functions the program will perform. Looking at the results of the mapping process, we immediately see that we must calculate Commissions Paid, Total Cost, and Profit. We also see that we will be providing totals for Sales Amount, Commissions Paid, Totals Cost, and Profit. We have already learned that whenever we print totals, we must first accumulate them. After reviewing the potential task list (see Exhibit 7–1 in Chapter 7) we make the following conclusions:

- *Record Selection*: Not needed for this program. All records will be processed.
- *Control-Break*: Not needed for this program. This program will have no control break processing. (This will be discussed in later chapters.)
- *Calculate*: This is required. We will calculate commissions paid, total cost, and profit.
- *Accumulation*: This is required since we will be producing totals for the report.
- *Write*: This is required since we will be producing output.
- *Read*: Always required as the last step of PROCESS.

As with the previous chapter, we need to look at those sections that can vary from program to program to determine if we need to further decompose any of the functions into more detail. Calculation should be broken down to indicate the three different fields (commissions paid, total cost, and profit) and the sequence in which these must be computed. The printer spacing chart and the data mapping process help us identify what totals are to be accumulated. On the structure chart, we may wish to decompose accumulation into more detail to ensure that we have accounted for all totals.

Determining the order of accumulation is not normally an issue. In most cases, there is no relative order in which these accumulations must be performed. Because accumulation consists of adding to a total field, order of addition is not important. Although we were required to compute commissions paid and total cost prior to computing profit, we are not required to accumulate commissions paid and total cost prior to accumulating profit. Because there is no relative sequence of importance, they can be accumulated in any order. The key item to remember in defining PROCESS is that accumulation must follow calculation. You cannot accumulate total cost if you do not first compute the total cost of the current item.

END-OF-JOB

After all of the records are processed, we need to print the report totals. Printing totals will be our first step of END-OF-JOB. Refer again to Exhibit 7–1. The first item on the EOJ task list is control break. Since this is not a control break program, this step is not necessary. The second task is to perform final calculations. Although this is not needed for this program, it may be necessary for others. We will discuss this shortly. The next task is printing report totals, which is required. Finally, we close our files. We are always required to close files.

The Structure Chart

Figure 10–1 contains the structure chart for the program we have just reviewed. As you can see, each functional component for the program was identified and placed in the structure chart in the order suggested by Exhibit 7–1. Further review will indicate that this structure chart is only slightly different from the one we built in Chapter 7 (same report except without the totals). The only difference is the inclusion of the ACCUMULATION procedure within PROCESS, and the step to print the report totals, which is added to END-OF-JOB.

Transition from the Structure Chart to the Flowchart

INITIALIZATION

As we already learned, INITIALIZATION has not changed from previous programs, with the exception of identifying the fields required for accumulating the totals. Figure 10–2 illustrates INITIALIZATION for this program.

This may be a good time to introduce the concept of *grouping the data* in INITIALIZATION. The annotation for INITIALIZE has the derived and logical data divided into four groups: FLAGS, COMPUTED-DATA, REPORT-TOTALS, and REPORT-CONTROL. When defining new data, such as derived and logical fields, it is always wise to provide meaningful names. Commission paid will be given the name COMM-PD. Profit will be named PROFIT. When identifying the report totals, one approach is to prefix the original field name with something meaningful. For report totals, we use the prefix RT. The field for accumulating the report total for commission paid is RT-COMM-PD. The field for accumulating the report total for profit is RT-PROFIT. Report Control will always contain the line counter and page counter for controlling the report. All status flags will be defined in the FLAGS area.

Figure 10–1
Structure chart for the accumulation program

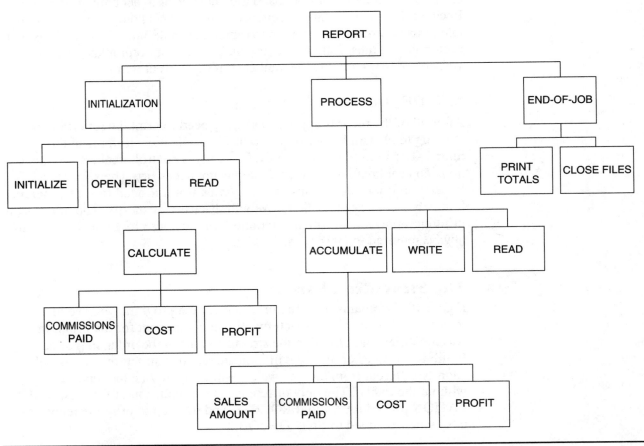

PROCESS

Figure 10–3 illustrates the PROCESS procedure of our program. Again, you will notice that the only difference in PROCESS from the original program in Chapter 8 is the inclusion of the ACCUMULATION procedure. Notice that PROCESS does not contain the accumulation logic, only the predefined process symbol for ACCUMULATION. The actual logic for accumulation will be located in the ACCUMULATION procedure to keep the PROCESS procedure clean and simple. It should be noted that this example does not illustrate all components of PROCESS. Since CALCULATE, WRITE, and READ have not changed from the previous program, they are not included. Later in this chapter, we will see an entire program.

END-OF-JOB

As we saw earlier, the only addition to EOJ is the logic required to print the report totals. Figure 10–4 illustrates how this is shown in a flowchart.

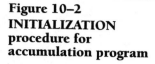

**Figure 10–2
INITIALIZATION
procedure for
accumulation program**

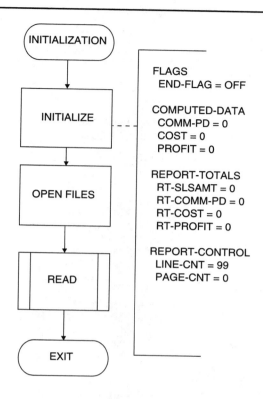

FLAGS
  END-FLAG = OFF

COMPUTED-DATA
  COMM-PD = 0
  COST = 0
  PROFIT = 0

REPORT-TOTALS
  RT-SLSAMT = 0
  RT-COMM-PD = 0
  RT-COST = 0
  RT-PROFIT = 0

REPORT-CONTROL
  LINE-CNT = 99
  PAGE-CNT = 0

PSEUDO CODE

```
initialization:
     INITIALIZE flags:          end-flag = off
                computed-data:  comm-pd = 0
                                cost = 0
                                profit = 0
                report-totals:  rt-slsamt = 0
                                rt-comm-pd = 0
                                rt-cost = 0
                                rt-profit = 0
                report-control: line-cnt = 99
                                page-cnt = 0
     OPEN files
     DO read
```

Figure 10–3
PROCESS and
ACCUMULATION
procedures for example
program

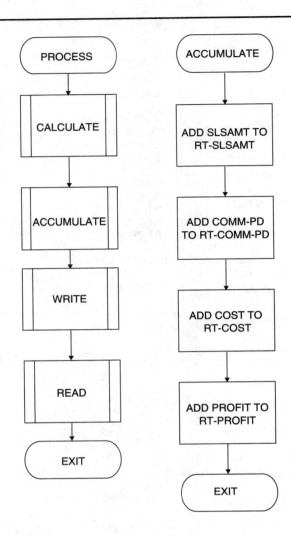

PSEUDO CODE

```
process:
  DO calculate
  DO accumulate
  DO write
  DO read

accumulate:
  ADD slsamt to rt-slsamt
  ADD comm-pd to rt-comm-pd
  ADD cost to rt-cost
  ADD profit to rt-profit
```

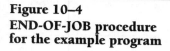

Figure 10–4
END-OF-JOB procedure
for the example program

PSEUDO CODE

```
end-of-job:
   MOVE report totals to output
   WRITE report totals
   CLOSE files
```

Performing Final Calculations

You will have occasions where some totals cannot be accumulated. For example, suppose you were calculating final grades for students in a class. During the quarter, each student completed six tests. The final grade for students will be determined by the average of their six test scores. Further, the instructor would like to know the final class average. The class has six students. The six test scores for each student and their average are as follows:

	1	2	3	4	5	6	Average
Tom	78	93	85	79	80	77	82
Bill	78	82	85	73	72	78	78
Mary	90	95	88	89	91	93	91
James	97	98	89	92	90	98	94
Karen	88	94	86	90	93	89	90
Kathy	78	81	77	90	81	79	81

You cannot accumulate the average of each student in order to determine the overall average for the class. If you accumulated the averages, you would have an average class score of 516 (82 + 78 + 91 + 94 + 90 + 81). We can safely assume this is an incorrect answer. In fact, the average score is 86 (516 divided by 6 students).

Therefore, we can safely say that not all totals can be accumulated. Some report totals, such as averages, must be computed just prior to printing.

Revising the Example Program

Let's make a small change to the program we just completed, and see how it affects the design. Exhibit 10–3 contains the example report we will consider next. Notice, in this example, that profit margin has been added. Profit margin is calculated as follows:

```
Profit Margin = (Profit / Sales Amount) * 100
```

Changes in PROCESS

The PROCESS procedure will require no changes to accommodate this report. We will, however, include the requirement for calculating the profit margin on the structure chart. This will be identified by another process added to CALCULATION. The calculation of profit margin must follow the calculation of profit, since we need the profit to compute the margin.

Accumulation would remain unchanged. We cannot accumulate profit margin in this report. In the sample report (Exhibit 10–3), if we were to accumulate profit margin, we would end up with a margin of 152.2%. Profit margin (a percentage), like the class average, cannot be accumulated. Instead, we must identify the data we need in order to calculate the overall profit margin and ensure that the required data is available at END-OF-JOB. To calculate the overall profit margin, we need total sales and total profit, both of which we are already accumulating.

Exhibit 10–3
REVISED REPORT CONTAINING PROFIT MARGIN

```
                                                                    1111111111111111111111111111111
            11111111112222222222333333333344444444445555555555666666666677777777778888888888999999999900000000001111111111222222222 3
   1234567890123456789012345678901234567890123456789012345678901234567890123456789012345678901234567890123456789012345678901234567890
```

| RUN MM/DD/YY HH:MM | | | | | | ACME DISTRIBUTORS | | | PAGE ZZZZ9 |
| | | | | | | SALES REPORT | | | |

SPORT CODE	EQUIP TYPE	ITEM NMBR	ITEM DESCRIPTION	QUANTITY SOLD	SALES AMOUNT	COMMISSIONS PAID	TOTAL COST	PROFIT	PROFIT MARGIN
01	01	1001A	RUNNING SHOE	120	4,800.00	336.00	1,560.00	2,904.00	60.5
01	02	2024S	TENNIS SHOE	193	9,650.00	675.50	4,053.00	4,921.50	50.0
01	20	6355F	SOCCER SHOE	95	3,515.00	386.65	1,662.50	1,465.85	41.7
			REPORT TOTALS		17,965.00	1,398.15	7,275.50	9,291.35	51.7

Changes to END-OF-JOB

Before printing the totals (including the total profit margin) we need to compute the total profit margin. When building the structure chart, this becomes the first step of EOJ. During the transition process to the flowchart, we will utilize the same formula we used at the detail level, only applying the calculation to the accumulated total fields for sales amount and profit.

The Entire Program

Figure 10–5 contains the complete structure chart for this final example. Figure 10–6 contains the entire flowchart and pseudo code for this program.

Figure 10–5
Structure chart for
final example program
including profit margin

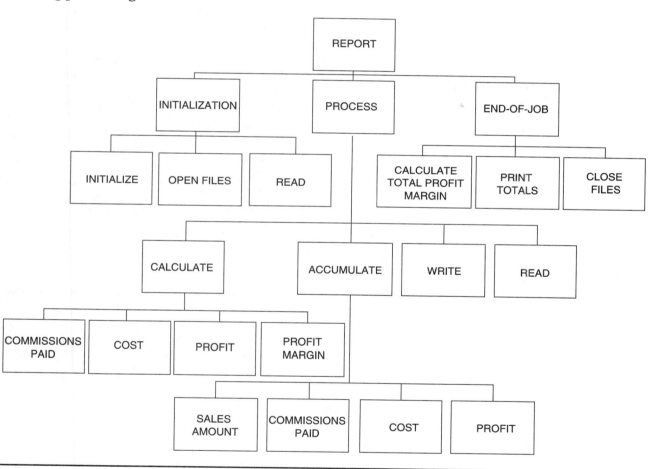

Figure 10–6
Flowchart for example program with profit margin

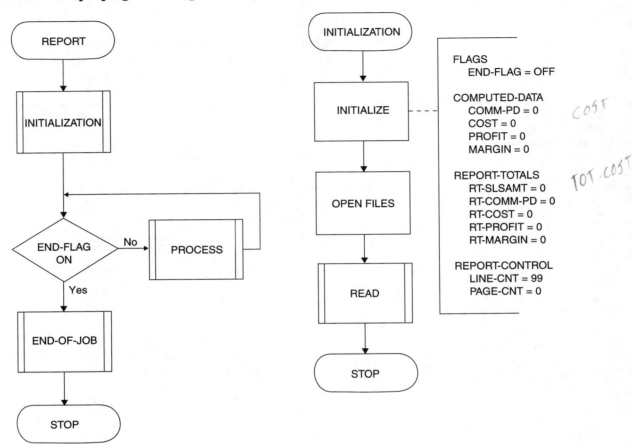

Figure 10–6
(continued)

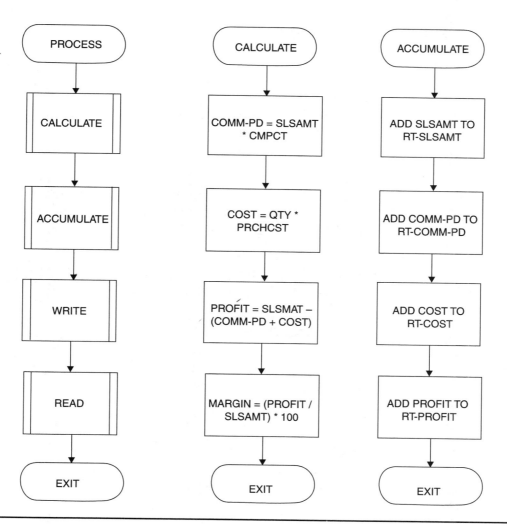

(continued on the next page)

Figure 10–6
(continued)

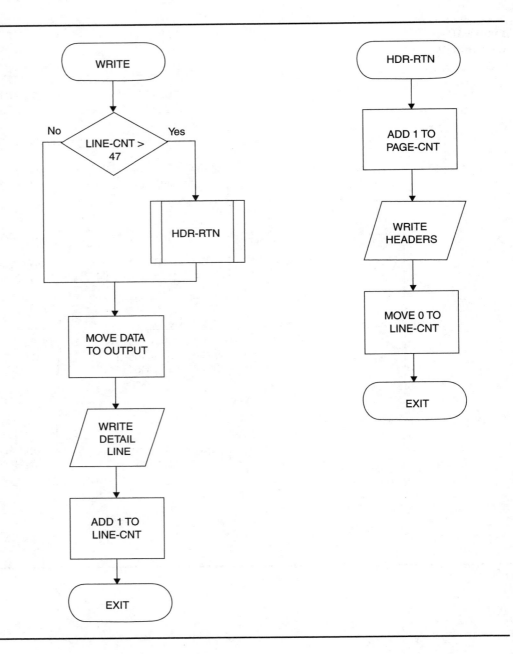

Figure 10–6
(continued)

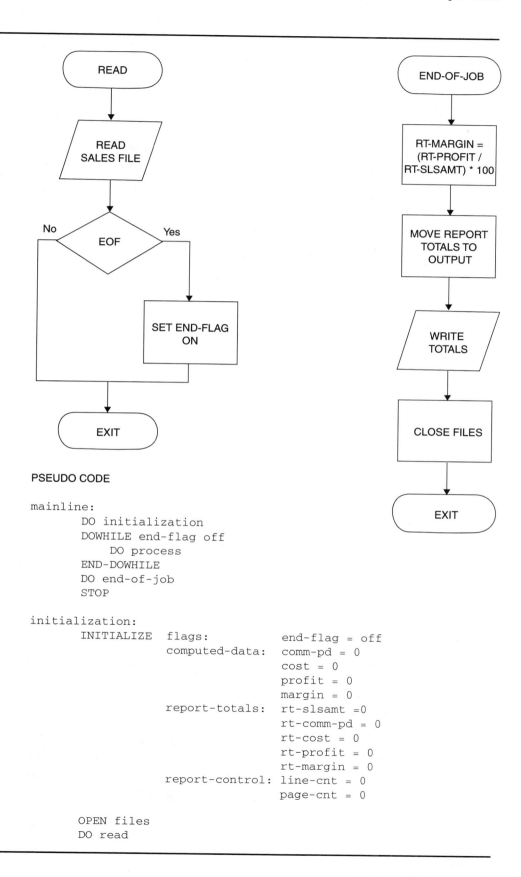

PSEUDO CODE

```
mainline:
      DO initialization
      DOWHILE end-flag off
         DO process
      END-DOWHILE
      DO end-of-job
      STOP


initialization:
      INITIALIZE  flags:          end-flag = off
                  computed-data:  comm-pd = 0
                                  cost = 0
                                  profit = 0
                                  margin = 0
                  report-totals:  rt-slsamt =0
                                  rt-comm-pd = 0
                                  rt-cost = 0
                                  rt-profit = 0
                                  rt-margin = 0
                  report-control: line-cnt = 0
                                  page-cnt = 0

      OPEN files
      DO read
```

(continued on the next page)

Figure 10–6
(continued)

```
process:
        DO calculate
        DO accumulate
        DO write
        DO read

calculate:
        LET comm-pd = slsamt * cmpct
        LET cost = qty * prchcst
        LET profit = slsamt - (comm-pd + cost)
        LET margin = (profit / slsamt) * 100

accumulate:
        ADD slsamt to rt-slsamt
        ADD comm-pd to rt-comm-pd
        ADD cost to rt-cost
        ADD profit to rt-profit

write:
        IF line-cnt > 47 THEN
                DO hdr-rtn
        END-IF
        MOVE data to output
        WRITE detail-line
        ADD 1 to line-cnt

hdr-rtn:
        ADD 1 to page-cnt
        WRITE headers
        LET line-cnt = 0

read:
        READ sales file
        IF end-of-file THEN
                LET end-flag = on
        END-IF

end-of-job:
        LET rt-margin = (rt-profit / rt-slsamt) * 100
        MOVE report totals to output
        WRITE totals
        CLOSE files
```

SUMMARY

In this chapter, we learned the concepts of accumulating data to obtain final totals. We saw how the basic structure of the program remained unchanged, and that the accumulation is just one more step to add to the basic PROCESS section. We learned that report totals are printed at EOJ. We discovered that some totals cannot be accumulated, but must be computed prior to printing. When final totals do require calculations, these calculations must be done prior to printing the totals.

REVIEW QUESTIONS	

REVIEW QUESTIONS

1. Why does the ACCUMULATE procedure follow the CALCULATE procedure?

2. Can all totals be accumulated? If not, which type of totals cannot be accumulated? How are these totals derived?

3. Why are final totals printed at END-OF-JOB, and not within PROCESS?

4. If we were to incorporate the accumulation function within a program that also has a record selection, would the ACCUMULATION procedure be dependent on the results of the selection, or would all records be accumulated regardless of whether they were selected?

EXERCISE

Refer back to the section of this chapter titled "Performing Final Calculations." This section of the chapter described the need to determine the average test scores for each student, as well as the overall average score for the class. This exercise will be to flowchart several procedures of the program to compute the student averages and overall class average. Remember, in order to compute the student averages, you must know the number of students. The example in "Performing Final Calculations" contained six students; however; you cannot plan on always having six. The program must be flexible to accommodate any number of students in the class.

Develop the flowchart or pseudo code the following procedures for this program:

INITIALIZATION (in order to identify the accumulation fields)
PROCESS
CALCULATE
ACCUMULATE
END-OF-JOB

Use the following field names from the file:

TEST1
TEST2
TEST3
TEST4
TEST5
TEST6

PROJECT 1

Objective

Produce a sales management report for Acme Distributors to better manage customer sales. This report will provide customer sales performance for the current year and prior year. Report will contain sales by customer.

Processing Requirements

1. Read and print all records on the file.

2. Use the following formulas:
   - Prior Year Sales = the sum of the sales for all twelve months of the prior year.
   - Current Year Sales = the sum of the sales for all twelve months of the current year.
   - Sales Increase = Current Year Sales – Prior Year Sales.
   - Percent Increase = (Sales Increase / Prior Year Sales) * 100.

3. Print the report as shown on the printer spacing chart.

4. The report will be single-spaced.

CUSTOMER SALES RECORD

01-02	REGION		CS-RGN
02-06	CUSTOMER NUMBER		CS-CUST
07-31	CUSTOMER NAME		CS-NAME
32-33	SPORT CODE		CS-SPRTCD
34-35	EQUIPMENT TYPE		CS-ETYP
36-43	CURRENT YEAR JANUARY	(8.2)	CS-CYJAN
44-51	CURRENT YEAR FEBRUARY	(8.2)	CS-CYFEB
52-59	CURRENT YEAR MARCH	(8.2)	CS-CYMAR
60-67	CURRENT YEAR APRIL	(8.2)	CS-CYAPR
68-75	CURRENT YEAR MAY	(8.2)	CS-CYMAY
76-83	CURRENT YEAR JUNE	(8.2)	CS-CYJUN
84-91	CURRENT YEAR JULY	(8.2)	CS-CYJUL
92-99	CURRENT YEAR AUGUST	(8.2)	CS-CYAUG
100-107	CURRENT YEAR SEPTEMBER	(8.2)	CS-CYSEP
108-115	CURRENT YEAR OCTOBER	(8.2)	CS-CYOCT
116-123	CURRENT YEAR NOVEMBER	(8.2)	CS-CYNOV
124-131	CURRENT YEAR DECEMBER	(8.2)	CS-CYDEC
132-139	PRIOR YEAR JANUARY	(8.2)	CS-PYJAN
140-147	PRIOR YEAR FEBRUARY	(8 2)	CS-PYFEB
148-155	PRIOR YEAR MARCH	(8.2)	CS-PYMAR
156-163	PRIOR YEAR APRIL	(8.2)	CS-PYAPR
164-171	PRIOR YEAR MAY	(8.2)	CS-PYMAY
172-179	PRIOR YEAR JUNE	(8.2)	CS-PYJUN
180-187	PRIOR YEAR JULY	(8.2)	CS-PYJUL
188-195	PRIOR YEAR AUGUST	(8.2)	CS-PYAUG
196-203	PRIOR YEAR SEPTEMBER	(8.2)	CS-PYSEP
204-211	PRIOR YEAR OCTOBER	(8.2)	CS-PYOCT
212-219	PRIOR YEAR NOVEMBER	(8.2)	CS-PYNOV
220-227	PRIOR YEAR DECEMBER	(8.2)	CS-PYDEC
228-250	Unused		

Printer Spacing Chart

```
                                                                              1111111111111111111111111111111111
                     111111111122222222223333333333444444444455555555556666666666777777777788888888889999999999000000000011111111112222222222
          1234567890123456789012345678901234567890123456789012345678901234567890123456789012345678901234567890123456789012345678901234567890123456789

RUN MM/DD/YY                                          ACME DISTRIBUTORS                                              PAGE ZZZZ9
TIME HH:MM                                         CUSTOMER SALES REPORT


                                    SPORT       EQUIP       CURR YEAR       PRIOR YEAR         SALES          PERCENT
          CUSTOMER    CUSTOMER NAME  CODE        TYPE        SALES           SALES              INCREASE       INCREASE
```

```
XXXXX     XXXXXXXXXXXXXXXXXXXXXXXXX     XX     XX     Z,ZZZ,ZZZ.99-     Z,ZZZ,ZZZ.99-     ZZZ,ZZZ.99-     ZZZZ.9-
XXXXX     XXXXXXXXXXXXXXXXXXXXXXXXX     XX     XX     Z,ZZZ,ZZZ.99-     Z,ZZZ,ZZZ.99-     ZZZ,ZZZ.99-     ZZZZ.9-
XXXXX     XXXXXXXXXXXXXXXXXXXXXXXXX     XX     XX     Z,ZZZ,ZZZ.99-     Z,ZZZ,ZZZ.99-     ZZZ,ZZZ.99-     ZZZZ.9-
XXXXX     XXXXXXXXXXXXXXXXXXXXXXXXX     XX     XX     Z,ZZZ,ZZZ.99-     Z,ZZZ,ZZZ.99-     ZZZ,ZZZ.99-     ZZZZ.9-

          REPORT TOTALS                                ZZZ,ZZZ,ZZZ.99-   ZZZ,ZZZ,ZZZ.99-   Z,ZZZ,ZZZ.99-   ZZZZ.9-
```

Assignment

1. Perform the mapping process.
2. Develop the structure chart for this program.
3. Flowchart or pseudo code the entire program.

PROJECT 2

Objective

Throughout the year, Acme Distributors must prepare for the beginning of each sporting season. That is, in the winter Acme prepares for baseball and soccer so that they have adequate inventory in the spring. In the summer, Acme stocks football and hockey equipment in preparation for the fall season.

Acme needs a program that can be requested by the sales manager for each sport (i.e., baseball, football, tennis, etc.) to identify what products need to be purchased in order to prepare for their upcoming season. The sport code to be reported will be provided via a parameter file.

Business Overview

Acme Distributors maintains current item and inventory data on the item master file. Current inventory levels are kept in the Quantity On Hand field (IM-QOH). As products are sold, this field is adjusted by the quantity sold to accurately reflect current inventory.

The item master file also has a field named Order Point (IM-ORDPT). This field represents the point at which the product is reordered. Whenever inventory level (IM-QOH) drops below that product's Order Point, it is time to reorder this item. This program must identify and report those items that must be reordered. Acme orders a predetermined quantity of the item whenever it is ordered. This quantity is contained in the field IM-ORD-QTY.

Processing Requirements

1. Read the sport code parameter file to obtain the sport code that is to be selected and printed.
2. Read the item master file and select all items that have the requested sport code and where the inventory level has dropped below the order point.
3. The following formulas will be required:
   - Extended Cost = Order Quantity * Purchase Cost.
   - Sales Tax = Extended Cost * 5%.
   - Total Cost = Extended Cost + Sales Tax.

4. The following fields should be printed on the report:
   - Vendor.
   - Item Number.
   - Description.
   - Order Quantity.
   - Purchase Price.
   - Extended Cost.
   - Sales Tax.
   - Total Cost.

5. Print report totals for the following:
   - Extended Cost.
   - Sales Tax.
   - Total Cost.

ITEM MASTER RECORD

01-05	ITEM NUMBER		IM-ITEM
06-20	DESCRIPTION		IM-DESC
21-22	SPORT CODE		IM-SPRTCD
23-24	EQUIPMENT TYPE		IM-ETYP
25-27	COMMISSION PERCENT	(3.3)	IM-PCT
28-33	VENDOR		IM-VNDR
34-40	PURCHASE COST	(7.2)	IM-COST
41-47	RETAIL PRICE	(7.2)	IM-PRICE
48-52	QUANTITY ON HAND	(5.0)	IM-QOH
53-57	ORDER POINT	(5.0)	IM-ORDPT
58-62	ORDER QUANTITY	(5.0)	IM-ORD-QTY
63-70	Unused		

SPORT CODE PARAMETER RECORD

01-02	SPORT CODE	PARM-SPRTCD

Assignment

1. Develop the printer spacing chart.
2. Perform the mapping process.
3. Build the structure chart for this program
4. Flowchart or pseudo code the entire program.

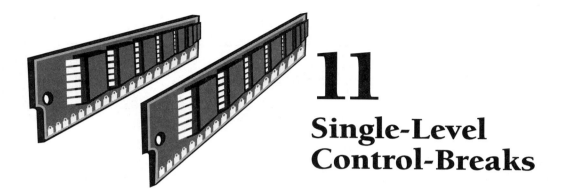

11
Single-Level Control-Breaks

OBJECTIVES

- Understanding the concepts of a control-break program.
- Understanding the use of hold fields.
- Understanding the fundamentals of the control-break process.

INTRODUCTION

In Chapter 10, we learned the process of accumulating final totals for a report. We did this by adding the appropriate value from each record of the file to an accumulation field, which was then printed at EOJ. In addition to final totals, many programs will be required to produce reports with subtotals following a logical *breakpoint* in the data. These breakpoints divide the report into logical groups. The final total would be the sum of all the subtotals.

To understand breakpoints, we need to better understand the data we will be using. From our example in Chapter 10, individual products are grouped by sport, and assigned a sport code. Equipment type designates the type of equipment, such as shoes, shirts/jerseys, and clubs. A control-break program would allow us to produce a report where products are grouped with similar products. In this chapter, we will be producing a sales report grouping all products by their sport code, and providing sales totals representing the total of all products used in that sport.

This chapter and Chapter 12 will explain the control-break process in three steps. First, here we will introduce control-breaks and diagram the single-level control-break program (program with only one level of subtotal). Chapter 12 will expand on this thought, and present multiple-level control-breaks. Chapter 12 will also illustrate some alternate program designs that might be required by some control-break programs.

SINGLE-LEVEL CONTROL-BREAK

A *single-level control-break* will present the user with one subtotal level in addition to the final totals. Exhibit 11–1 illustrates an example of such a report. In this example, a subtotal is printed for each sport code. Exhibit 11–2 contains the program specification associated with this report.

Exhibit 11–1
SAMPLE REPORT WITH SINGLE-LEVEL CONTROL-BREAK

```
                                                                      1111111111111111111111111111111
                           1111111111222222222233333333334444444444555555555566666666667777777777888888888899999999990000000000111111111122222222222
         1234567890123456789012345678901234567890123456789012345678901234567890123456789012345678901234567890123456789012345678901234567890123456789

RUN  06/30/94  14:43                              ACME DISTRIBUTORS                                              PAGE    1
                                                   SALES REPORT

        SPORT    ITEM                    QUANTITY        SALES       COMMISSIONS        TOTAL
        CODE     NMBR    ITEM DESCRIPTION   SOLD         AMOUNT         PAID            COST           PROFIT

         01      1001A   WHT BBALL SHOE     120         4,800.00       336.00         1,560.00        2,904.00
         01      2024S   BLK BBALL SHOE     193         9,650.00       675.50         4,053.00        4,921.50
         01      6355F   ALUMINUM BAT        95         3,515.00       386.65         1,662.50        1,465.85

                         SPORT CODE TOTAL              17,965.00     1,397.65         7,275.50        9,291.35

         02      81155   TENNIS BALLS     2,650         7,950.00        79.50         3,975.00        3,895.50
         02      3284L   ALM TENNIS RCKT    170        13,515.00     2,027.25         4,377.50        7,110.25
         02      6355F   FGL TENNIS RCKT    220        17,589.00     2,638.37         6,490.00        8,460.63

                         SPORT CODE TOTAL              39,054.00     4,745.12        14,842.50       19,466.38

                         REPORT TOTAL                  57,019.00     6,142.77        22,118.00       28,757.73
```

File Sequence

In order to produce the report, the input file must be sorted in the sequence required for the report. In this case, the file must be in sport code sequence. That is, sport code 01 will be first, followed by sport code 02, followed by sport code 03, and so on. Within each sport code, the item numbers must be in sequence. When we refer to the *sequence* of the file, we will say the file is sorted by item number within sport code. Within this text, we will work from the presumption that the process of sorting the file (*sorting* is the process of putting the records into the proper sequence) occurs outside the program we are designing. This sort will precede our program; therefore we can design and develop assuming the file is already in the proper sequence. An example of the sorted data can be seen in Exhibit 11–3.

Exhibit 11–2
PROGRAM SPECIFICATION FOR EXAMPLE PROGRAM WITH SINGLE-LEVEL CONTROL-BREAK

Objective

Produce a sales report showing profitability by item, and provide total profitability by sport code.

Processing Requirements

1. Read and print all records on the file.
2. Report format shown on printer spacing chart.
3. Use the following formulas:
   - Commissions Paid = Sales Amount * Commission Rate.
   - Total Cost = Quantity Sold * Purchase Cost.
   - Profit = Sales Amount – (Commissions Paid + Total Cost).
4. Provide control-breaks and subtotals for sport code.

5. Provide report totals.

6. Report will be single-spaced.

SALES RECORD

01-02	SPORT CODE		SPRTCD
03-04	EQUIPMENT TYPE		ETYP
05-09	ITEM NUMBER		ITEM
10-24	ITEM DESCRIPTION		DESC
25-29	QUANTITY SOLD	(5.0)	QTY
30-38	SALES AMOUNT	(9.2)	SLSAMT
39-41	COMMISSION PERCENT	(3.3)	CMPCT
42-48	PURCHASE COST	(7.2)	PRCHCST
49-60	Unused		

Printer Spacing Chart

```
                                                                    111111111111111111111111111111
          11111111112222222222333333333344444444445555555555666666666677777777778888888888999999999900000000001111111111222222222
123456789012345678901234567890123456789012345678901234567890123456789012345678901234567890123456789012345678901234567890123456789

RUN  MM/DD/YY   HH:MM                           ACME DISTRIBUTORS                                    PAGE ZZZZ9
                                                  SALES REPORT

      SPORT    ITEM
      CODE     NMBR    ITEM DESCRIPTION      QUANTITY     SALES        COMMISSIONS     TOTAL
                                               SOLD       AMOUNT         PAID          COST         PROFIT
       XX     XXXXX    XXXXXXXXXXXXXX         ZZ,ZZZ-    Z,ZZZ,ZZZ.99-   ZZZ,ZZZ.99-   ZZZ,ZZZ.99-  ZZZ,ZZZ.99-
       XX     XXXXX    XXXXXXXXXXXXXX         ZZ,ZZZ-    Z,ZZZ,ZZZ.99-   ZZZ,ZZZ.99-   ZZZ,ZZZ.99-  ZZZ,ZZZ.99-
       XX     XXXXX    XXXXXXXXXXXXXX         ZZ,ZZZ-    Z,ZZZ,ZZZ.99-   ZZZ,ZZZ.99-   ZZZ,ZZZ.99-  ZZZ,ZZZ.99-

                      SPORT CODE TOTAL                   ZZ,ZZZ,ZZZ.99- Z,ZZZ,ZZZ.99- Z,ZZZ,ZZZ.99- Z,ZZZ,ZZZ.99-

                      REPORT TOTAL                       ZZ,ZZZ,ZZZ.99- Z,ZZZ,ZZZ.99- Z,ZZZ,ZZZ.99- Z,ZZZ,ZZZ.99-
```

Exhibit 11–3
SORTED INPUT DATA FOR EXAMPLE PROGRAM

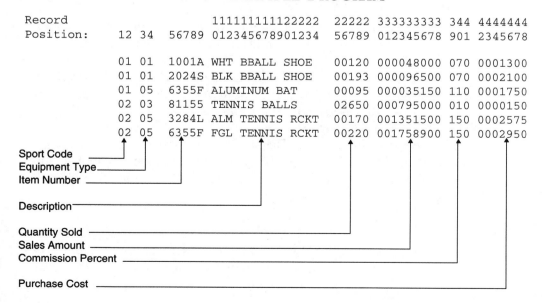

```
Record                          111111111122222   22222 333333333 344 4444444
Position:   12 34  56789 012345678901234  56789 012345678 901 2345678

            01 01  1001A WHT BBALL SHOE   00120 000048000 070 0001300
            01 01  2024S BLK BBALL SHOE   00193 000096500 070 0002100
            01 05  6355F ALUMINUM BAT     00095 000035150 110 0001750
            02 03  81155 TENNIS BALLS     02650 000795000 010 0000150
            02 05  3284L ALM TENNIS RCKT  00170 001351500 150 0002575
            02 05  6355F FGL TENNIS RCKT  00220 001758900 150 0002950
```

Sport Code
Equipment Type
Item Number

Description

Quantity Sold
Sales Amount
Commission Percent

Purchase Cost

Fundamental Logic

As we discussed in earlier chapters, a computer has no intelligence of its own. Computers have memory, but the only thing they can remember is what we have put in their memory as the program executes. Therefore, as we look at the different steps of this process, let's keep in mind what we must store in memory, in order to achieve our objective.

You will notice that we are printing subtotals at the sport code level, as well as the report total at the end of the report. This requires two sets of totals. We will need to accumulate totals at the sport code level, as well as report totals.

How will the program know when to print the totals? As you can see in the report example (Exhibit 11–1), totals are printed each time the sport code changes. In control-break programs, we call fields like sport code *control fields*. So how do we know when a control field changes? We must look at the sport code control field of the record we are processing and compare it to the control field of the previous record. When the two are no longer the same, we have a control-break. When a control-break occurs, we perform a *break routine process*, which we will discuss shortly.

Unfortunately, it is not as simple as comparing the control field of the current record to the control field of the previous record. Remember the concept of the *destructive read?* When one record is read, the contents of the previous record will be destroyed. If we need to use any data from that previous record, we must save the contents before the next read. Because we require the control field from that previous record, we must save the control field in a *hold field*. By saving the control field in a hold area, the value of the control field of one record is available for the comparison to the control field of the next record.

Initialization of the totals and the hold fields are accomplished in the INITIALIZATION section of the program.

Programming Concepts

Let's take a look at the major components of the program. First, let's look at the program from a high level, and then we can decompose to a lower level of detail.

As before, the first step in designing a program is to identify what functions the program will perform. As stressed in Chapter 7, we want to concentrate on what the program must do, and not how to do it. We will cover the how to later in the chapter.

Refer back to Exhibit 7–1 in Chapter 7. This listed all the major components found in the typical business program. The components are listed in the order they will be executed. Let's use this as a guide to outlining the key steps of this program.

INITIALIZATION

Initialize: Always required. When we flowchart this program, you will see how we initialize the hold areas and total fields.

Open File:	Always required. This program will be no exception.
Read Special File:	Not required in this program.
Read Input File:	Always the last step of INITIALIZATION. This program will be no exception.

PROCESS

Record Selection:	Not required. All records will be processed in our example. If this program required record selection, then the record selection process (described in Chapter 9) would go here.
Control-Break:	Required. We will need to incorporate control-break logic in this program. We will cover the logic of the control-break later in this chapter.
Calculate:	Required. We will need to calculate commissions paid, total cost, and profit.
Accumulation:	This is always required whenever you are accumulating and printing totals.
Write:	Required. Because we will be writing the records being read, we will need this.
Read Input File:	Always required as the last step of PROCESS. This program will be no exception.

END-OF-JOB

Control-Break:	This is required for this program. We will see why and how later in this chapter.
Final Calculations:	Not required for this program.
Print Final Totals:	Required for this program.
Close Files:	Always required. This program will be no exception.

The final task list looks like this:

INITIALIZATION:	Initialize Open files Read input file
PROCESS:	Control-break Calculate Accumulate Write Read
END-OF-JOB:	Control-break Print final totals Close file

If you refer to Chapter 10 (Accumulation and Final Totals), you will see that only processing required for control-breaks has been added to the task list. Otherwise, this program is basically the same as before. This reinforces the concept that all programs are built from the same basic set of building blocks. Selection and organization of the blocks may vary from program to program, but the basic program architecture remains consistent. Figure 11–1 illustrates the structure chart for this program.

Details of the Control-Break

Let's look at the components within the control-break logic. Control-break logic can be divided into two steps. The first step is to decide whether a control-break has occurred and the second step consists of the tasks to be performed when a control-break has occurred.

Identifying When a Control-Break Occurs

As mentioned earlier in this chapter, we will determine when a control-break occurs by comparing the control field of the current record to the control field of the previous record. In the program we are designing, the control field is sport code, or SPRTCD, as it is defined in the record layout. In the beginning of this chapter, the concept of hold fields was introduced. Hold fields are portions of memory defined by the program for containing

Figure 11–1
Structure chart for example program single-level control-break

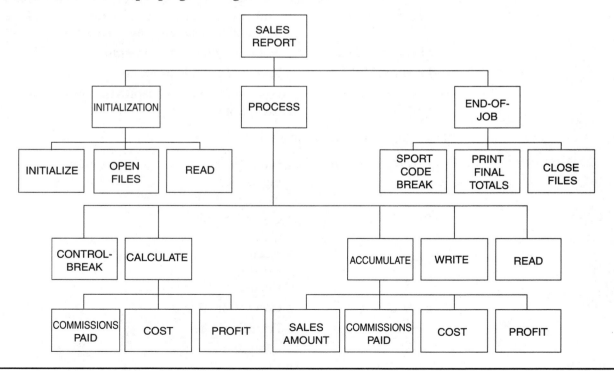

the content of the control field(s). For example, when developing the report shown in Exhibit 11–3, the hold fields will contain the value 01 for the first three records processed. Once we reach the first record for the sport code 02, the program will recognize that a control-break has occurred. After printing the totals (and doing a few other tasks), the hold area will contain the new sport code, 02.

Tasks Performed When a Control-Break Occurs

There are five tasks performed whenever the program determines that the value in the control field changes (i.e., we have completed sport code 01 and are now processing the first record of sport code 02).

1. Determine if the control-break is the result of the first record.
2. Print the totals.
3. Roll the totals to the next highest level.
4. Zero the totals for this control-break level.
5. Move the new control field value to the hold field.

Determine if the Control-Break Is the Result of the First Record

In INITIALIZATION, we create and define the logical data field FRST-RCD-FLAG. We initialize FRST-RCD-FLAG to ON to indicate that we are processing the first record. We also set the initial value of the hold area, HOLD-SPRTCD, to spaces. When we read the first record, the program will trigger a control-break. This is because sport code 01 in the first record is not equal to spaces; thus the program will think we are processing the first record of a new control-break. In reality we are processing the first record of the file. This first step is to avoid printing totals prior to processing the first record. To do this we will check the logical field FRST-RCD-FLAG to see if it is ON. If the flag is ON, we will know that we are processing the first record, and thus bypass the tasks related to processing the control-break. In the event that the flag is ON, we will turn the flag OFF, since we want the computer to recognize that we have already processed the first record.

Print Totals

This is the task of printing the control totals on the report. In our example, this is printing the sport code totals.

Roll Totals to the Next Highest Level

There will be more on this later in the chapter. For now, recognize that each time the sport code changes, we need to add the sport code total to the report total. This is known as *rolling* the totals. We will always *roll* to the next higher level.

Zero the Totals for this Control-Break Level

After the totals have been rolled to the next highest level, we need to zero the totals we have been accumulating. This allows the next control-break total, in this case sport code 02, to start at zero. Looking back at the sample report in Exhibit 11–1, we see that the sales total for sport code 01 was $17,965. If we did not zero the totals, the value of the total sales for sport code 02 would remain $17,965, corrupting the total at the next control-break.

Move the New Control Field Value to the Hold Area

After processing the main steps of the control-break, we need to set the hold area to the new control field value. This allows subsequent records to be compared to this record to determine when the next control-break occurs.

As we review the flowchart for the control-break logic, pay close attention to the placement of these five components.

FLOWCHART FOR THE CONTROL-BREAK PROGRAM

Figure 11–2 illustrates the INITIALIZATION procedure. Notice how the hold field and control totals have been defined. You will find it easier if you give the hold area a name that represents the data field being stored. Because we are going to hold sport code, we will name the field HOLD-SPRTCD. We have also added FRST-RCD-FLAG to the list of FLAGS.

Also, look closely at the two areas defined for maintaining totals. These areas, SPORT-TOTALS and REPORT-TOTALS, will be used to accumulate and store the totals for the report as the program executes. You will notice that within each total group, the four fields for which we will be printing totals must be identified.

Figure 11–3 illustrates PROCESS. The only difference between this program and previous programs is the inclusion of the control-break predefined process. Notice that this is the first step of PROCESS. This is because we need to determine if a control-break has occurred before we perform any calculation, accumulations, or printing of the record that we just read.

Calculation and Accumulation

CALCULATE remains the same as in the previous program. CALCULATE will contain the statements required to compute commission paid, cost, and profit. Because this procedure did not change, the flowchart has not been included in this discussion. However, ACCUMULATE will change. Remember that we always accumulate to the lowest level totals. In the previous program, the lowest level was the report totals. In this program, the lowest level is the sport code totals. Therefore, we must accumulate to the sport code totals. Figure 11–4 illustrates the new ACCUMULATE procedure.

Figure 11-2
INITIALIZATION
procedure for example
program

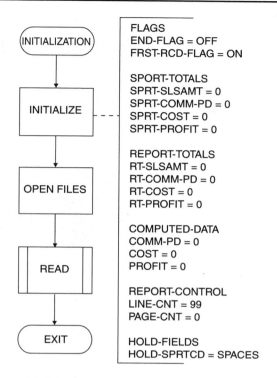

```
FLAGS
END-FLAG = OFF
FRST-RCD-FLAG = ON

SPORT-TOTALS
SPRT-SLSAMT = 0
SPRT-COMM-PD = 0
SPRT-COST = 0
SPRT-PROFIT = 0

REPORT-TOTALS
RT-SLSAMT = 0
RT-COMM-PD = 0
RT-COST = 0
RT-PROFIT = 0

COMPUTED-DATA
COMM-PD = 0
COST = 0
PROFIT = 0

REPORT-CONTROL
LINE-CNT = 99
PAGE-CNT = 0

HOLD-FIELDS
HOLD-SPRTCD = SPACES
```

PSEUDO CODE

```
initialization:
    INITIALIZE flags:          end-flag = off
                               frst-rcd-flag = off
               sport-totals:   sprt-slsamt = 0
                               sprt-comm-pd = 0
                               sprt-cost = 0
                               sprt-profit = 0
               report-totals:  rt-slsamt = 0
                               rt-comm-pd = 0
                               rt-cost = 0
                               rt-profit = 0
               computed-data:  comm-pd = 0
                               cost = 0
                               profit = 0
               report-control: line-cnt = 99
                               page-cnt = 0
               hold-fields:    hold-sprtcd = spaces
    OPEN files
    DO read
    STOP
```

Determine If a Control-Break Has Occurred

Figure 11-5 illustrates CONTROL-BREAK. At this time we are comparing
the value of SPRTCD for the record currently being processed with the
hold area, HOLD-SPRTCD. Notice that when a control-break occurs (the
two fields are not equal) we perform a procedure entitled SPRTCD-BREAK.

**Figure 11–3
PROCESS procedure for
example program**

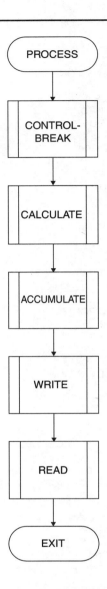

PSEUDO CODE

```
process:
    DO control-break
    DO calculate
    DO accumulate
    DO write
    DO read
```

To keep the program easy to follow, you would be wise to name the procedures after the control field that changed. Notice that after control is returned from SPRTCD-BREAK, we perform the fifth and last step of the control-break process, moving the new control field value to the hold area. This is not done within SPRTCD-BREAK. We will see why when we discuss end-of-job processing.

Figure 11–4
ACCUMULATE procedure
for example program

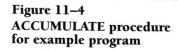
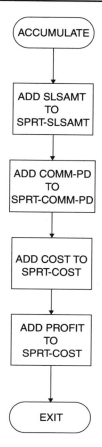

PSEUDO CODE

```
accumulate:
  ADD slsamt to sprt-slsamt
  ADD comm-pd to sprt-comm-pd
  ADD cost to sprt-cost
  ADD profit to sprt-profit
```

The Break Routine

Figure 11–6 illustrates the flowchart required to perform tasks 1, 2, 3, and 4 of the control-break. Notice that the first decision is to determine if FRST-RCD-FLAG is ON. This is to determine if we are processing the first record. If this condition is true, we do not want to write any control totals.

If this is a legitimate control-break (FRST-RCD-FLAG is off), then we will print the totals, roll the totals to the next highest level, and zero out the sport code totals. Let's take a look at each of these steps in detail.

Printing the Totals   In the procedure shown in Figure 11–6, the first three steps of the control relate to printing the totals. The first step is to move the totals to the output, or total line. The second step is to print the totals. The third and final step is to add to the line

**Figure 11–5
CONTROL-BREAK
procedure for example
program**

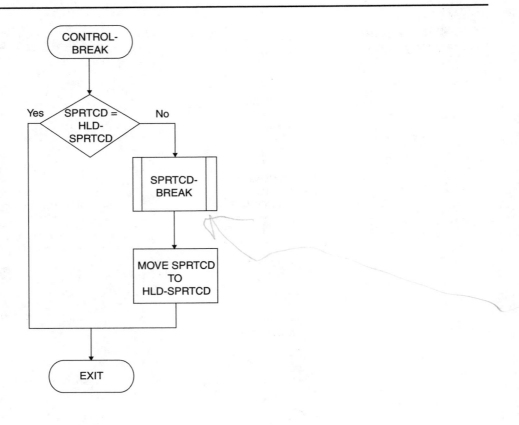

```
PSEUDO CODE

control-break:
   IF sprtcd not = hld-sprtcd THEN
      DO sprtcd-break
      LET hld-sprtcd = sprtcd
   END-IF
```

counter the number of lines consumed by the totals. In this example, we must add three to the line count. This accounts for the blank line before the totals, the totals themselves, and the blank line after the totals.

Rolling the Totals After printing the totals, the next step is to roll, or add the current level totals to the next highest level. In this example, the next highest level is the report totals. So, for this procedure, the rolling step is to add the sport totals to the report totals.

Zero the Totals The third and final step of the break procedure is setting the totals of the current control-break level, in this case sport totals, to zero.

END-OF-JOB

Figure 11–7 shows how the END-OF-JOB is changed to accommodate the control-break logic. The first step in EOJ must be to perform

**Figure 11–6
SPRTCD-BREAK
procedure for example
program**

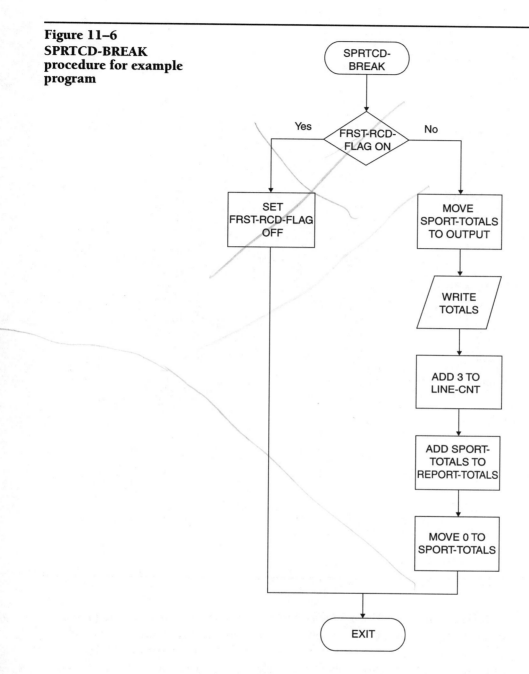

PSEUDO CODE

```
sprtcd-break:
  IF frst-rcd-flag = on THEN
     LET frst-rcd-flag = off
   ELSE
     MOVE sport-totals to output
     WRITE totals
     ADD 3 to line-cnt
     ADD sport-totals to report-totals
     MOVE zero to sport-totals
  END-IF
```

Figure 11–7
END-OF-JOB procedure
for example program

PSEUDO CODE

```
end-of-job:
    DO sprtcd-break
    MOVE report-totals to output
    WRITE totals
    CLOSE files
```

SPRTCD-BREAK. Since EOJ is performed when we have reached the end of the file, we cannot trigger the final control-break in the usual fashion. That is, if there is no record to process, we will not perform PROCESS; thus, we never perform CONTROL-BREAK. In order to get the final sport code totals, we must force the execution of SPRTCD-BREAK.

Refer again to Figure 11–5. Notice that we moved the new control-break value to the hold field after we performed SPRTCD-BREAK. We did this because SPRTCD-BREAK is performed at EOJ, and EOJ is performed when we have no more records. If we placed the process of setting the hold field to the new value of the control field within SPRTCD-BREAK, we could have a problem at EOJ. A problem could occur because the value of sport code would be unpredictable since we have no more data. Manipulating or processing any fields from the input record area after the end of the file has been reached can cause your program to fail.

Let's complete our review of Figure 11–7. When control is returned from SPRTCD-BREAK, we need to print the report totals. Finally, as with any program, we will close our files.

The following exercise walks you through this process record by record. To illustrate the processing, we will use the data contained in Exhibit 11–4. (Exhibit 11–4 also contains this sample file of six records.) As you walk through this process, be prepared to refer back to the several examples we have covered thus far.

Exhibit 11–4
SAMPLE DATA FOR LOGIC WALK-THROUGH

	Sprt Cd	Equip Type	Item	Description	Qty	Sales	Comm Pct	Cost
Record 1	01	01	1001A	WHT BBALL SHOE	00120	000480000	070	0001300
Record 2	01	01	2024S	BLK BBALL SHOE	00193	000965000	070	0002100
Record 3	01	10	6355F	ALUMINUM BAT	00095	000351500	110	0001750
Record 4	02	03	81155	TENNIS BALLS	02650	000795000	010	0000150
Record 5	02	05	3284L	ALM TENNIS RCKT	00170	001351500	150	0002575
Record 6	02	05	6355F	FGL TENNIS RCKT	00220	001758900	150	0002950

Processing

INITIALIZATION sets the starting values for all of our derived fields. Step 1 below shows the initial values set for each field. Refer to Figure 11–2 to see how the fields were initialized.

	FRST-RCD FLAG	HOLD-SPRTCD	****** Sport Totals ****** Sls	Comm	Cost	Profit	***** Report Totals ***** Sls	Comm	Cost	Profit
1.	ON	spaces	0	0	0	0	0	0	0	0

The final step of INITIALIZATION is to read the contents of the first record:

	Sport Code	Equip Type	Item	Description	Qty	Sales	Comm Pct	Cost
Record 1	01	01	1001A	WHT BBALL SHOE	00120	000480000	070	0001300

After INITIALIZATION, the program moves on to PROCESS. Figure 11–3 shows PROCESS. The first step of process is to perform CONTROL-BREAK. Refer to Figure 11–5. The first step of CONTROL-BREAK is to compare the control field of the input record (SPRTCD) to the hold field for the sport code (HOLD-SPRTCD). Since SPRTCD is 01 and HOLD-SPRTCD is spaces, the program will follow the NO path from the decision and perform SPRTCD-BREAK. The first step of SPRTCD-BREAK is to check if FRST-RCD-FLAG is turned ON. This is to determine if we are processing the first record. Since the flag is on, we know that we are processing the first record and therefore will not print the totals. We do, however, set the flag OFF. We exit SPRTCD-BREAK and move the new sport code to HOLD-SPRTCD. Below are the results of this:

	FRST-RCD FLAG	HOLD-SPRTCD	****** Sport Totals ****** Sls	Comm	Cost	Profit	***** Report Totals ***** Sls	Comm	Cost	Profit
2.	OFF	01	0	0	0	0	0	0	0	0

After exiting CONTROL-BREAK, we return to PROCESS. Our next step in PROCESS is to perform CALCULATE where we compute Commission Paid, Total Cost, and Profit. (This is not shown in this chapter because it is the same as in previous chapters.) The results of CALCULATE are as follows:

Commission Paid	336.00	(4800.00 × .070)
Total Cost	1560.00	(120 × 13.00)
Profit	2904.00	[(4800.00 − (336.00 + 1560.00)]

After CALCULATE, we proceed to ACCUMULATE. As we discussed in Chapter 10, we accumulate by adding the appropriate data to the lowest level control totals. In this case, the lowest level is the sport code. Below are the values of the fields after we accumulate to the sport totals:

	HOLD-SPRTCD	******** Sport Totals ********				******* Report Totals *******			
		Sls	Comm	Cost	Profit	Sls	Comm	Cost	Profit
3.	01	4800.00	336.00	1560.00	2904.00	0	0	0	0

After writing the results of the first record, we read the second record and pass control back to MAINLINE.

The contents of the second records are as follows:

	Sport Code	Equip Type	Item	Description	Qty	Sales	Comm Pct	Cost
Record 2	01	01	2024S	BLK BBALL SHOE	00193	000965000	070	0002100

MAINLINE is not shown, but has not changed from any other program. Again, MAINLINE passes control back to PROCESS. Once in PROCESS, the first task is to perform CONTROL-BREAK. CONTROL-BREAK compares the value of SPRTCD in the input record to HOLD-SPRTCD. Since both fields have the value 01, no control-break occurs. As with the previous record, CALCULATION and ACCUMULATE are performed. The results of CALCULATE are as follows:

Commission Paid	675.50	(9659.00 × .070)
Total Cost	4053.00	(193 × 21.00)
Profit	4921.50	(9650.00 − (675.50 + 4053.00))

Below are the results of our totals field and HOLD-SPRTCD after ACCUMULATE:

	HOLD-SPRTCD	******** Sport Totals ********				******* Report Totals *******			
		Sls	Comm	Cost	Profit	Sls	Comm	Cost	Profit
4.	01	14450.00	1011.50	5613.00	7825.50	0	0	0	0

After writing the results of this record, we read the next record on the file (record 3) and return control back to MAINLINE. The contents of record 3 are as follows:

	Sport Code	Equip Type	Item	Description	Qty	Sales	Comm Pct	Cost
Record 3	01	05	6355F	ALUMINUM BAT	00095	000035150	110	0001750

Because we have not reached the end of the file, control is passed backed to PROCESS. Again the first task encountered is CONTROL-BREAK. As with the previous record processed, SPRTCD is still 01, so no control-break occurs. As before, control is returned to PROCESS where

we perform CALCULATE and ACCUMULATE. The results of CALCU-
LATE are as follows:

Commission Paid	386.65	(3515.00 × .110)
Total Cost	1662.50	(95 × 17.50)
Profit	1465.85	(3515.00 − (386.65 + 1662.50))

The results after ACCUMULATE are shown below:

```
              ******** Sport Totals ********    ******* Report Totals *******
   HOLD-SPRTCD    Sls      Comm      Cost     Profit    Sls    Comm    Cost   Profit
5.    01       17965.00  1398.15   7275.50   9291.35     0      0       0       0
```

After writing the results of this record, we read the next record on the
file (record 4) and return control back to MAINLINE.

The contents of the next record are as follows:

```
            Sport  Equip                                          Comm
            Code   Type   Item   Description    Qty     Sales     Pct   Cost
Record 4     02     03    81155  TENNIS BALLS  02650  000795000   010  0000150
```

Because we have not reached the end of the file, control is again passed
back to PROCESS. This time, however, we will have a different result
when we perform CONTROL-BREAK. This time, SPRTCD is 02, while
HOLD-SPRTCD is 01. The program now recognizes that a control-break
has occurred. Before continuing to process record 4, we must first complete the processing related to sport code 01. This is done when we perform
SPRTCD-BREAK. SPRTCD-BREAK will first examine the FIRST-
RECORD-FLAG to determine if this is a real control-break, or simply the
result of the first record. In this case, the first record flag has been turned
off. Next we will move our Sport Totals to the total line and print the sport
totals on the report. (Refer to the report sample in Exhibit 11–1.) When this
is complete, the program will roll the sport totals into the report totals, and
zero the sport totals. The results are shown below:

```
              ******** Sport Totals ********     ******** Report Totals ********
   HOLD-SPRTCD   Sls      Comm     Cost    Profit      Sls      Comm     Cost   Profit
6.    01          0        0        0        0      17965.00  1397.65  7275.50  9291.35
```

Finally, when control is passed back to CONTROL-BREAK, we update
the hold area HOLD-SPRTCD with the new SPRTCD value.

```
              ******** Sport Totals ********     ******** Report Totals **********
   HOLD-SPRTCD   Sls      Comm     Cost    Profit      Sls      Comm     Cost   Profit
7.    02          0        0        0        0      17965.00  1397.65  7275.50  9291.35
```

Processing for records 4, 5, and 6 will occur just like 1, 2, and 3. That is,
SPRTCD of each record will be compared to HOLD-SPRTCD to determine
if control-break has occurred. Following that check, each CALCULATE and
ACCUMULATE will be performed for each record. When we have completed with ACCUMULATE for record 6, our fields will be as shown below:

```
              ******** Sport Totals ********      ******* Report Totals ********
   HOLD-SPRTCD    Sls      Comm      Cost     Profit     Sls      Comm     Cost   Profit
8.    02       39054.00  4745.12  14842.50  19466.38  17965.00  1397.65  7275.50  9291.35
```

After we have completed ACCUMULATE for record 6, we will print
the results and read the seventh record. At this time, we will obtain the
end-of-file condition since there is no seventh record. MAINLINE will

pass control to END-OF-JOB. Refer to Figure 11–6 for EOJ processing. The first task EOJ performs is SPRTCD-BREAK. Notice we have yet to print the totals for sport code 02. Forcing SPRTCD-BREAK at EOJ will allow us to print these totals. As before, the first thing SPRTCD-BREAK will do is print the totals for sport code 02. After printing the totals, we roll the sport code totals to the report totals, and zero the sport code totals. The results are shown below:

		Sport Code Totals				Report Totals		
HOLD-SPRTCD	Sls	Comm	Cost	Profit	Sls	Comm	Cost	Profit
9. 02	0	0	0	0	57019.00	6142.77	22118.00	28757.73

Following the completion of SPRTCD-BREAK, control is returned to EOJ, where we can now print the report totals.

Take the time necessary to fully understand the single-level control-break logic before moving on to multiple-level control-breaks.

SUMMARY

Control-breaks are a technique to break a report into manageable and logical subsets. Often, each subset of the report will be followed by the appropriate subtotals. The program identifies these control breaks by determining when the value of the control field changes from one record to the next, through the use of hold fields. When these control-breaks occur, the program performs a break routine that prints the totals, rolls the totals to the next highest level, zeroes the totals, and moves the new control field value to a hold field. In order to avoid printed subtotals for the first record, we employ the use of a FRST-RCD-FLAG. At END-OF-JOB, we force the printing of the final set of subtotals before printing the report totals.

REVIEW QUESTIONS

1. What is a control-break?
2. How do you determine when a control-break occurs?
3. What are the steps of a control-break?
4. What is a control field?
5. What is a hold field?
6. What is the importance of the FRST-RCD-FLAG?
7. Why do we force the break routine at END-OF-JOB?
8. Why does CONTROL-BREAK precede WRITE?

EXERCISE

This exercise is a simple program to compute and print payroll data. The report will list all employees. It will have a control-break when the department changes, and it will print totals for Gross Pay, Taxes, and Net Pay. Also, print report totals at the end. Use the following formulas:

- Gross Pay = Hours Worked * Hourly Rate.
- Taxes = Gross Pay * 15% (.15).
- Net Pay = Gross Pay − Taxes.

Use the following fields:

DEPT for department

GRSPAY for gross pay

TAX for taxes

NETPAY for net pay

Flowchart the following procedures:

INITIALIZATION (to identify all accumulation fields)
PROCESS
CONTROL-BREAK and the appropriate break routine, DEPT-BREAK
CALCULATE
ACCUMULATE
END-OF-JOB

PROJECT 1

Objective

Throughout the year, Acme Distributors must prepare for the beginning of each sporting season. That is, in the winter Acme prepares for baseball and soccer so that they have adequate inventory in the spring. In the summer, Acme stocks football and hockey equipment in preparation for the fall season.

Acme needs a program that can be requested by the sales manager for each sport (i.e., baseball, football, tennis, etc.) that will identify what products need to be purchased in order to prepare for their upcoming season. The sport code to be reported will be provided via a parameter file.

Acme Distributors maintains current merchandise inventory levels using the *Quantity-On-Hand* field (IM-QOH) in the item master file. As products are sold, this field is adjusted by the quantity sold. For that reason we can assume IM-QOH will always reflect an accurate current inventory.

The item master file also has a field named Order Point (IM-ORDPT). Whenever inventory level (IM-QOH) drops below the Order Point, it is time to reorder this item. This program must identify and report those items that must be ordered. The report will list all products to be purchased and the vendor from which the products are ordered. Acme orders a predetermined quantity of the item whenever it is ordered. This quantity is contained in the field IM-ORD-QTY.

Processing Requirements

1. Read the sport code parameter file to obtain the sport code that is to be selected and printed.

2. Read the Item Master file and select all items that have the requested sport code and where the inventory level has dropped below the order point.

3. The following formulas will be required:
   ■ Extended Cost = Order Quantity * Purchase Cost.
   ■ Sales Tax = Extended Cost * 5%.
   ■ Total Cost = Extended Cost + Sales Tax.

4. Provide a control-break and subtotals by vendor. Provide report totals. File will be sorted by vendor prior to being used by this program.

ITEM MASTER RECORD

01-05	ITEM NUMBER		IM-ITEM
06-20	DESCRIPTION		IM-DESC
21-22	SPORT CODE		IM-SPRTCD
23-24	EQUIPMENT TYPE		IM-ETYP
25-27	COMMISSION PERCENT	(3.3)	IM-PCT
28-33	VENDOR		IM-VNDR
34-40	PURCHASE COST	(7.2)	IM-COST
41-47	RETAIL PRICE	(7.2)	IM-PRICE
48-52	QUANTITY ON HAND	(5.0)	IM-QOH
53-57	ORDER POINT	(5.0)	IM-ORDPT
58-62	ORDER QUANTITY	(5.0)	IM-ORD-QTY
63-70	Unused		

SPORT CODE PARAMETER RECORD

01-02	SPORT CODE	PARM-SPRTCD

Printer Spacing Chart

```
                                                                                 111111111111111111111111111111111
             11111111112222222222333333333344444444445555555555666666666677777777778888888888999999999900000000001111111111222222222233
1234567890123456789012345678901234567890123456789012345678901234567890123456789012345678901234567890123456789012345678901234567890

DATE RUN:  MM/DD/YY                          ACME DISTRIBUTORS                                            PAGE ZZZZ9
TIME RUN:  HH:MM                        PRODUCT REPLENISHMENT REPORT
                                           FOR SPORT CODE XX

                  ITEM              ORDER     PURCHASE      EXTENDED      SALES       TOTAL
         VENDOR   NUMBER  DESCRIPTION  QTY       COST          COST        TAX        COST

         XXXXXX   XXXXX   XXXXXXXXXXXXXX  ZZ,ZZZ   Z,ZZZ.99    ZZZ,ZZZ.99   Z,ZZZ.99   ZZZ,ZZZ.99
         XXXXXX   XXXXX   XXXXXXXXXXXXXX  ZZ,ZZZ   Z,ZZZ.99    ZZZ,ZZZ.99   Z,ZZZ.99   ZZZ,ZZZ.99
         XXXXXX   XXXXX   XXXXXXXXXXXXXX  ZZ,ZZZ   Z,ZZZ.99    ZZZ,ZZZ.99   Z,ZZZ.99   ZZZ,ZZZ.99
         XXXXXX   XXXXX   XXXXXXXXXXXXXX  ZZ,ZZZ   Z,ZZZ.99    ZZZ,ZZZ.99   Z,ZZZ.99   ZZZ,ZZZ.99

                         VENDOR TOTALS                      Z,ZZZ,ZZZ.99  ZZ,ZZZ.99  Z,ZZZ,ZZZ.99

                         REPORT TOTALS                      Z,ZZZ,ZZZ.99  ZZ,ZZZ.99  Z,ZZZ,ZZZ.99
```

Assignment

1. Complete the mapping process.
2. Develop the structure chart.
3. Develop the flowchart or pseudo code for the entire program.

PROJECT 2

Objective

This program will provide sales management for Acme Distributors sales information for all customers, subtotaled by region.

Processing Requirements

1. Read and report all records on the file.
2. Print the report shown on the printer spacing chart.
3. Use the following formulas:
   - Sales Increase = Current Year Sales – Prior Year Sales.
   - Percent of Increase = (Sales Increase / Prior Year Sales) * 100.
4. Provide subtotals (control-breaks) at the region level.
5. Input file will be sorted by customer number within region number.

CUSTOMER SALES SUMMARY RECORD

01-02	REGION		CSS-RGN
03-07	CUSTOMER NUMBER		CSS-CUST
08-32	CUSTOMER NAME		CSS-NAME
33-41	CURRENT YEAR SALES	(9.2)	CSS-CYSLS
42-50	PRIOR YEAR SALES	(9.2)	CSS-PYSLS

Handwritten notes: ALPHA NUMERIC; REGION; RGN-HLD=BLANK

Printer Spacing Chart

```
          1111111111222222222233333333334444444444555555555566666666667777777777888888888899999999990011111111111111111111111111111
123456789012345678901234567890123456789012345567890123456789012345678901234567890123456789012345678901234567890123456789

RUN MM/DD/YY                                    ACME DISTRIBUTORS                                              PAGE ZZZZ9
TIME HH:MM                                    REGIONAL SALES REPORT

          CUSTOMER                              CURRENT         PRIOR          SALES         PERCENT OF
REGION    NUMBER    CUSTOMER NAME              YEAR SALES     YEAR SALES      INCREASE        INCREASE

  XX      XXXXX     XXXXXXXXXXXXXXXXXXXXXXXXX  Z,ZZZ,ZZZ.99-  Z,ZZZ,ZZZ.99-  Z,ZZZ,ZZZ.99-    ZZZ.9-
  XX      XXXXX     XXXXXXXXXXXXXXXXXXXXXXXXX  Z,ZZZ,ZZZ.99-  Z,ZZZ,ZZZ.99-  Z,ZZZ,ZZZ.99-    ZZZ.9-
  XX      XXXXX     XXXXXXXXXXXXXXXXXXXXXXXXX  Z,ZZZ,ZZZ.99-  Z,ZZZ,ZZZ.99-  Z,ZZZ,ZZZ.99-    ZZZ.9-
  XX      XXXXX     XXXXXXXXXXXXXXXXXXXXXXXXX  Z,ZZZ,ZZZ.99-  Z,ZZZ,ZZZ.99-  Z,ZZZ,ZZZ.99-    ZZZ.9-

  XX      REGION TOTALS                        ZZ,ZZZ,ZZZ.99- ZZ,ZZZ,ZZZ.99- ZZ,ZZZ,ZZZ.99-    ZZZ.9-

  XX      XXXXX     XXXXXXXXXXXXXXXXXXXXXXXXX  Z,ZZZ,ZZZ.99-  Z,ZZZ,ZZZ.99-  Z,ZZZ,ZZZ.99-    ZZZ.9-
  XX      XXXXX     XXXXXXXXXXXXXXXXXXXXXXXXX  Z,ZZZ,ZZZ.99-  Z,ZZZ,ZZZ.99-  Z,ZZZ,ZZZ.99-    ZZZ.9-
  XX      XXXXX     XXXXXXXXXXXXXXXXXXXXXXXXX  Z,ZZZ,ZZZ.99-  Z,ZZZ,ZZZ.99-  Z,ZZZ,ZZZ.99-    ZZZ.9-
  XX      XXXXX     XXXXXXXXXXXXXXXXXXXXXXXXX  Z,ZZZ,ZZZ.99-  Z,ZZZ,ZZZ.99-  Z,ZZZ,ZZZ.99-    ZZZ.9-

  XX      REGION TOTALS                        ZZ,ZZZ,ZZZ.99- ZZ,ZZZ,ZZZ.99- ZZ,ZZZ,ZZZ.99-    ZZZ.9-

          REPORT TOTALS                        ZZ,ZZZ,ZZZ.99- ZZ,ZZZ,ZZZ.99- ZZ,ZZZ,ZZZ.99-    ZZZ.9-
```

Assignment:

1. Perform the mapping process.
2. Develop the program structure chart.
3. Develop the flowchart or pseudo code for the entire program.

12
Multiple-Level Control-Breaks

OBJECTIVES

■ Understanding the concepts of the multiple-level control-break.

■ Understanding the differences between a single-level control-break and a multiple-level control-break.

■ Understanding summary reporting.

INTRODUCTION

Now that we understand the single-level control-break, let's take a look at the multiple-level control-break. This chapter will concentrate on the difference between them, and, for the most part, you will discover that the concepts and program design are the same. The basic difference between the two is that, while you still do the same fundamental tasks, you perform them more often for a multiple-level control-break.

What Is a Multiple-Level Control-Break?

In a multiple-level control-break program, the report is divided into smaller sections. In our example of a single-level control-break, the sales report had a control-break on the sport code. According to our data dictionary, products can be viewed in multiple ways. First, they are associated with a type of sport, such as tennis, football, or hockey. This sport association is defined by the sport code. Another way of grouping products is by equipment type. The equipment type defines the type of item, such as a shoe, jersey, or racket. In a multiple-level control-break report, we can organize the items by equipment type within sport code. In doing so, we can provide subtotals at these different levels. Exhibit 12–1 illustrates an example of this report, and Exhibit 12–2 is the program specification for this report.

Exhibit 12–1
SAMPLE MULTIPLE-LEVEL CONTROL-BREAK REPORT

```
                                                               1111111111111111111111111111111
         1111111111222222222233333333334444444444555555555566666666667777777777888888888899999999990000000000111111111222222222
123456789012345678901234567890123456789012345678901234567890123456789012345678901234567890123456789012345678901234567890123456789

RUN  06/30/94   14:43                        ACME DISTRIBUTORS                                        PAGE    1
                                             SALES REPORT
```

SPORT CODE	EQUIP TYPE	ITEM NMBR	ITEM DESCRIPTION	QUANTITY SOLD	SALES AMOUNT	COMMISSIONS PAID	TOTAL COST	PROFIT
01	01	1001A	WHT BBALL SHOE	120	4,800.00	336.00	1,560.00	2,904.00
01	01	2024S	BLK BBALL SHOE	193	9,650.00	675.50	4,053.00	4,921.50
			EQUIPMENT TYPE TOTAL		14,450.00	1,011.50	5,613.00	7,825.50
01	05	6355F	ALUMINUM BAT	95	3,515.00	386.65	1,662.50	1,465.85
			EQUIPMENT TYPE TOTAL		3,515.00	386.65	1,662.50	1,465.85
			SPORT CODE TOTAL		17,965.00	1,397.65	7,275.50	9,291.35
02	03	81155	TENNIS BALLS	2,650	7,950.00	79.50	3,975.00	3,895.50
			EQUIPMENT TYPE TOTAL		7,950.00	79.50	3,975.00	3,895.50
02	05	3284L	ALM TENNIS RCKT	170	13,515.00	2,027.25	4,377.50	7,110.25
02	05	6355F	FGL TENNIS RCKT	220	17,589.00	2,638.37	6,490.00	8,460.63
			EQUIPMENT TYPE TOTAL		31,104.00	4,665.62	10,867.50	15,570.88
			SPORT CODE TOTAL		39,054.00	4,745.12	14,842.50	19,466.38
			REPORT TOTAL		57,019.00	6,142.77	22,118.00	28,757.73

Exhibit 12–2
PROGRAM SPECIFICATION FOR MULTIPLE-LEVEL CONTROL-BREAK EXAMPLE

Objective

Produce a sales report showing profitability by item. File will be sorted prior to the execution of the program. Input file will be sorted by:

Sport code – major sort field.

Equipment type – intermediate sort field.

Item number – minor sort field.

Processing Requirements

1. Read and print all records on the file.
2. Report format shown on printer spacing chart.
3. Use the following formulas:
   - Commission Paid = Sales Amount * Commission Percent.
   - Total Cost = Quantity Sold * Purchase Cost.
   - Profit = Sales Amount – (Commission Paid + Total Cost).
4. Provide control-breaks and subtotals for equipment type and sport code.
5. Provide report totals.
6. Report will be single-spaced.

SALES RECORD

01-02	SPORT CODE		SPRTCD
03-04	EQUIPMENT TYPE		ETYP
05-09	ITEM NUMBER		ITEM
10-24	ITEM DESCRIPTION		DESC
25-29	QUANTITY SOLD	(5.0)	QTY
30-38	SALES AMOUNT	(9.2)	SLSAMT
39-41	COMMISSION PERCENT	(3.3)	CMPCT
42-48	PURCHASE COST	(7.2)	PRCHCST
49-60	Unused		

Printer Spacing Chart

```
                                                                                        11111111111111111111111111111111
          1111111111222222222233333333334444444444555555555566666666667777777777888888888899999999990000000000111111111122222222223
123456789012345678901234567890123456789012345678901234567890123456789012345678901234567890123456789012345678901234567890

RUN  MM/DD/YY   HH:MM                                ACME DISTRIBUTORS                                                 PAGE ZZZZ9
                                                       SALES REPORT

     SPORT      EQUIP       ITEM                      QUANTITY      SALES          COMMISSIONS       TOTAL
     CODE       TYPE        NMBR    ITEM DESCRIPTION     SOLD       AMOUNT            PAID           COST            PROFIT

      XX         XX        XXXXX    XXXXXXXXXXXXXX     ZZ,ZZZ-    Z,ZZZ,ZZZ.99-    ZZZ,ZZZ.99-    ZZZ,ZZZ.99-    ZZZ,ZZZ.99-
      XX         XX        XXXXX    XXXXXXXXXXXXXX     ZZ,ZZZ-    Z,ZZZ,ZZZ.99-    ZZZ,ZZZ.99-    ZZZ,ZZZ.99-    ZZZ,ZZZ.99-
      XX         XX        XXXXX    XXXXXXXXXXXXXX     ZZ,ZZZ-    Z,ZZZ,ZZZ.99-    ZZZ,ZZZ.99-    ZZZ,ZZZ.99-    ZZZ,ZZZ.99-

                             EQUIPMENT TYPE TOTAL    ZZ,ZZZ,ZZZ.99-  Z,ZZZ,ZZZ.99-  Z,ZZZ,ZZZ.99-  Z,ZZZ,ZZZ.99-

                             SPORT CODE TOTAL        ZZ,ZZZ,ZZZ.99-  Z,ZZZ,ZZZ.99-  Z,ZZZ,ZZZ.99-  Z,ZZZ,ZZZ.99-

                             REPORT TOTAL            ZZ,ZZZ,ZZZ.99-  Z,ZZZ,ZZZ.99-  Z,ZZZ,ZZZ.99-  Z,ZZZ,ZZZ.99-
```

Programming Fundamentals

File Sequence

As with the single-level control-break, the file must be sorted in the proper sequence. For the report shown in Exhibit 12-1, the input sales file will be sorted by item number, within equipment type, within sport code.

Determining If a Control-Break Has Occurred

Next, let's look at the logic that determines if a control-break has occurred. In the single-level control-break program we simply compared the value of the control field from the input record to the hold field we used to store the value of the previous record(s). This will not change, except that we now have more than one field to check for the occurrence of a control-break. In our example, we must now check to see if the equipment type has changed in addition to the sport code.

In multiple-level control-break programs, we can identify control-breaks as "major," "intermediate," and "minor" level breaks. The major break will be the control-break of greatest significance, in this case sport code. The minor break is the control-break of least significance, in this case equipment type. Intermediate breaks are the breaks between the major and minor. This example has no intermediate breaks.

When determining if a control-break occurs, we first determine if a major break has occurred. If it has, we perform the same basic tasks we did when a single-level control-break occurred, with only minor alterations (more on this in just a moment). If the major control field did not change, we check the intermediate, and then the minor. We always check the control fields from major to minor. The reason for the major to minor check is that if the major changes, we will automatically force the intermediate and minor control totals to print. In the example report illustrated in Exhibit 12–1, notice that when the sport code changed, we printed the equipment type totals.

Now let's take a look at the tasks we perform when a control-break has occurred. In this discussion, we will keep the control-breaks generic (minor, intermediate, and major). The flowchart related to the program specifications provided in Exhibit 12–2 will be illustrated later in the chapter.

MINOR-LEVEL CONTROL-BREAK TASKS

1. Print the minor totals.
2. Roll the totals to the next highest level (intermediate level).
3. Zero the totals for this control-break level (minor totals).
4. Move the value of the new minor control field to the minor hold field.

Notice that these are the same steps performed for the single-level control-break except that we do not check to see if the control-break is the result of the first record. This first record test will be performed as part of the major control-break.

INTERMEDIATE-LEVEL CONTROL-BREAK

1. Perform minor-level control-break.
2. Print the intermediate totals.
3. Roll the totals to the next highest level (major level).
4. Zero the totals for this control-break level (intermediate totals).
5. Move the value of the new intermediate control field to the intermediate hold field.

Again, notice that these steps are still the same, except for the first step. Whenever the intermediate control-break occurs, we will force the minor-level control-break. This will print the minor-level subtotal before the intermediate subtotals.

MAJOR-LEVEL CONTROL-BREAK

1. Determine if the control-break is a result of the first record.
2. Perform intermediate-level control-break.
3. Print the major totals.
4. Roll the totals to the next highest level (report totals).
5. Zero the totals for this control-break level (major totals).
6. Move the value of the new major control field to the major hold field.

Notice that the first step of the major-level control-break will determine if the first record is the cause of the control-break situation. Whenever the major control-break occurs, our first task is to force the intermediate control-break. This in turn forces the minor break. After the minor totals are printed, the intermediate totals are printed. Finally, the major totals are printed.

Let's take a look at the flowchart for this generic example.

FLOWCHARTING MULTIPLE CONTROL-BREAKS

As we look at the generic flowcharting examples, keep in mind that only the portions of the program impacted by a multiple control-break are illustrated. Because control breaks do not affect READ, WRITE, and CALCULATE, these procedures will not be shown.

Figure 12–1 illustrates the INITIALIZATION section. Look at how the hold areas, totals, and the general configuration of the memory area for

Figure 12–1
**Generic example of
INITIALIZATION for a
multiple-level control-
break program**

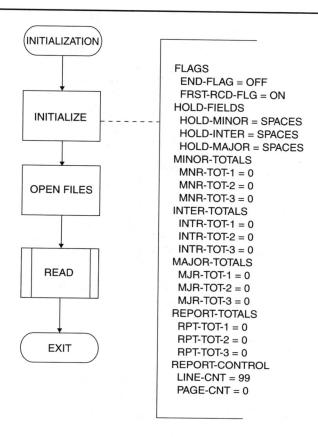

FLAGS
  END-FLAG = OFF
  FRST-RCD-FLG = ON
HOLD-FIELDS
  HOLD-MINOR = SPACES
  HOLD-INTER = SPACES
  HOLD-MAJOR = SPACES
MINOR-TOTALS
  MNR-TOT-1 = 0
  MNR-TOT-2 = 0
  MNR-TOT-3 = 0
INTER-TOTALS
  INTR-TOT-1 = 0
  INTR-TOT-2 = 0
  INTR-TOT-3 = 0
MAJOR-TOTALS
  MJR-TOT-1 = 0
  MJR-TOT-2 = 0
  MJR-TOT-3 = 0
REPORT-TOTALS
  RPT-TOT-1 = 0
  RPT-TOT-2 = 0
  RPT-TOT-3 = 0
REPORT-CONTROL
  LINE-CNT = 99
  PAGE-CNT = 0

PSEUDO CODE

```
initialization:
    INITIALIZE flags:          end-flag = off
                               frst-rcd-flag = off
               hold-fields:    hold-minor = spaces
                               hold-inter = spaces
                               hold-major = spaces
               minor-totals:   mnr-tot-1 = 0
                               mnr-tot-2 = 0
                               mnr-tot-3 = 0
               inter-totals:   intr-tot-1 = 0
                               intr-tot-2 = 0
                               intr-tot-3 = 0
               major-totals:   mjr-tot-1 = 0
                               mjr-tot-2 = 0
                               mjr-tot-3 = 0
               report-totals:  rt-tot-1 = 0
                               rt-tot-2 = 0
                               rt-tot-3 = 0
               report-control: line-cnt = 99
                               page-cnt = 0
    OPEN files
    DO read
    STOP
```

the program have been laid out. It is important to keep this design simple, yet complete.

Figure 12–2 shows the revised CONTROL-BREAK procedure. Notice that the first check is to determine if the major control-break has occurred. If so, the MAJOR-BREAK procedure is performed. Notice that all three

Figure 12–2
Generic example of the CONTROL-BREAK procedure for a multiple-level control-break program

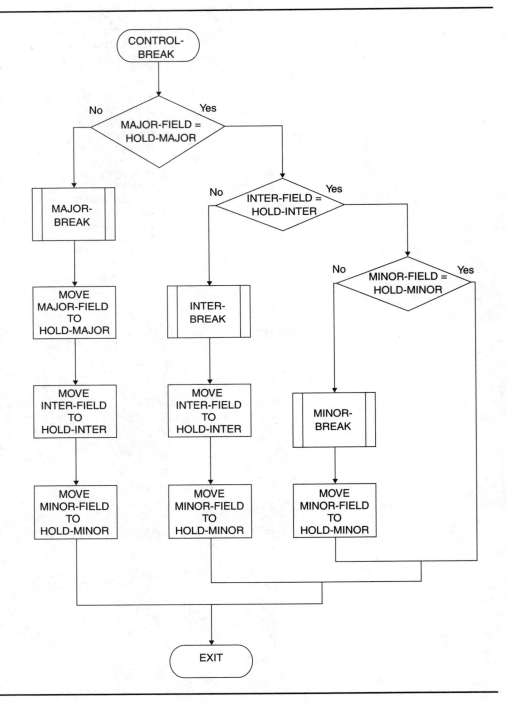

Figure 12–2
(continued)

PSEUDO CODE

```
control break:
        IF major-field not = hold-major THEN
                DO major-break
                LET hold-major = major-field
                LET hold-inter = inter-field
                LET hold-minor = minor-field
           ELSE
             IF inter-field not = hold-inter THEN
                     DO inter-break
                     LET hold-inter = inter-field
                     LET hold-minor = minor-field
             ELSE
               IF minor-field not = hold-minor THEN
                       DO minor-break
                       LET hold-minor = minor-field
               END-IF
           END-IF
        END-IF
```

hold areas are set after control is returned from MAJOR-BREAK. Because we will ultimately perform all control-break levels at this time, we need to be sure that we set all hold areas to their new values. As with the single level break, this resetting of the hold areas cannot occur within the MAJOR-BREAK procedure. If the major break did not occur, we next check the intermediate, and perform the appropriate tasks if it changed. If the intermediate break did not occur, we check the minor control level.

Figure 12–3 shows the three levels of control-breaks. Look first at the MINOR-BREAK. The only difference from this and the single-level control-break is that we do not check to see if this break occurred because of the first record. The first record check is now performed in the MAJOR-BREAK. Next, take a look at the INTERMEDIATE-BREAK. As explained earlier, the first task performed is the minor level control break. After control is returned from the minor break, we print the intermediate totals, roll them to the next level, and zero the intermediate totals. Finally, take a look at MAJOR-BREAK. Here we check to see if the control-break was a result of the first record. If this is an actual control break (not caused by the first record), then we invoke the procedure to print the intermediate totals, print the major totals, roll the major totals to the next level (report totals), and zero the major totals.

Finally, we reach END-OF-JOB. In the single-level control-break program, we executed the break routine as the first step of EOJ. Here we will perform MAJOR-BREAK as the first task. Figure 12–4 illustrates END-OF-JOB.

Figure 12–5 contains the complete flowchart for the program specification provided in Exhibit 12-2.

Figure 12–3
Generic break routines (MINOR, INTERMEDIATE, and MAJOR) for multiple-level control-break program

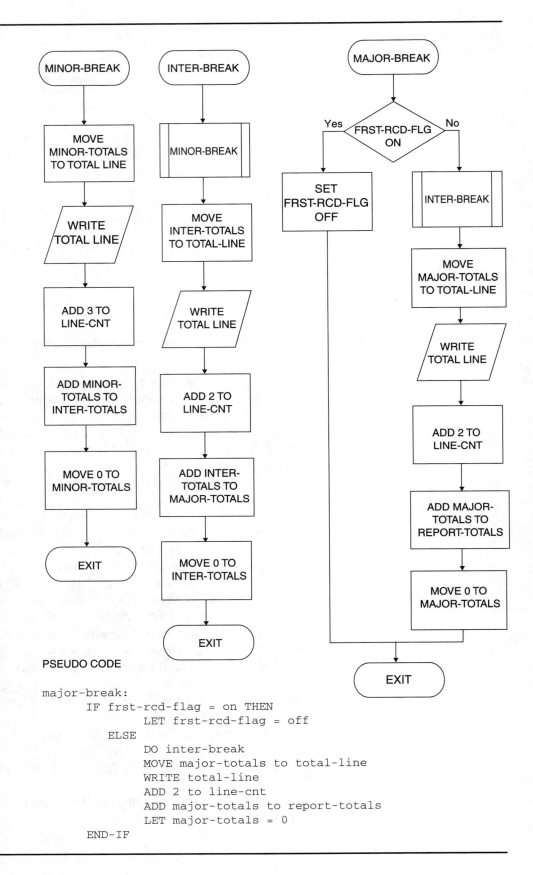

PSEUDO CODE

```
major-break:
        IF frst-rcd-flag = on THEN
                LET frst-rcd-flag = off
           ELSE
                DO inter-break
                MOVE major-totals to total-line
                WRITE total-line
                ADD 2 to line-cnt
                ADD major-totals to report-totals
                LET major-totals = 0
        END-IF
```

Figure 12–3
(continued)

```
inter-break:
        DO minor-break
        MOVE inter-totals to total-line
        WRITE total-line
        ADD 2 to line-cnt
        ADD inter-totals to major totals
        LET inter-totals = 0

minor-break:
        MOVE minor-totals to total-line
        WRITE total-line
        ADD 2 to line-cnt
        ADD minor-totals to inter-totals
        LET minor-totals = 0
```

Figure 12–4
**Generic END-OF-JOB
procedure for multiple-
level control-break
programs**

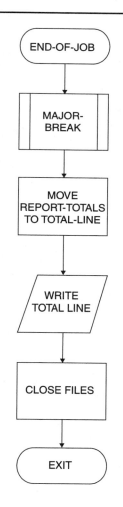

PSEUDO CODE

```
end-of-job:
        DO major-break
        MOVE report-totals to total-line
        WRITE total-line
        CLOSE files
```

Figure 12–5
Flowchart for program specification provided in Exhibit 12–2

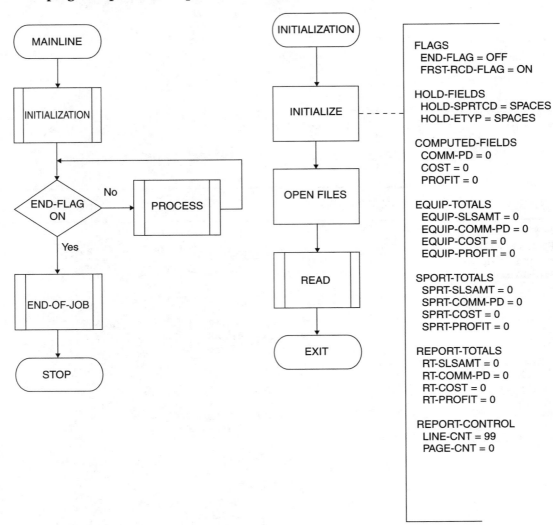

Figure 12–5
(*continued*)

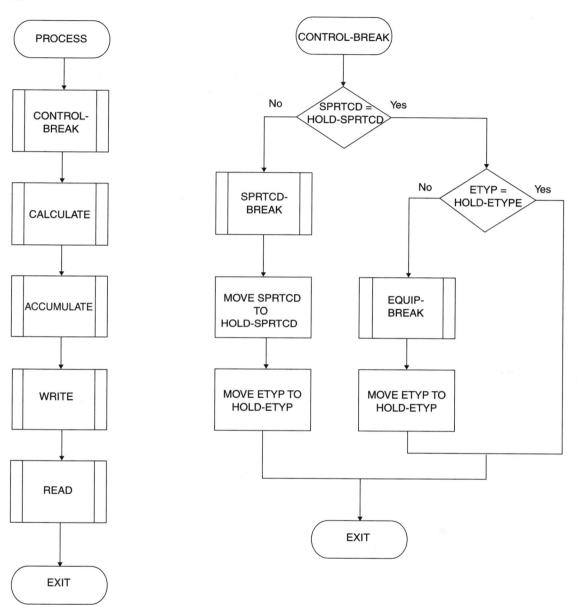

(*continued on the next page*)

Figure 12–5
(continued)

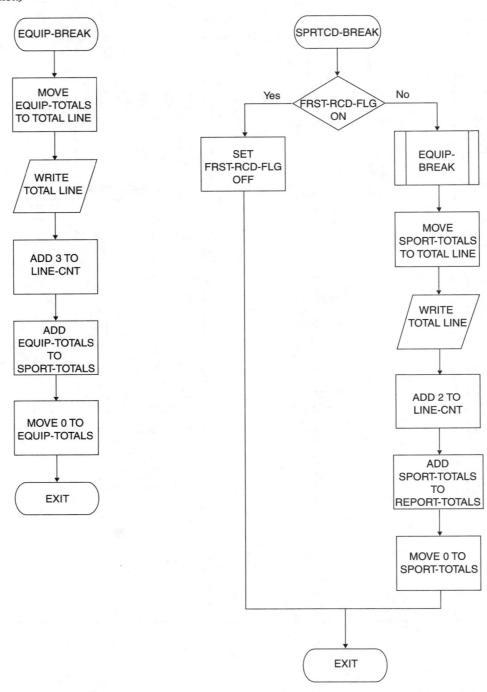

Figure 12–5
(continued)

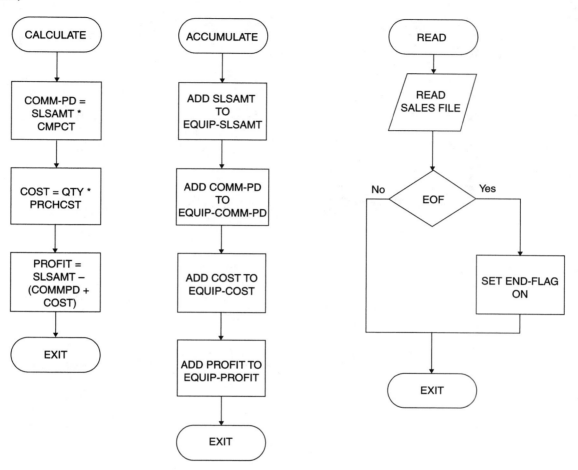

(continued on the next page)

Figure 12–5
(*continued*)

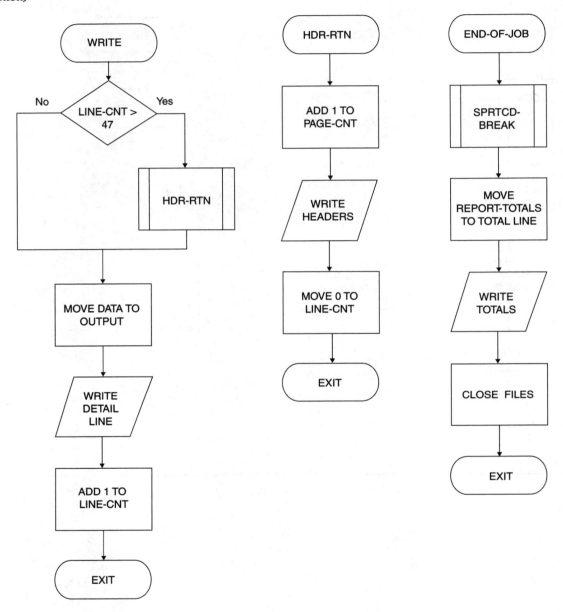

PSEUDO CODE

```
mainline:
      DO initialization
      DOWHILE end-flag off
         DO process
      END-DOWHILE
      DO end-of-job
      STOP
```

Figure 12–5
(continued)

```
initialization:
        INITIALIZE  flags:           end-flag = off
                                     frst-rcd-flag = on
                    hold-fields:     hold-sprtcd = spaces
                                     hold-etyp = spaces
                    computed-fields: comm-pd = 0
                                     cost = 0
                                     profit = 0
                    equip-totals:    equip-slsamt = 0
                                     equip-comm-pd = 0
                                     equip-cost = 0
                                     equip-profit = 0
                    sport-totals:    sprt-slsamt = 0
                                     sprt-comm-pd = 0
                                     sprt-cost = 0
                                     sprt-profit = 0
                    report-totals:   rt-slsamt = 0
                                     rt-comm-pd = 0
                                     rt-cost = 0
                                     rt-profit = 0
                    report-control:  line-cnt = 99
                                     page-cnt = 0
        OPEN files
        DO read

process:
        DO control-break
        DO calculate
        DO accumulate
        DO write
        DO read

control-break:
        IF sprtcd not = hold-sprtcd THEN
            DO sprtcd-break
            LET hold-sprtcd = sprtcd
            LET hold-etyp = etyp
          ELSE
            IF etyp not = hold-etyp THEN
                    DO equip-break
                    LET hold-etyp = etyp
            END-IF
        END-IF
```

(continued on the next page)

Figure 12–5
(continued)

```
sprtcd-break:
        IF frst-rcd-flag = on THEN
             LET frst-rcd-flag = off
          ELSE
             DO equip-break
             MOVE sport-totals to total-line
             WRITE total-line
             ADD 2 to line-cnt
             ADD sport-totals to report-totals
             LET sport-totals = 0
        END-IF

equip-break:
        MOVE equip-totals to total-line
        WRITE total-line
        ADD 2 to line-cnt
        ADD equip-totals to sport-totals
        LET equip-totals = 0

calculate:
        LET comm-pd = slsamt * cmpct
        LET cost = qty * prchcst
        LET profit = slsamt - (comm-pd + cost)

accumulate:
        ADD slsamt to equip-slsamt
        ADD comm-pd to equip-comm-pd
        ADD cost to equip-cost
        ADD profit to equip-profit

write:
        IF line-cnt > 47 THEN
                DO hdr-rtn
        END-IF
        MOVE data to output
        WRITE detail-line
        ADD 1 to line-cnt

hdr-rtn:
        ADD 1 to page-cnt
        WRITE headers
        LET line-cnt = 0

read:
        READ sales-file
        IF end-of-file THEN
                LET end-flag = on
        END-IF

end-of-job:
        DO sprtcd-break
        MOVE report-totals to total-line
        WRITE totals-line
        CLOSE files
```

OTHER CONTROL-BREAK PROCESSES

With the basics of control-break processing well in hand, let's discuss two final topics that you may encounter. First, we will discuss computations that occur at control-break; and secondly, we will look at processing in cases where only summarized data is printed.

Control-Break Computations

To gain maximum benefit from the report we just designed, the client has requested that we include the profit margin. Profit margin will represent the percentage of the sales amount that represents profit. We are told that the formula for computing the profit margin is (PROFIT / SALES AMOUNT) * 100. This is what the new report will look like:

```
RUN  06/30/94   14:43                         ACME DISTRIBUTORS                              PAGE    1
                                                SALES REPORT


SPORT    EQUIP                            QUANTITY        SALES      COMMISSIONS      TOTAL                    PROFIT
CODE     TYPE    NMBR   ITEM DESCRIPTION     SOLD        AMOUNT          PAID          COST       PROFIT       MARGIN

 01       01     1001A  WHT BBALL SHOE        120       4,800.00       336.00       1,560.00     2,904.00       60.5
 01       01     2024S  BLK BBALL SHOE        193       9,650.00       675.50       4,053.00     4,921.50       51.0

                        EQUIPMENT TYPE TOTAL          14,450.00     1,011.50       5,613,00     7,825.50       54.2

 01       05     6355F  ALUMINUM BAT           95       3,515.00       386.65       1,662.50     1,465.85       41.7

                        EQUIPMENT TYPE TOTAL           3,515.00       386.65       1,662.50     1,465.85       41.7

                        SPORT CODE TOTAL             17,965.00     1,397.65       7,275.50     9,291.35       51.7

 02       03     81155  TENNIS BALLS        2,650       7,950.00        79.50       3,975.00     3,895.50       49.0

                        EQUIPMENT TYPE TOTAL           7,950.00        79.50       3,975.00     3,895.50       49.0

 02       05     3284L  ALM TENNIS RCKT       170      13,515.00     2,027.25       4,377.50     7,110.25       52.6
 02       05     6355F  FGL TENNIS RCKT       220      17,589.00     2,638.37       6,490.00     8,460.63       48.1

                        EQUIPMENT TYPE TOTAL          31,104.00     4,665.62      10,867.50    15,570.88       50.1

                        SPORT CODE TOTAL             39,054.00     4,745.12      14,842.50    19,466.38       49.8

                        REPORT TOTAL                 57,019.00     6,142.77      22,118.00    28,757.73       50.4
```

Notice that the only difference is the inclusion of the profit margin on the right-hand side of the report. As you would expect, the calculation of the margin for each item will be in the CALCULATION procedure. However, we cannot accumulate the profit margin, as this would give us an inflated and incorrect answer. Let's take a look at the first equipment type total printed. This total indicates that we have total sales of $14,450.00 with profits of $7,825.50. This is a profit margin of 54.2%, which we compute using calculation (7825.50/14450.00) * 100. In this example we must compute the margin at the time of control-break. Again, we cannot accumulate the margin. If we tried to accumulate Margin as we do Sales, Cost, Commissions Paid, and Profit, we would show a profit margin of 111.5% (60.5 + 51.0).

Figure 12–6 illustrates the new CALCULATE procedure. The only change is the step to compute the margin percent.

Figure 12–7 illustrates the revised EQUIP-BREAK and SPORT-BREAK procedures. You will see in Figure 12–7, that we have added the calculation for the margin percentages to the beginning of these break procedures. This

Figure 12–6
Revised CALCULATE
procedure to include
computation of Margin
Percent

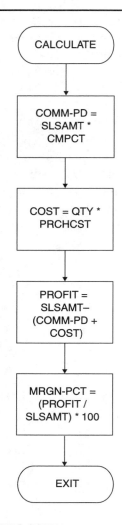

PSEUDO CODE

```
calculate:
    LET comm-pd = slsamt * cmpct
    LET cost = qty * prchcst
    LET profit = slsamt - (comm-pd + cost)
    LET mrgn-pct = (profit / slsamt) * 100
```

is because we must compute the margin percentage before we can print the totals. The INITIALIZE step of INITIALIZATION is modified so that MRGN-PCT is initialized to zero. MRGN-PCT would be placed under computed-fields. Likewise, SPORT-MRGN-PCT, EQUIP-MRGN-PCT, and RPT-MRGN-PCT are added to the appropriate total groupings.

END-OF-JOB is also be modified, as shown in Figure 12–8, to compute the final margin percentage using RPT-SLSAMT and RPT-PROFIT. This calculation is placed after SPORT-BREAK is executed and before printing the report totals.

Figure 12–7
Revised break routines that now include computation of margin percentage to be printed with each control-break total

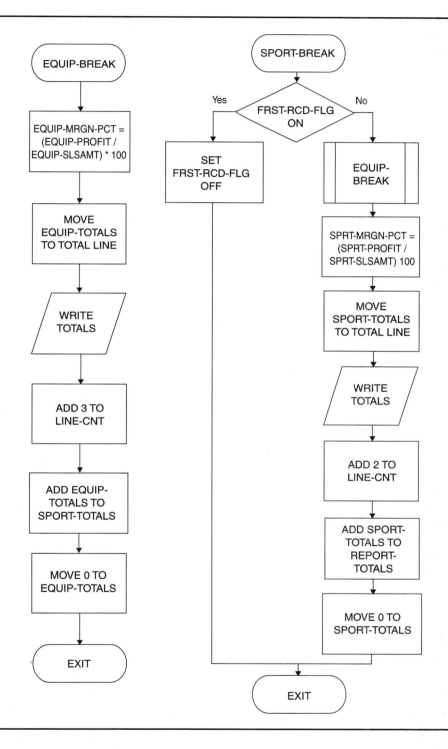

(continued on the next page)

**Figure 12–7
(continued)**

PESUDO CODE

```
sport-break:
        IF frst-rcd-flag not = on THEN
                LET frst-rcd-flag = off
            ELSE
                DO equip-break
                LET sprt-mrgn-pct = (sprt-profit / sprt-slsamt) * 100
                MOVE sport-totals to total-line
                WRITE total-line
                ADD 2 to line-cnt
                ADD sport-totals to report-totals
                LET sport-totals = 0
        END-IF

equip-break:
        LET equip-mrgn-pct = equip-profit / equip-slsamt) * 100
        MOVE equip-totals to total-line
        WRITE total-line
        ADD 3 to line-cnt
        ADD equip-totals to sport-totals
        LET equip-totals = 0
```

Print Only the Summary Data

Our client has returned to us again. This time they no longer require the item-level detail of the report. Because Acme sells thousands of products, the reports have become large and unusable. They have requested the following *summary* report instead:

```
RUN  06/30/94   14:43                        ACME DISTRIBUTORS                           PAGE    1
                                              SALES REPORT
```

SPORT CODE	EQUIP TYPE	SALES AMOUNT	COMMISSIONS PAID	TOTAL COST	PROFIT	PROFIT MARGIN
01	01	14,450.00	1,011.50	5,613,00	7,825.50	54.2
01	05	3,515.00	386.65	1,662.50	1,465.85	41.7
SPORT CODE TOTAL		17,965.00	1,397.65	7,275.50	9,291.35	51.7
02	03	7,950.00	79.50	3,975.00	3,895.50	49.0
02	05	31,104.00	4,665.62	10,867.50	15,570.88	50.1
SPORT CODE TOTAL		39,054.00	4,745.12	14,842.50	19,466.38	49.8
REPORT TOTAL		57,019.00	6,142.77	22,118.00	28,757.73	50.4

The structure of this program will deviate slightly from earlier programs. In each of the previous programs that we designed, we printed a detail line on the report for every record we processed. If you refer back to the previous report, you will see detail lines for every item we sold, with each item being a separate record on the sales file. For summary reports, however, we do not write out a line for each record read. We will only write the report when a control-break occurs. Therefore, WRITE will not be performed within the PROCESS procedure. Instead WRITE will be performed within EQUIP-BREAK. *The WRITE procedure is always performed at the*

Figure 12–8
END-OF-JOB procedure,
revised to compute the
report total margin
percent

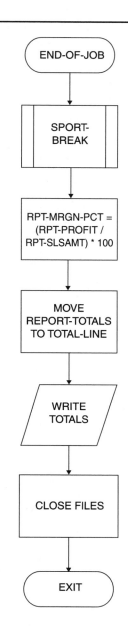

PSEUDO CODE

```
end-of-job:
    DO sport-break
    LET rpt-mrgn-pct = (rpt-profit / rpt-slsamt) *  100
    MOVE report-toals to total-line
    WRITE total-line
    CLOSE files
```

lowest level of the report. Until now, the lowest level has always been the detail level (each record). This time, the lowest level of information on the report is the equipment total. Other than that, this program remains the same.

Figure 12–9 illustrates the new PROCESS and EQUIP-BREAK procedures. All other procedures remain the same.

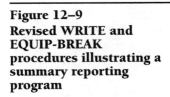

Figure 12–9
Revised WRITE and
EQUIP-BREAK
procedures illustrating a
summary reporting
program

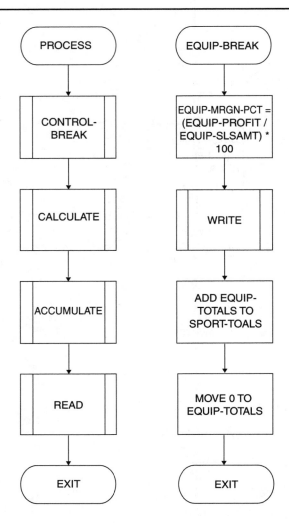

PSEUDO CODE

```
process:
    DO control-break
    DO calculate
    DO accumulate
    DO read


equip-break
    LET equip-mrgn-pct =
         (equip-profit / equip-slsamt) * 100
    DO write
    ADD equip-totals to sport-totals
    LET equip-totals = 0
```

SUMMARY

Programs with multiple-level control-breaks are designed similarly to programs with single-level control-breaks. The main difference is that we must check additional control fields to see if a control-break has occurred. As we learned in Chapter 10, not all totals can be accumulated. If total lines contain percentages or averages, these must be computed prior to printing. This is true of report totals, single-level control-breaks, and multiple-level control-breaks. Finally, some reports are not written at the detail level. In some cases, the lowest level of detail on the report may be at the minor control-break. In this case, WRITE is removed from PROCESS and relocated to the minor control field's break routine.

REVIEW QUESTIONS

1. Why are the control-break fields check performed in major/ intermediate/minor sequence when determining a control-break?

2. Why do higher-level control-breaks (i.e., major and intermediate) force the break routine of the next control-break lower?

3. What is a summary report? How is PROCESS changed to allow the summary report to be produced?

4. Which type of total cannot be accumulated with other control-break totals? How are these types of totals derived if they cannot be accumulated?

EXERCISE

This exercise will expand on the exercise we did in Chapter 10 to include the procedures required to provide two control-breaks.

To complete this exercise, you will need to flowchart several procedures of the program to compute the average for each student, and provide the appropriate average at each level of control-break. The major break will be instructor, and the minor break will be the class number. You are also expected to print the average for the entire report. As with the exercise in Chapter 10, the program must be flexible to accommodate any number of students in the class.

Flowchart the following procedures for this program:

INITIALIZATION (to identify the accumulation fields)

PROCESS

CONTROL-BREAK and the appropriate break routines

CALCULATE

ACCUMULATE

END-OF-JOB

Use the following field names from the file:

INSTRUCTOR

CLASS

TEST1

TEST2

TEST3

TEST4

TEST5

TEST6

PROJECT

Objective

This program will provide sales information for Acme Distributors sales management department. This report will print total sales by equipment type, sport code, and region. The input file will sort equipment type (minor), within sport code (intermediate), within region (major), prior to this program being executed.

Processing Requirements

1. Read and process all records on the file.

2. Do not report at the customer level. The lowest reporting level is the equipment type summary.

3. Print the report shown on the printer spacing chart.

4. Use the following formula:
   - Sales Increase = Current Year Sales – Prior Year Sales.

5. Provide subtotals (control-breaks) at the equipment type, sport code, and region level.

CUSTOMER SALES SUMMARY RECORD

Position	Field	Name
01-02	REGION	CSS-RGN
03-07	CUSTOMER NUMBER	CSS-CUST
08-32	CUSTOMER NAME	CSS-NAME
33-34	SPORT CODE	CSS-SRPTCD
35-36	EQUIPMENT TYPE	CSS-ETYPE
37-45	CURRENT YEAR SALES (9.2)	CSS-CYSLS
46-54	PRIOR YEAR SALES (9.2)	CSS-PYSLS
55-60	Unused	

Printer Spacing Chart

```
                                                                                                      1
          111111111122222222223333333333444444444455555555556666666666777777777788888888889999999999 0
123456789012345678901234567890123456789012345678901234567890123456789012345678901234567890123456789 0

RUN MM/DD/YY                        ACME DISTRIBUTORS                        PAGE ZZZZ9
TIME HH:MM                          REGIONAL SALES REPORT


                SPORT  EQUIP          CURRENT          PRIOR           SALES
       REGION   CODE   TYPE         YEAR SALES       YEAR SALES      INCREASE

         XX      XX     XX         Z,ZZZ,ZZZ.99-    Z,ZZZ,ZZZ.99-   Z,ZZZ,ZZZ.99-
                        XX         Z,ZZZ,ZZZ.99-    Z,ZZZ,ZZZ.99-   Z,ZZZ,ZZZ.99-
                        XX         Z,ZZZ,ZZZ.99-    Z,ZZZ,ZZZ.99-   Z,ZZZ,ZZZ.99-


                SPORT CODE TOTALS  ZZ,ZZZ,ZZZ.99-  ZZ,ZZZ,ZZZ.99-  ZZ,ZZZ,ZZZ.99-

         XX      XX     XX         Z,ZZZ,ZZZ.99-    Z,ZZZ,ZZZ.99-   Z,ZZZ,ZZZ.99-
                        XX         Z,ZZZ,ZZZ.99-    Z,ZZZ,ZZZ.99-   Z,ZZZ,ZZZ.99-
                        XX         Z,ZZZ,ZZZ.99-    Z,ZZZ,ZZZ.99-   Z,ZZZ,ZZZ.99-
```

```
            SPORT CODE TOTALS    ZZ,ZZZ,ZZZ.99-   ZZ,ZZZ,ZZZ.99-   ZZ,ZZZ,ZZZ.99-

            REGION TOTALS        ZZ,ZZZ,ZZZ.99-   ZZ,ZZZ,ZZZ.99-   ZZ,ZZZ,ZZZ.99-

XX     XX       XX               Z,ZZZ,ZZZ.99-    Z,ZZZ,ZZZ.99-    Z,ZZZ,ZZZ.99-
                XX               Z,ZZZ,ZZZ.99-    Z,ZZZ,ZZZ.99-    Z,ZZZ,ZZZ.99-

            SPORT CODE TOTALS    ZZ,ZZZ,ZZZ.99-   ZZ,ZZZ,ZZZ.99-   ZZ,ZZZ,ZZZ.99-

       XX       XX               Z,ZZZ,ZZZ.99-    Z,ZZZ,ZZZ.99-    Z,ZZZ,ZZZ.99-
                XX               Z,ZZZ,ZZZ.99-    Z,ZZZ,ZZZ.99-    Z,ZZZ,ZZZ.99-

            SPORT CODE TOTALS    ZZ,ZZZ,ZZZ.99-   ZZ,ZZZ,ZZZ.99-   ZZ,ZZZ,ZZZ.99-

            REGION TOTALS        ZZ,ZZZ,ZZZ.99-   ZZ,ZZZ,ZZZ.99-   ZZ,ZZZ,ZZZ.99-

            REPORT TOTALS        ZZ,ZZZ,ZZZ.99-   ZZ,ZZZ,ZZZ.99-   ZZ,ZZZ,ZZZ.99-
```

Assignment

1. Perform the mapping process.

2. Develop the program structure chart.

3. Develop the flowchart or pseudo code for the entire program.

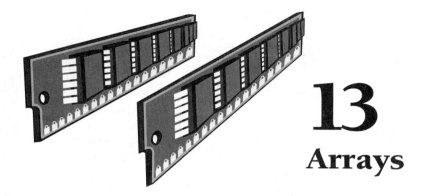

13
Arrays

OBJECTIVES

- Understanding array concepts.
- Understanding the looping process.
- Understanding the different methods of accessing an array.
- Understanding the different techniques of loading arrays.

INTRODUCTION

You will be using arrays in many of the programs you will develop in the future. An *array* is best described as having multiple occurrences of the same data field concurrently. Each occurrence of the field will use the same data name as the other occurrences. These fields may be contained within the input record or built within the program's working area.

UNDERSTANDING THE ARRAY

Let's take a look at a file we have already used and see how an array could be employed. Project 1 in Chapters 7 and 8 used the customer sales file. The file definition we used is shown in Exhibit 13–1. Note that each month is individually named. We have specific fields for January, February, March, and so on. If we take a look at this from a different angle, we can say we have 24 sales fields, 12 for each year. Therefore, we have 12 current-year sales fields, and 12 prior-year sales fields. Because we have, in effect, 12 fields with the same name (i.e., current-year sales) and another 12 called prior-year sales, we could consider these two arrays.

Exhibit 13–2 illustrates an alternate record layout with two arrays: one array for current year and the second array for prior year. Notice the wording in the record definition for the array. You will see the field name, and the term "OCCURS 12 TIMES." This indicates that there will be 12 fields called CS-CYSLS, each with a format of 8.2. Likewise, we have 12 fields called CS-PYSLS, also with a format of 8.2.

Exhibit 13–1
ORIGINAL LAYOUT OF THE CUSTOMER SALES RECORD

CUSTOMER SALES RECORD

01-02	REGION		CS-RGN
02-06	CUSTOMER NUMBER		CS-CUST
07-31	CUSTOMER NAME		CS-NAME
32-33	SPORT CODE		CS-SPRTCD
34-35	EQUIPMENT TYPE		CS-ETYP
36-43	CURRENT YEAR JANUARY	(8.2)	CS-CYJAN
44-51	CURRENT YEAR FEBRUARY	(8 2)	CS-CYFEB
52-59	CURRENT YEAR MARCH	(8.2)	CS-CYMAR
60-67	CURRENT YEAR APRIL	(8.2)	CS-CYAPR
68-75	CURRENT YEAR MAY	(8.2)	CS-CYMAY
76-83	CURRENT YEAR JUNE	(8.2)	CS-CYJUN
84-91	CURRENT YEAR JULY	(8.2)	CS-CYJUL
92-99	CURRENT YEAR AUGUST	(8.2)	CS-CYAUG
100-107	CURRENT YEAR SEPTEMBER	(8.2)	CS-CYSEP
108-115	CURRENT YEAR OCTOBER	(8.2)	CS-CYOCT
116-123	CURRENT YEAR NOVEMBER	(8.2)	CS-CYNOV
124-131	CURRENT YEAR DECEMBER	(8.2)	CS-CYDEC
132-139	PRIOR YEAR JANUARY	(8.2)	CS-PYJAN
140-147	PRIOR YEAR FEBRUARY	(8.2)	CS-PYFEB
148-155	PRIOR YEAR MARCH	(8.2)	CS-PYMAR
156-163	PRIOR YEAR APRIL	(8.2)	CS-PYAPR
164-171	PRIOR YEAR MAY	(8.2)	CS-PYMAY
172-179	PRIOR YEAR JUNE	(8.2)	CS-PYJUN
180-187	PRIOR YEAR JULY	(8.2)	CS-PYJUL
188-195	PRIOR YEAR AUGUST	(8.2)	CS-PYAUG
196-203	PRIOR YEAR SEPTEMBER	(8.2)	CS-PYSEP
204-211	PRIOR YEAR OCTOBER	(8.2)	CS-PYOCT
212-219	PRIOR YEAR NOVEMBER	(8.2)	CS-PYNOV
220-227	PRIOR YEAR DECEMBER	(8.2)	CS-PYDEC
228-250	Unused		

Exhibit 13–2
LAYOUT OF THE CUSTOMER SALES RECORD USING ARRAYS

CUSTOMER SALES RECORD

01-02	REGION	CS-RGN
02-06	CUSTOMER NUMBER	CS-CUST
07-31	CUSTOMER NAME	CS-NAME
32-33	SPORT CODE	CS-STRPCD
34-35	EQUIPMENT TYPE	CS-ETYP
36-131	CURRENT YEAR SALES	CS-CYSLS
	OCCURS 12 TIMES (8.2)	
132-227	PRIOR YEAR SALES	CS-PYSLS
	OCCURS 12 TIMES (8.2)	
228-250	Unused	

Accessing the Array

Suppose we wanted to sum the values of each month for the current year. If we refer to the current year sales field as CS-CYSLS, the computer will not know which field we want—remember we have 12 CS-CYSLS fields. As a result, we need to be specific as to which CS-CYSLS we want. To do this, we will need to use a *subscript*. A subscript is a pointer into an array that tells the computer which occurrence we want to access. To reference the fifth occurrence of CS-CYSLS, we would say CS-CYSLS(5). The eleventh occurrence is defined as CS-CYSLS(11).

Subscripts

Any numeric field can be used as a subscript. The only requirement is that the value of the subscript must be greater than zero, and cannot exceed the size of the array. For example, you could not refer to CS-CYSLS(15) because there are not 15 occurrences of this field. Throughout this chapter, we will use the field SUB to represent the subscript.

Looping Through an Array

Nearly all arrays you will use in the future will require the program to *loop* though the data. A loop is described as a method by which you repeatedly execute the same instructions. Loops are controlled by the DO WHILE and DO UNTIL structures. For example, MAINLINE is a DO WHILE loop. In the MAINLINE loop you repeatedly execute the instructions of PROCESS while END-FLAG is turned off.

There are four components of typical DO WHILE and DO UNTIL loops:

1. Initialization: Getting the loop ready to execute.
2. Process: Perform the purpose of the loop.
3. Modification: Normally, this is setting a logical data field to indicate that execution of the loop should be discontinued.
4. Testing: Check the value of the logical data field to see if execution of the loop should be continued.

In MAINLINE these four steps are as follows:

1. Initialization: This is the INITIALIZATION procedure. We set END-FLAG off in INITIALIZATION.
2. Process: This is the PROCESS procedure.
3. Modification: This takes place in the READ procedure when we turn END-FLAG on.
4. Testing: This is the decision within MAINLINE where we test to see if END-FLAG is on or off. Depending on the result of this decision, we either continue PROCESS or proceed to END-OF-JOB.

Applying the Loop to an Array

Now let's take a look at how we might use a loop to add together the sales in each of the 12 months for the current year. First, let's determine what each of the four components of the loop must do:

Initialization   We must tell the computer to start at the beginning of the array. Because we will be using a subscript (SUB) to identify which occurrence we want, we will initialize SUB to 1 (the first occurrence).

Process	The purpose of the loop will be to add the value of the current sales field (CS-CYSLS) to a field call TOTAL-SALES.
Modification	Here, we must increment SUB by 1, in order to instruct the program to use the next occurrence during the next cycle in the loop.
Testing	We know we are finished with the loop after all 12 months have been added to TOTAL-SALES. Therefore, the test will be to see if the value of SUB exceeds 12.

Figure 13–1 contains the flowchart for this looping process. Let's take a look at the logic.

Figure 13–1
Sample DO WHILE loop to sum the 12 months sales for the year

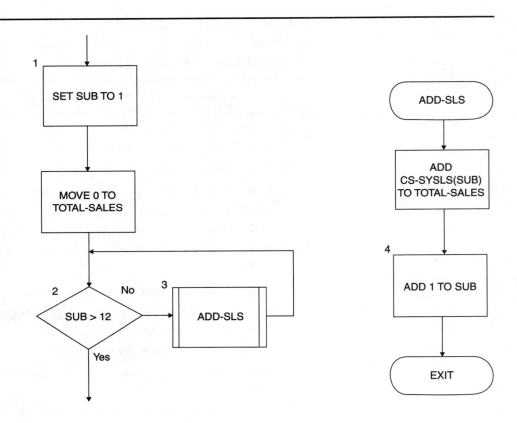

PSEUDO CODE

```
LET sub = 1
LET total-sales = 0
DOWHILE sub not > 12
   DO add-sls
END-DOWHILE

add-sls:
   ADD cs-cysls(sub) to totals-sales
   ADD 1 to sub
```

Following the Loop

First, the initialization step (1) sets SUB to 1. This is required in order to tell the computer to start at the beginning of the array. Not only do we initialize the subscript, but we also need to initialize TOTAL-SALES to zero. Notice that in this loop, just as in MAINLINE, the initialization step is performed only one time.

Next, we perform the testing step of the loop (2). Here we check to see if SUB is greater than 12. If so, we exit the looping process.

If the testing step decides to continue the loop, we perform the processing portion of the loop (3). Here we add the value of CS-CYSLS to TOTAL-SALES. Notice that we use the subscript SUB to indicate which of the 12 CS-CYSLS should be added in. The modification tasks (4) is within the process step. The modification step occurs after we add the sales to the total sales, when we increment the SUB by 1.

Finally, we perform the testing step again. Here we check to see if SUB, which was modified in the processing step, is greater than 12. If so, we exit the looping process. If SUB is not greater than 12, we continue the loop by performing the processing procedure, ADD-SLS, again.

Incorporating Arrays into a Program

Now let's see how we incorporate this logic into a simple program. To keep this example simple, we will be producing an output file, and not a report. Exhibit 13–3 contains the specification for this program.

A review of the program specification reveals that we have a parameter record that will contain the current processing date. We will use the month provided to set the upper boundary of the looping process. In our first example we performed the loop until SUB was greater than 12. In this example, however, we do not necessarily want all 12 months. We want only the number of months represented by the parameter record. If the parameter record specified that we were to build the output based on year-to-date June sales (month of 06), then we would stop the looping process when SUB exceeds 6. To do this, we replace the constant 12 we used earlier with a variable that represents the upper limit (PARM-MONTH).

Figure 13–2 contains the complete sample program.

Exhibit 13–3
PROGRAM SPECIFICATIONS FOR CALCULATION EXAMPLE

Objective

This program will build the customer sales summary file that will be used for sales reporting. The input to the program will be the customer sales record. A parameter file will be used to supply the program with the current month number. The output file will contain the total year-to-date sales for the current year and prior year.

Processing Requirements

1. Read the parameter file to obtain the current month.
2. Read the customer sales file and calculate year-to-date sales totals for the current year and prior year by summing the appropriate months in the sales file.
3. Create the file as shown below in the Customer Sales Summary.

CUSTOMER SALES RECORD

01-02	REGION	CS-RGN
03-07	CUSTOMER NUMBER	CS-CUST
08-32	CUSTOMER NAME	CS-NAME
33-34	SPORT CODE	CS-SPRTCD
35-36	EQUIPMENT TYPE	CS-ETYP
37-134	CURRENT YEAR SALES	CS-CYSLS
	OCCURS 12 TIMES (8.2)	
135-230	PRIOR YEAR SALES	CS-PYSLS
	OCCURS 12 TIMES (8.2)	

PARAMETER RECORD

01-02	PARM-MONTH	PARM-MTH

CUSTOMER SALES SUMMARY RECORD

01-02	REGION		CSS-RGN
03-07	CUSTOMER NUMBER		CSS-CUST
08-32	CUSTOMER NAME		CSS-NAME
33-34	SPORT CODE		CSS-SPRTCD
35-36	EQUIPMENT TYPE		CSS-ETYP
37-45	CURRENT YEAR SALES	(9.2)	CSS-CYSLS
46-54	PRIOR YEAR SALES	(9.2)	CSS-PYSLS
55-60	Unused		

Figure 13–2
Flowchart for example program defined in Exhibit 13–3

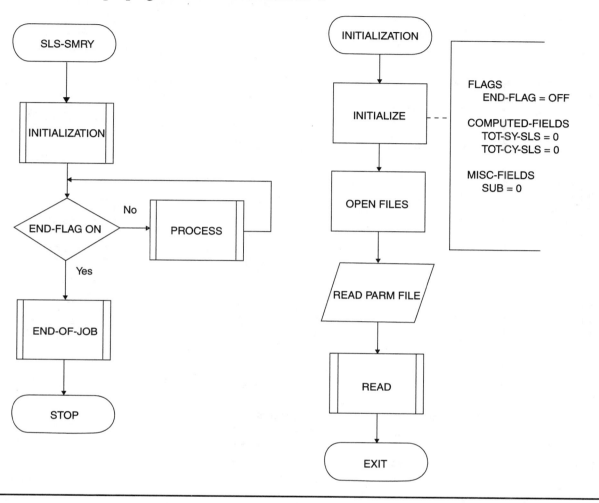

(continued on the next page)

Figure 13–2
(continued)

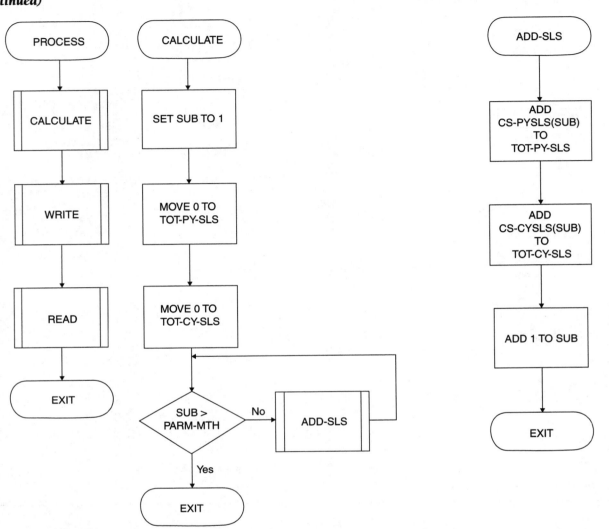

Figure 13–2
(continued)

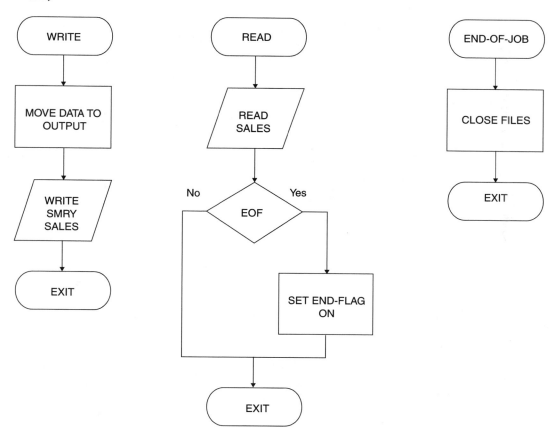

PSEUDO CODE

```
mainline:
        DO initialization
        DOWHILE end-flag off
            DO process
        END-DOWHILE
        DO end-of-job
        STOP

initialization:
        INITIALIZE    flags:          end-flag = off
                      computed-data:  tot-py-sls = 0
                                      tot-cy-sls = 0
                      misc-fields:    sub = 0
        OPEN files
        READ parameter file
        DO read

process:
        DO calculate
        DO write
        DO read
```

(continued on the next page)

Figure 13–2
(continued)

```
calculate:
        LET sub = 1
        LET tot-py-sls = 0
        LET tot-cy-sls = 0
        DOWHILE sub not > parm-mth
            DO add-sls
        END-DOWHILE

add-sls:
        ADD cs-pysls(sub) to tot-py-sls
        ADD cs-cysls(sub) to tot-cy-sls
        ADD 1 to sub

write:
        MOVE data to output
        WRITE smry sales

read:
        READ sales file
            IF end-of-file THEN
                    LET end-flag = on
            END-IF
        END-READ

end-of-job:
        CLOSE files
```

USING ARRAYS IN PROGRAMS

Now that we have learned the basic principles of array processing, let's see how we can use arrays in our programs. Later in this chapter, we will see how we can employ arrays during the record selection and accumulation. First, let's see how arrays are built within programs.

Loading and Using Arrays

In most cases, an array will not be presented to us in a ready-to-use format, as it was in the previous example with the customer sales file. Instead, we will probably read a sequential file and build an array one occurrence at a time from the data contained in each record. There are two common methods used to load arrays. These are the *pre-process load* and the *in-process load.*

Pre-Process Load

The pre-process load is the most common method of loading an array. First, let's see how the load works and then we will see how we can use the array after it has been loaded. As the name implies, the pre-process load takes place prior to PROCESS. Because the only procedure executed prior to PROCESS is INITIALIZATION, it stands to reason that the pre-process load technique must be performed here.

Loading the Array

To illustrate how we might employ this technique, review the brief program specification in Exhibit 13–4. (See page 192.)

In this specification, we have been instructed to build a program that will select customers based on region. However, as the instructions state, we will have multiple regions to consider. Therefore, we must be able to accommodate more than one PARM-RGN field. Remember, whenever we have multiple fields with the same name, we have an array. According to the specification, we will have only one region per parameter record, so we must store each region within an array as we read each record. Let's see how this load is accomplished. Figure 13–3 illustrates this processing.

Figure 13–3

Logic required to load data to an array for example program defined in Exhibit 13–4

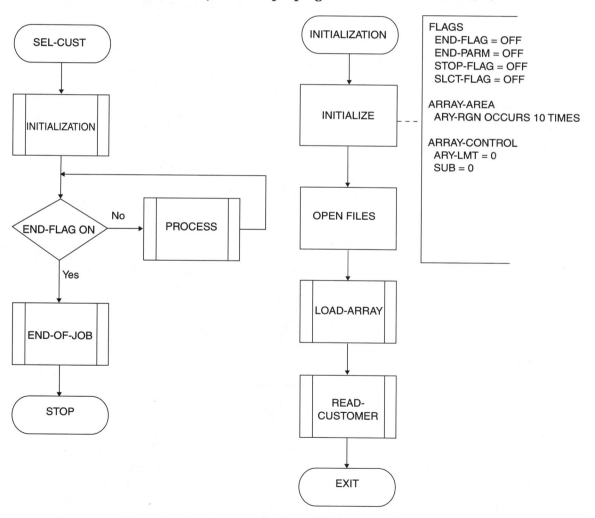

(continued on the next page)

Figure 13–3
(continued)

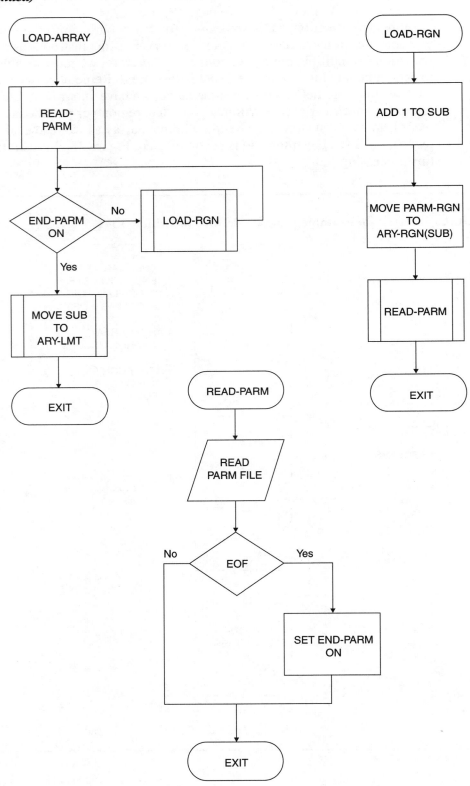

Figure 13–3
(continued)

PSEUDO CODE

```
mainline:
        DO initialization
        DOWHILE end-flag off
            DO process
        DO end-of-job
        STOP

initialization:
        INITIALIZE      flags:              end-flag = off
                                            end-parm = off
                                            stop-flag = off
                                            slct-flag = off
                        array-area:     ary-rgn occurs 10 times
                        array-control: ary-lmt = 0
                                            sub = 0
        OPEN files
        DO load-array
        DO read-customer

load-array:
        DO read-parm
        DOWHILE end-parm off
            DO load-rgn
        END-DOWHILE
        LET ary-lmt = sub

load-rgn:
        ADD 1 to sub
        MOVE parm-rgn to ary-rgn(sub)
        DO read-parm

read-parm:
        READ parmfile
            IF end-of-file
                    LET end-parm = on
            END-IF
```

Take notice of the following:

1. Two new entries have been added to the FLAGS group: STOP-FLAG and END-PARM. STOP-FLAG will almost always be included in programs with arrays. END-PARM is the end-flag for the parameter file. You will see how STOP-FLAG and END-PARM are used shortly.

2. We have defined an array in the working area of our program. This array contains the regions that will be specified by the parameter file. We can have up to 10 regions.

3. We have added a group to the working area called ARRAY-CONTROL. This contains the fields SUB and ARY-LMT. You already know what SUB is, but what is ARY-LMT? ARY-LMT will serve as the upper boundary of the array. As you will see, we will set ARY-LMT to reflect the number of active occurrences of the array that we are using.

4. We have added a procedure called LOAD-ARRAY to INITIALIZA-TION. This new procedure will contain all the instructions needed to read the parameter file and load the contents to the array.

5. Notice that LOAD-ARRAY is a DO WHILE loop that looks very similar to MAINLINE in its structure. This loop will read the parameter file and load the region to the array. Because it is a looping process, it must contain all four components of the loop. This loop will do the following:

- Read the first parameter record. Notice that within the procedure READ-PARM we set the flag END-PARM. As mentioned earlier, END-PARM is the end-flag for the parameter file.

- If END-PARM is not turned on, then we perform the LOAD-RGN procedure.

- The first step of LOAD-RGN is to increment SUB by 1. Because we initialized SUB to 0 at the beginning, we must now increment it so that SUB points to the next open position of the array.

- We now move the PARM-RGN to the next open position of the array using SUB as the pointer to that occurrence.

- Read the next parameter record and exit from the procedure.

6. When we have completed the load process (i.e., END-PARM is turned on) we terminate the loop. The final step is to set ARY-LMT to the value of SUB. In doing so, the program will now know how many regions have actually been loaded. Remember, according to the array definition, we can have *up to* ten regions. Because we may not always have 10 regions supplied by the parameter file, ARY-LMT tells us how many of these ten are actually used.

Exhibit 13–4
PROGRAM
SPECIFICATIONS FOR
RECORD SELECTION
EXAMPLE

Objective

This program will supply the Marketing department with key customers when new products are introduced. The program will be written so that the selection criteria will be supplied from the parameter file. Marketing will supply the requested regions each time the program is processed. More than one region can be selected. Allow for a maximum of ten regions.

Processing Requirements

1. Read the parameter file and load the requested regions to an array.

2. Read the customer master file and select the customers whose regions match one of the regions supplied in the parameter file.

3. Print report shown on the printer spacing chart.

CUSTOMER MASTER RECORD

01-05	CUSTOMER NUMBER	CUST-NO
06-30	CUSTOMER NAME	NAME
31-50	STREET ADDRESS	ADDR

```
        51-65 CITY                            CITY
        66-67 STATE                           ST
        68-72 ZIP CODE                        ZIP
        73-74 CUSTOMER TYPE                   CTYPE
        75-76 REGION                          RGN
        77-78 AREA                            AREA
        79-83 HEADQUARTER ID                  HQ
        84-91 LAST PURCHASE (YYYYMMDD)        LSTPRCH
        92-100 Unused
```

PARAMETER RECORD

```
        01-02 REGION NUMBER                   PARM-RGN
        03-80 Unused
```

Printer Spacing Chart

```
                                                                                        111111111111111111111
          11111111112222222222333333333344444444445555555555666666666677777777778888888888999999999900000000000011111111112
123456789012345678901234567890123456789012345678901234567890123456789012345678901234567890123456789012345678901234567890
RUN  MM/DD/YY   HH:MM                               ACME DISTRIBUTORS                                    PAGE ZZZZ9
                                                   TARGET CUSTOMER REPORT

       CUSTOMER
       NUMBER   NAME                        STREET ADDRESS        CITY              STATE   ZIP    REGION

       XXXXX    XXXXXXXXXXXXXXXXXXXXXXXXX    XXXXXXXXXXXXXXXXXXX   XXXXXXXXXXXXXX      XX    XXXXX    XX
       XXXXX    XXXXXXXXXXXXXXXXXXXXXXXXX    XXXXXXXXXXXXXXXXXXX   XXXXXXXXXXXXXX      XX    XXXXX    XX
       XXXXX    XXXXXXXXXXXXXXXXXXXXXXXXX    XXXXXXXXXXXXXXXXXXX   XXXXXXXXXXXXXX      XX    XXXXX    XX
```

Using the Array

Before continuing, let's make sure we understand how this program is going to work. We have already loaded the regions from the parameter file to an array defined within the program. As we read in each customer record, we will search the array to see if the region number in that customer's record is also in the array. If the region is in the array, we will know that the region was one that was specified within the parameter file and we want it. If the region is not within the array, then we do not want the customer. The process of searching the array will be simple. We look at the first region in the array and compare it to the customer's region. If the first region in the array matches the customer's region, we stop looking. If they are different, we move on to the second occurrence of the array, then on to the third, and so on. We continue until we have found the region we are searching for or exhaust the regions we loaded from the parameter file.

Now, let's see how we design this process using the structure chart and flowchart design tools. First let's take a look at the program's structure chart. (See Figure 13–4.) Again, notice that for the most part this has not changed. We do recognize, however, that since multiple regions are expected, INITIALIZATION has been modified to reflect that an array will be loaded.

We have already flowcharted INITIALIZATION (Figure 13–3), so let's move on to PROCESS. Figure 13–5 contains the PROCESS procedure. As you can see, PROCESS has not changed. Because we will be using an array to support our record selection process, the SELECT procedure will change. Figure 13–6 illustrates the revised SELECT procedure, which contains two key components. These will become known as the *search loop* and the *search procedure*.

Figure 13–4
Structure chart for example program defined in Exhibit 13–4

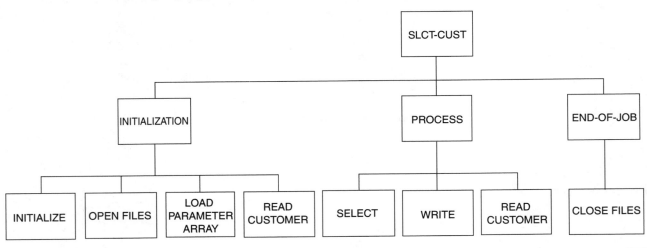

The Search Loop

The guiding principle that has arisen many times in this textbook is the basic premise that all data processing programs are structurally alike. That applies also to the search loop and the search procedure. The examples we will review for this program can serve as the foundation for future array searches that you need to perform. With only minimal changes required by each program, these can be considered standard routines.

The first step in any SELECT procedure is to set SLCT-FLAG off. We learned this in Chapter 9, and it never changes. Now, the search loop. Remember the four components of the loop? Let's apply these to SELECT (Figure 13–6):

1. *Initialize* the variables that will support the looping process. The subscript, SUB, is set to 1. Because SUB acts as a pointer to the array and we want to start at the beginning of the array, we set this pointer to the first occurrence. We also set STOP-FLAG off. As you will see shortly, STOP-FLAG is a logical field we turn on when we decide to stop the looping process.

2. Next, we *test* to see if the loop should continue. If STOP-FLAG has been turned on, we discontinue the looping process.

3. Perform the *process* portion of the loop, which in this case is the SEARCH procedure.

4. As before, the *modification* step of the loop will occur within this processing procedure. In this example, the modification step is the where we set STOP-FLAG on.

Now let's move on to the search procedure. Figure 13–7 illustrates SEARCH. As with SELECT, let's study the components of SEARCH one at a time.

1. Our first step of all search procedures is to compare the subscript, SUB, to ARY-LMT. As you recall, the last step of the array loading process

Figure 13–5
PROCESS procedure for
example program

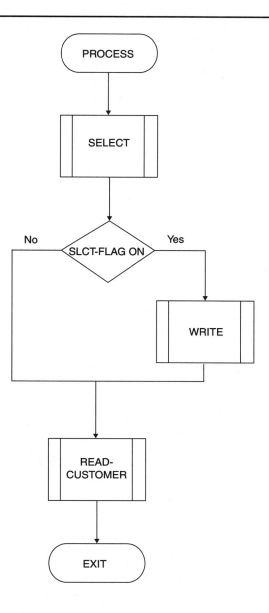

PSEUDO CODE

```
process:
    DO select
    IF slct-flag on
       DO write
    END-IF
    DO read-customer
```

was to move SUB to ARY-LMT. We did this so we would know how many occurrences of the array were in use even after we reset SUB to a different value. When the value of SUB exceeds the value of ARY-LMT, we know we have exhausted the loaded portion of the array, thus there is no need to continue. Let's follow the YES path of this decision.

Figure 13–6
SELECT procedure
containing search loop
for example program

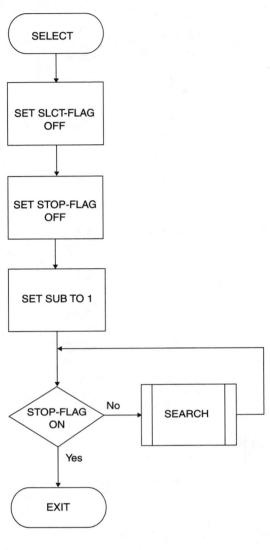

PSEUDO CODE

```
select:
    LET slct-flag = off
    LET stop-flag = off
    LET sub = 1
    DOWHILE stop-flag off
      DO search
    END-DOWHILE
```

2. If SUB is greater than ARY-LMT, we turn STOP-FLAG on and exit the search procedure. This will discontinue the search loop, and leave SLCT-FLAG off.

3. If we follow the NO path of SUB > ARY-LMT decision (step 1), we need to compare the value of the customer's region to that of the region in the array that SUB points to. If the values are equal, we follow the YES path. If they are not equal, we follow the NO path.

Figure 13–7
SEARCH procedure for
example program

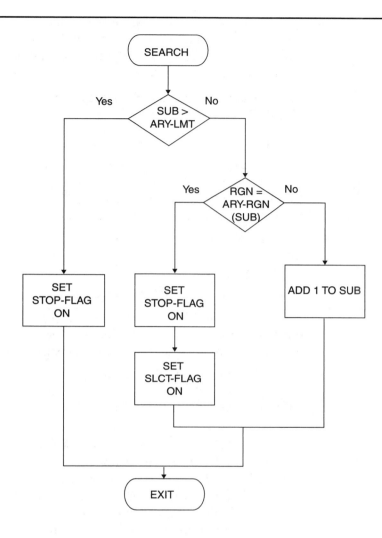

PSEUDO CODE

```
search:
    IF sub > ary-lmt THEN
         LET stop-flag = on
       ELSE
         IF rgn = ary-rgn(sub) THEN
            LET stop-flag = on
            LET slct-flag = on
          ELSE
            ADD 1 to sub
         END-IF
    END-IF
```

4. Let's first follow the YES path from step 3. When the customer's region matches the region in the array, we want to turn SLCT-FLAG on (we want this record). We turn STOP-FLAG on (we found what we are looking for, no need to continue looking) and exit the search procedure.

5. Following the NO path of the decision from step 3, we see what we need to do if the regions are not equal. In this case, we increment SUB by 1 and exit. The next time we enter the search procedure we will be looking at the next occurrence.

In this example, steps 2 and 4 were the modification steps where we turned STOP-FLAG ON.

Following the Logic

Now, let's see if the theory we have discussed really works. Consider the following example. Let's suppose the parameter file supplied three regions for selection. These regions were 02, 03, and 05. We loaded the array with these regions, and the array now looks like this:

Occurrence 1: 02
Occurrence 2: 03
Occurrence 3: 05

ARY-LMT: 3 (we loaded three regions)

We have read the first customer master record. Let's assume this customer's region is 03. We enter SELECT and set SLCT-FLAG and STOP-FLAG OFF. We also set SUB to 1. The variables are as follows:

RGN (Customer's region) = 03
SLCT-FLAG = OFF
STOP-FLAG = OFF
SUB = 1

Next is the loop's testing decision. We check to see if STOP-FLAG is ON. Because STOP-FLAG is not ON we perform SEARCH. We first compare SUB to ARY-LMT. SUB has a value of 1 and is not greater than ARY-LMT, which has a value of 3 so we follow the NO path. We compare the customer's region (with a value of 03) to the region in the array pointed to by SUB. Because SUB is 1, we look at the first region in the array, which contains the value of 02. Since customer's region does not equal the region in the array (03 does not equal 02), we take the NO path. We add 1 to SUB and exit. The variables are now:

RGN = 03
SLCT-FLAG = OFF
STOP-FLAG = OFF
SUB = 2

We return to the search loop and check to see if STOP-FLAG is turned ON. It is not, we perform SEARCH again.

We again follow the NO leg of the SUB > ARY-LMT (2 is not greater than 3). Next, we compare the customer's region with the second occurrence of the array (SUB is 2). This time they are equal (3 equals 3) so we take the YES leg. Here we turn STOP-FLAG ON and SLCT-FLAG ON and exit. The testing decision of our search loop tests to see if STOP-FLAG has been turned ON. Since it has, we stop the loop and exit SELECT. Also, since we turned SLCT-FLAG ON, PROCESS will follow the YES path of the SLCT-FLAG ON decision and write the selected record.

We then read the next customer in the file. Let's assume this customer has a region of 07. Again we enter SELECT. The first step is to initialize the loop. The values of the variables are as follows:

RGN = 07
SLCT-FLAG = OFF
STOP-FLAG = OFF
SUB = 1

ARY-LMT is still 3

We test to see if STOP-FLAG is ON. It is not, so we perform SEARCH. Our first decision again, is to see if SUB is greater than ARY-LMT. Because 1 is not greater than 3, we move onto compare the regions. The regions are not the same (07 is not equal 02) so we follow the NO path, adding 1 to SUB and exit.

SUB now equals 2.

We again check to see if STOP-FLAG has been turned ON. It hasn't, so we perform SEARCH. We check to see if SUB is greater than ARY-LMT. It is not, so we again follow the NO path. We check the customer's region (which is 07) to the second occurrence of the array (remember SUB = 2) and we see that the regions are still not equal. We add 1 to SUB and exit. SUB is now equal to 3.

Back in SELECT we see that STOP-FLAG has not been turned ON, so we again execute SEARCH. We check again to see if SUB > ARY-LMT. They are equal, but SUB is not greater than ARY-LMT so we take the NO path. We compare the customer's region to the third occurrence of the array. Again, no match, so we increment SUB by 1 and exit. SUB is now equal to 4.

Once again, STOP-FLAG is not ON, so we perform SEARCH. This time, however, SUB is greater than ARY-LMT (4 > 3) so we take the YES path of this decision. We set STOP-FLAG ON and exit.

Now that STOP-FLAG is turned ON, we discontinue the loop and exit SELECT. Because SLCT-FLAG was never turned ON, PROCESS will disregard this record, and read the next customer record.

Does the Search Procedure Ever Change?

The structure of the search procedure never changes. The only portion of the search that may vary from program to program is what you do when you find a match in the array, and what you do when you do not. In the example we just completed, we turned SELECT-FLAG ON because we were using the loop to select records. In a later example, you will see how we use the loop to drive an accumulation procedure. The loop performs the same tasks, up to the point of what it does when it encounters a *hit* in the array. As you will see, the *structure* of the search procedure remains the same. The only difference will be in the actions we perform when 1) the search finds the data that we are looking for, or 2) the search determines that the array does not contain the data that we are searching for.

Using an Array for Accumulation

Review the program specifications in Exhibit 13–5. In this example, we are going to accumulate total sales by sport code and print the results. However, notice that the specifications indicate that the sales file is not in sport code sequence, but rather in item sequence. We have also been asked to print the sport code description, which is not in the item sales file, but rather in the sport code description file.

What will this program have to do? First, it will need to load an array from the sport code description file. This will enable us to have the sport code descriptions available for the report. Next, we need to accumulate sales amount by sport code (but remember the file is not in sport code sequence, so we cannot use a control-break); therefore, we will be required to perform the accumulation within an array. Finally, since the report contains only the totals, we will dump the array at the end. This may sound complicated, but it is really quite simple.

Exhibit 13–5
**PROGRAM
SPECIFICATIONS FOR
AN ACCUMULATION
EXAMPLE**

Objective

This program will print a report showing sales totals by sport code. The input file will not be in sport code sequence, so the totals must be accumulated within an array. Sport code descriptions will be printed, and are available in the sport code description file.

Processing Requirements

1. Using a pre-process load, read the sport code description file and load the sport code number and description to an array.
2. Read the item sales file, processing all records on the file.
3. Search the array and find the sport code in the array that matches the sport code in the item sales record. Add the sales amount in the sales record to the array. In the event that no matching entry in the array is found, add the sales amount to a field dedicated for undefined sport code.
4. When the sales file is exhausted, print the sales totals in the array as shown in the printer spacing chart.

SALES RECORD

01-02	SPORT CODE		SPRTCD
03-04	EQUIPMENT TYPE		ETYP
05-09	ITEM NUMBER		ITEM
10-24	ITEM DESCRIPTION		DESC
25-29	QUANTITY SOLD	(5.0)	QTY
30-38	SALES AMOUNT	(9.2)	SLSAMT
39-41	COMMISSION PERCENT	(3.3)	CMPCT
42-48	PURCHASE COST	(7.2)	PRCHCST
49-60	Unused		

SPORT CODE DESCRIPTION RECORD

01-02 SPORT CODE   SCD-SPRTCD
03-27 SPORT CODE DESCRIPTION   SCD-DESC

Printer Spacing Chart

```
                                                                         1111111111111111111111
           1111111111222222222233333333334444444444555555555566666666667777777777888888888899999999990000000000011111111112
 123456789012345678901234567890123456789012345678901234567890123456789012345678901234567890123456789012345678901234567890

RUN  MM/DD/YY   HH:MM                        ACME DISTRIBUTORS                                    PAGE ZZZZ9
                                          SPORT CODE SALES REPORT

                   SPORT                                         SALES
                   CODE      DESCRIPTION                         AMOUNT

                    XX      XXXXXXXXXXXXXXXXXXXXXXXXX       Z,ZZZ,ZZZ.99-
                    XX      XXXXXXXXXXXXXXXXXXXXXXXXX       Z,ZZZ,ZZZ.99-
                    XX      XXXXXXXXXXXXXXXXXXXXXXXXX       Z,ZZZ,ZZZ.99-
                    XX      XXXXXXXXXXXXXXXXXXXXXXXXX       Z,ZZZ,ZZZ.99-
                            UNDEFINED SPORT CODES           Z,ZZZ,ZZZ.99-
```

The Accumulating Array

First, let's look at the structure chart for this program as shown in Figure 13–8.

Figure 13–9 illustrates MAINLINE and INITIALIZATION for this program. Figure 13–10 illustrates the procedure to load the sport code description array. Notice how we define the array. We indicate that the array occurs 99 times (we could have up to 99 different sport codes) and we have also specified that each occurrence of the array has three fields: sport code, description, and the sales amount. We have included the sales amount in the array so that we have a place to accumulate total sales for each sport code. Remember, because we can have up to 99 different sport codes, we could have up to 99 different sport code totals. Therefore, the sport code totals that we will be accumulating need to be in the same array as the sport code and the corresponding description. Within the FLAGS grouping, we have included END-SPRTCD and STOP-FLAG.

Figure 13–8
Structure chart for accumulation example

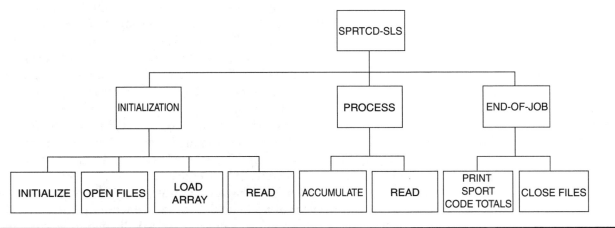

Figure 13–9
MAINLINE and INITIALIZATION procedures for accumulation example

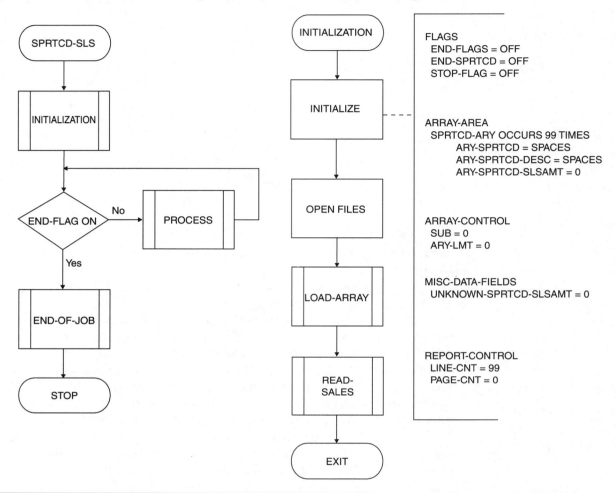

The array load works as before, so let's move on to PROCESS.

Figure 13–11 contains the PROCESS and ACCUMULATE procedures. As you can see, PROCESS is not affected. However, ACCUMULATE does change. In previous versions of ACCUMULATE, we simply added one variable to another, such as ADD SLSAMT TO SPRTCD-SLSAMT. However, in this case, we have 99 SPRTCD-SLSAMTs. Therefore, we must search the array to find which occurrence of sport code matches the sport code of the item we are processing.

ACCUMULATE contains the search loop, which is very similar to the loop we saw when selecting the customers based on their region. As before, we initialize the loop by setting STOP-FLAG OFF and setting SUB to 1. The only change to the SEARCH procedure is the tasks we perform once we either have a match in the array or determine that the sport code is not in the array. In the event of no matching entry, we were instructed by the specifications to add the sales amount to a field dedicated to holding the total of unknown sport codes. This field is defined as UNKNOWN-

Figure 13–10
Procedures required for loading the array for the accumulation example

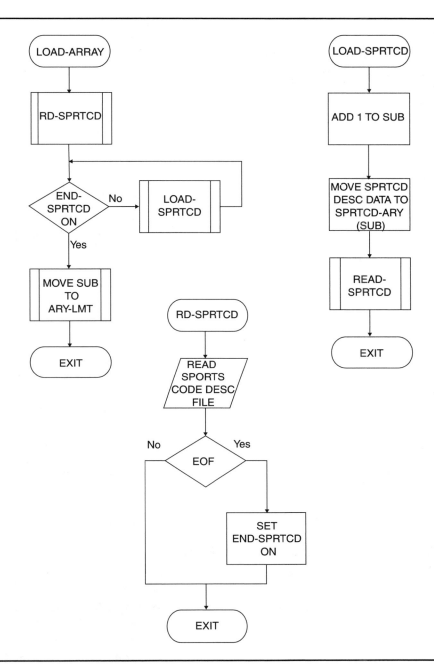

SPRTCD-SLSAMT. As you can see in Figure 13–12, the structure of the SEARCH procedure did not change.

What did change, however slightly, was the logic. When we found a matching sport code, we added the sales amount to the SPRTCD-SLSAMT field in the array, using SUB to point to the same relative occurrence of SPRTCD-SLSAMT as the sport code we matched on. When we determined there was no matching sport code, we added the sales amount to UNKNOWN-SPRTCD-SLSAMT. Following Figure 13–12 is Figure 13–13 containing the pseudo code for the flowcharts in Figures 13–9 through 13–12.

Figure 13–11
PROCESS procedure
and ACCUMULATION
procedure with search
loop for accumulation
example

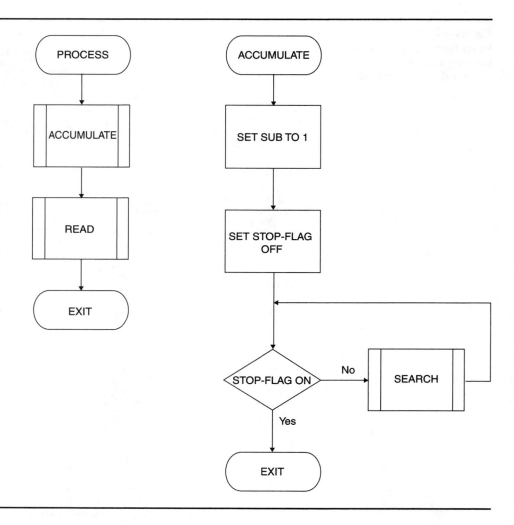

Dumping the Array

After processing the final record, we will perform END-OF-JOB, as always.
As we can see in the structure chart shown in Figure 13–18, we need to print
the array containing the sport code totals. To do this, we invoke a loop that
will start at the beginning of the array, and print each occurrence until we have
printed the last occurrence. Figure 13–14 shows the revised END-OF-JOB
procedure, complete with the routine used to print the sport code sales array.

Summary of the Pre-Process Load

This concludes the section on loading and searching arrays using the pre-
process technique. We learned the looping techniques and learned how
to apply the loop to the searching process. Now that we have a good understanding of the pre-process technique, let's move on to the in-process load.

Figure 13–12
SEARCH procedure for accumulation example program

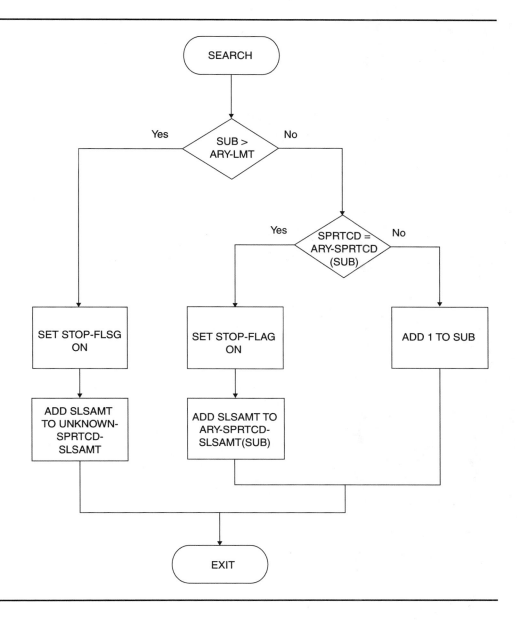

Figure 13–13
Pseudo code for example program

```
mainline:
        DO initialization
        DOWHILE end-flag off
            DO process
        END-DOWHILE
        DO end-of-job
        STOP

initialization:
        INITIALIZE    flags:      end-flag = off
                                  end-sprtcd = off
                                  stop-flag = off
```

(continued on the next page)

Figure 13–13
(*continued*)

```
                                        sprtcd-ary occurs 99 times:
                                                    ary-sprtcd = spaces
                                                    ary-sprtcd-desc = spaces
                                                    ary-sprtcd-slsamt = 0
                                        array-control:  sub = 0
                                                        ary-lmt = 0
                                        misc-fields:    unknown-sprtcd-slsamt = 0
                                        report-control: line-cnt = 99
                                                        page-cnt = 0
                    OPEN files
                    DO load-array
                    DO read-sales

        load-array:
                    DO rd-sprtcd
                    DOWHILE end-sprtcd off
                         DO load-sprtcd
                    END-DOWHILE
                    LET ary-lmt = sub

        load-sprtcd:
                    ADD 1 to sub
                    MOVE sprtcd desc data to sprtcd-ary(sub)
                    DO rd-sprtcd

        rd-sprtcd:
                    READ sportcode desc file
                        IF end-of-file THEN
                             LET end-sprtcd = on
                        END-IF
                    END-READ

        process:
                    DO accumulate
                    DO read

        accumulate:
                    LET sub = 1
                    LET stop-flag = off
                    DOWHILE stop-flag off
                         DO search
                    END-DOWHILE

        search:
                    IF sub > ary-lmt THEN
                         LET stop-flag = on
                         ADD slsamt to unknown-sprtcd-slsamt
                       ELSE
                         IF sprtcd = ary-sprtcd(sub) THEN
                                 LET stop-flag = on
                                 ADD slsamt to ary-sprtcd-slsamt(sub)
                             ELSE
                                 ADD 1 to sub
                         END-IF
                    END-IF
```

Figure 13–14
END-OF-JOB and related procedures to dump the array in the accumulation example

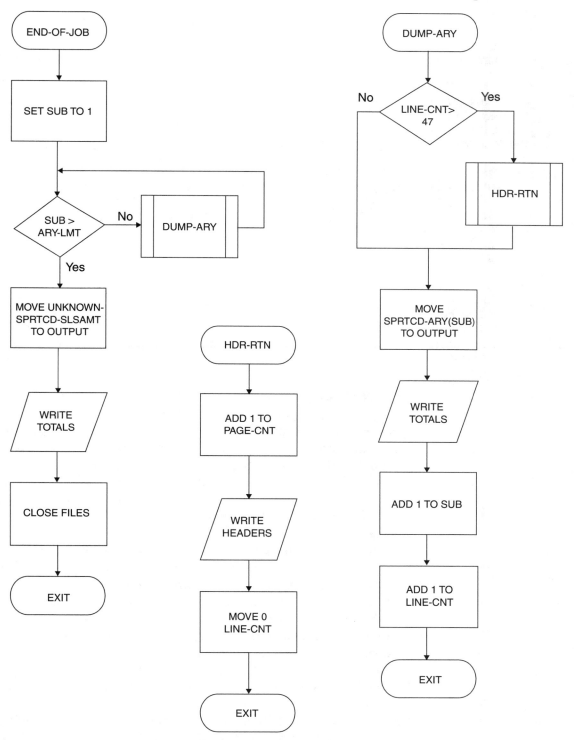

(continued on the next page)

Figure 13–14
(*continued*)

PSEUDO CODE

```
end-of-job:
        LET sub = 1
        DOWHILE sub not > ary-lmt
            DO dump-ary
        END-DOWHILE
        MOVE unknown-sprtcd-slsamt to output
        WRITE totals
        CLOSE files

dump-ary:
        IF line-cnt > 47
            DO hdr-rtn
        END-IF
        MOVE sprtcd-ary(sub) to output
        WRITE totals
        ADD 1 to sub

hdr-rtn:
        ADD 1 to page-cnt
        WRITE headers
        LET line-cnt = 0
```

In-Process Load

There will be occasions when we do not have a file from which to build an array prior to processing. In the previous examples, we had a parameter file that contained selected regions or a file containing all known sport codes and their descriptions. Suppose, however, that we were asked to read through the item sales file, and accumulate sales by sport code and print totals. No descriptions were needed, and no sport codes were considered unknown. In this event, we may choose to process the file using an in-process load.

In the in-process load technique, the array is built within PROCESS. We invoke the search loop and search procedures as before in ACCUMULATE. The difference will be in our actions when we do not find the sport code in the array. With the in-process load technique, we build the array as we process the records. If we cannot locate the sport code we are looking for in the array, we add another occurrence to the array containing the new sport code. The loop and search structures remain unchanged, and the only difference occurs in the YES leg of the SUB > ARY-LMT decision of the search procedure. Figure 13–15 illustrates the revised version of ACCUMULATE.

Notice the only difference in this search procedure from the previous one. On the YES leg of the SUB > ARY-LMT decision, we move the new sport code to the array, move the value of SUB to ARY-LMT (to reflect the fact that another occurrence is now in use), and add the sales to the sales amount in the array.

Figure 13–15
ACCUMULATE and SEARCH procedure if in-process load technique were used

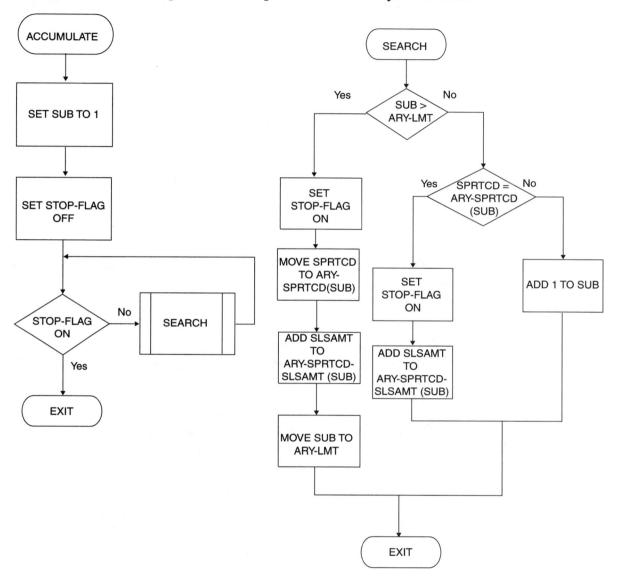

PSEUDO CODE

```
accumulate:
        LET sub = 1
        LET stop-flag = off
        DOWHILE stop-flag off
            DO search
        END-DOWHILE
```

(continued on the next page)

Figure 13–15
(*continued*)

```
search:
            IF sub > ary-lmt THEN
                LET stop-flag = on
                MOVE sprtcd to ary-sprtcd(sub)
                ADD slsamt to sprtcd-slsamt(sub)
                LET ary-lmt = sub
            ELSE
                IF sprtcd = ary-sprtcd(sub) THEN
                        LET stop-flag = on
                        ADD slsamt to sprtcd-slsamt(sub)
                ELSE
                        ADD 1 to sub
                END-IF
            END-IF
```

Dumping the array in END-OF-JOB would not change from the method shown in Figure 13–14.

The in-process technique is normally used only when accumulating.

Direct Access to Arrays

Finally, let's take a look at one more method of array access. This works best when the array has been loaded using the pre-process method.

At the beginning of this chapter, we learned that a subscript can be any numeric field. In all examples so far, we have created a logical data field called SUB. But what if the sport code field, SPRTCD, is numeric? Could we use SPRTCD as the subscript to an array? We can, as long as it conforms to the three rules for a subscript:

1. The subscript must be numeric.

2. The subscript must contain a value greater than zero.

3. The subscript cannot contain a value that is greater than the size (number of occurrences) of the array.

Let's look at a revised version of the specification we used earlier. Exhibit 13–6 (see page 212) contains a different version of the specification we saw in Exhibit 13–5. In this example, the specifications instruct you to use the sport code field as the subscript. This makes loading the array easier, and searching the array later unnecessary. Let's see why. If we use the sport code field as the subscript, to which occurrence within the array would sport code 18 be stored? It would be in the 18th occurrence. Likewise, sport code 37 would be in the 37th occurrence within the array. Because the sport code acts as the subscript, the sport code will point to the occurrence equal to its own value. Thus, the loading of the array will change, as illustrated in Figure 13–16.

ACCUMULATE becomes much easier, as shown in Figure 13–17. We no longer need to search the array since the sport code is the subscript. We

Figure 13–16
Procedures required to load array in using the direct access technique

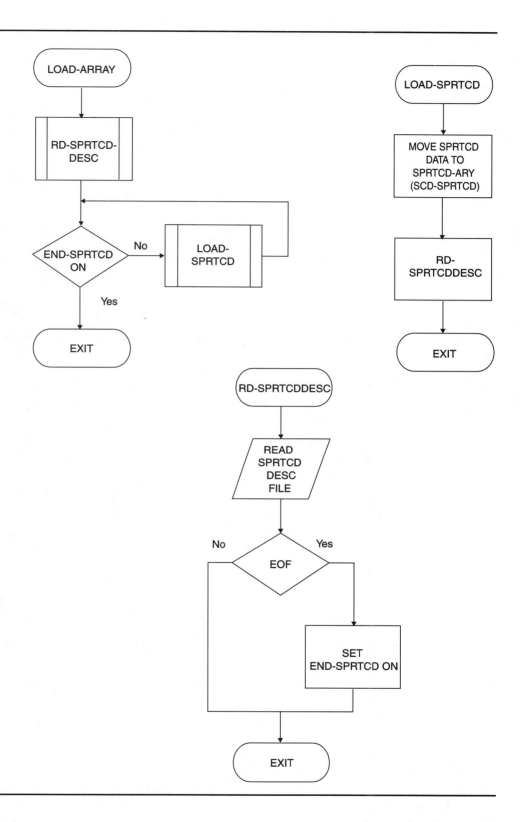

(continued on the next page)

**Figure 13–16
(continued)**

PSEUDO CODE

```
load-array:
        DO rd-sprtcddesc
        DOWHILE end-sprtcd off
            DO load-sprtcd
        END-DOWHILE

load-sprtcd:
        MOVE sprtcd data to sprtcd-ary(scd-sprtcd)
        DO rd-sprtcddesc

rd-sprtcddesc:
        READ sprtcd desc file
            IF end-of-file THEN
                    LET end-sprtcd = on
            END-IF
        END-READ
```

**Figure 13–17
ACCUMULATION for
direct access technique**

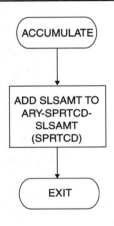

PSEUDO CODE

```
accumulate:
    ADD slsamt to ary-sprtcd-slsamt(sprtcd)
```

do not need to go looking for sport code 18, since it will always be in the 18th occurrence.

Exhibit 13–6
**PROGRAM
SPECIFICATIONS FOR
DIRECT ACCESS
TECHNIQUE**

Objective

This program will print a report showing total sales by sport code. The input file will not be in sport code sequence, so the totals must be accumulated within an array. Sport code descriptions will be printed, and are available in the sport code description file.

Processing Requirements

1. Using a pre-process load, read the sport code description file and load the sport code number and description to an array. Use the sport code as the subscript.

2. Read the item sales file, processing all records on the file.

3. Accumulate the sales in each item sales record to the array. Use the sport code as the subscript to the array.

4. When the sales file is exhausted, print the sales totals in the array as shown in the printer spacing chart. Print only active sport codes. These can be determined as sport codes that have sales volume.

SALES RECORD

Range	Field	Format	Name
01-02	SPORT CODE		SPRTCD
03-04	EQUIPMENT TYPE		ETYP
05-09	ITEM NUMBER		ITEM
10-24	ITEM DESCRIPTION		DESC
25-29	QUANTITY SOLD	(5.0)	QTY
30-38	SALES AMOUNT	(9.2)	SLSAMT
39-41	COMMISSION PERCENT	(3.3)	CMPCT
42-48	PURCHASE COST	(7.2)	PRCHCST
49-60	Unused		

SPORT CODE DESCRIPTION RECORD

Range	Field	Name
01-02	SPORT CODE	SCD-SPRTCD
03-27	SPORT CODE DESCRIPTION	SCD-DESC
27-80	Unused	

Printer Spacing Chart

```
                                                                                  1111111111111111111111
          11111111112222222222333333333344444444445555555555666666666677777777778888888888999999999900000000001111111111112
 123456789012345678901234567890123456789012345678901234567890123456789012345678901234567890123456789012345678901234567890

RUN MM/DD/YY  HH:MM                     ACME DISTRIBUTORS                                      PAGE ZZZZ9
                                     SPORT CODE SALES REPORT

                        SPORT                                          SALES
                        CODE    DESCRIPTION                            AMOUNT

                         XX     XXXXXXXXXXXXXXXXXXXXXXXXX      Z,ZZZ,ZZZ.99-
                         XX     XXXXXXXXXXXXXXXXXXXXXXXXX      Z,ZZZ,ZZZ.99-
                         XX     XXXXXXXXXXXXXXXXXXXXXXXXX      Z,ZZZ,ZZZ.99-
                         XX     XXXXXXXXXXXXXXXXXXXXXXXXX      Z,ZZZ,ZZZ.99-
```

Dumping the Array

Dumping the array will change only slightly. Because we may not have 99 active product categories, we need only print the ones that are active. In the specification, we defined *active* as those product categories defined in the description array (regardless of whether there were sales) or an undefined sport code with sales.

The looping process through the array remains unchanged. As before, we start at the beginning and continue through to the end. We must still use SUB as the pointer for a loop, and we know that any of the 99 entries could have data, so we stop the loop when SUB exceeds 99. In this example, we also check to see if we have any sales for the next occurrence in the array before printing the next total line. See Figure 13–18 for the revised END-OF-JOB.

Figure 13–18
Dumping an array built using the direct access technique

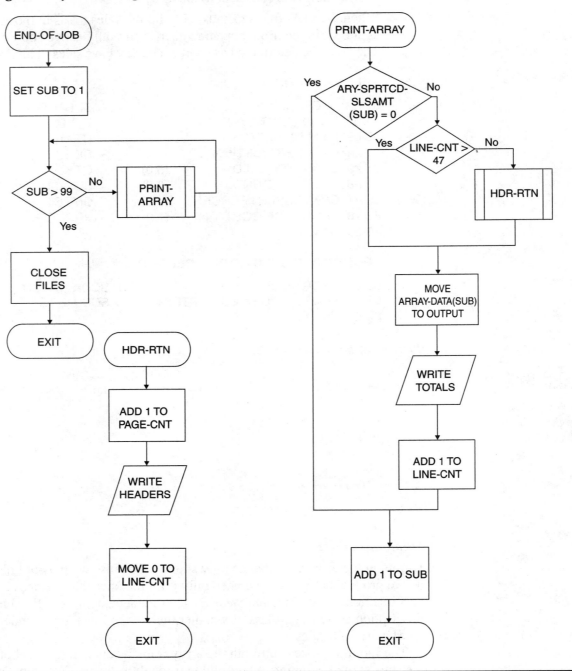

Figure 13–18
(continued)

```
end-of-job:
        LET sub = 1
        DOWHILE sub not > 99
            DO print-array
        END-DOWHILE
        CLOSE files

print-array:
        IF ary-sprtcd-slsamt(sub) not = 0 THEN
            IF line-cnt > 47 THEN
                    DO hdr-rtn
            END-IF
            MOVE array-data(sub) to output
            WRITE totals
            ADD 1 to line-cnt
        END-IF
        ADD 1 to sub

hdr-rtn:
        ADD 1 to page-cnt
        WRITE headers
        LET line-cnt = 0
```

Notice that the PRINT-ARRAY routine has now changed. Rather than just printing the occurrence, we first need to see if it needs to be printed. If the sales amount is not 0, we know that we have sales for this sport code.

SUMMARY

There was a lot packed into this chapter! First, we learned that an array consists of multiple occurrences of the same data field. In order to access one specific occurrence of the data field within an array, we must point to the occurrence we want using a subscript. A subscript can be any numeric field, with a value greater than zero but not exceeding the size of that array.

We learned the looping process and how it is applied to arrays. Specifically, we learned that the four components of a loop are initialize, process, modification, and testing. We learned how the search loop works and how the search routine is employed. That is, we learned that the search loop will continue to execute until we either find a match or determine that no matching entry exists. We learned that the search procedure will be used to determine if we have a match, or we have exceeded the portion of the array being used.

We learned that there are two methods of loading arrays. The pre-process load is used when we have an external file containing data that gets loaded to an array. The in-process load is used when the data for an array is developed from the input file being processed. Finally, we learned that we can directly access an array by using a data field on the input file as the subscript.

REVIEW QUESTIONS	1. What is ARY-LMT used for?
	2. How do we use STOP-FLAG?
	3. What is a subscript? What are the requirements of a subscript?
	4. What is the difference between a pre-process load and an in-process load?
	5. What are the four components of a loop?

PROJECT

Objective

Sales Management requires two reports to assist them in evaluating sales nationwide. The first report is a standard sales report showing customer sales, subtotaled by region. The second report is a summary of the regions showing each region's contribution to the total sales.

Processing Requirements

1. Using pre-process load, load the region description file to an array.
2. Read and process all records on the file.
3. Provide a control-break, and print the appropriate totals for each region.
4. At each region break, store the regional sales total to the array.
5. At the end of the report, print the sales in the array, and compute the region's contribution to the final total. Use the following formula:
   - Contribution = (Region Total/Report Total) * 100.
6. File will be sorted by customer number (minor) within region (major).

SALES RECORD

1-2	Region		RGN
3-8	Customer Number		CUST
9-28	Customer Name		NAME
29-38	Customer Sales	(9.2)	SLS

REGION DESCRIPTION RECORD

1-2	Region	RD-RGN
3-17	Region Desc.	RD-DESC

Printer Spacing Chart

```
          1111111111222222222233333333334444444444555555555566666666667
 1234567890123456789012345678901234567890123456789012345678901234567890

RUN MM/DD/YY               REGIONAL SALES REPORT            PAGE ZZZZ9
TIME HH:MM:SS                  CUSTOMER SALES

     REGION   CUSTOMER                                 SALES
     NUMBER   NUMBER    CUSTOMER NAME                  AMOUNT

       XX     XXXXX     XXXXXXXXXXXXXXXXXXXX      Z,ZZZ,ZZZ.99-
       XX     XXXXX     XXXXXXXXXXXXXXXXXXXX      Z,ZZZ,ZZZ.99-
       XX     XXXXX     XXXXXXXXXXXXXXXXXXXX      Z,ZZZ,ZZZ.99-
       XX     XXXXX     XXXXXXXXXXXXXXXXXXXX      Z,ZZZ,ZZZ.99-
```

```
                    REGION TOTAL          ZZ,ZZZ,ZZZ.99-

        XX      XXXXX    XXXXXXXXXXXXXXXXXXX    Z,ZZZ,ZZZ.99-
        XX      XXXXX    XXXXXXXXXXXXXXXXXXX    Z,ZZZ,ZZZ.99-
        XX      XXXXX    XXXXXXXXXXXXXXXXXXX    Z,ZZZ,ZZZ.99-

                    REGION TOTAL          ZZ,ZZZ,ZZZ.99-

                    REPORT TOTAL         ZZZ,ZZZ,ZZZ.99-



             1111111111222222222233333333334444444444555555555566666666667
    1234567890123456789012345678901234567890123456789012345678901234567890

RUN  MM/DD/YY            REGIONAL SALES REPORT            PAGE ZZZZ9
TIME HH:MM:SS            REGIONAL CONTRIBUTION


        REGION   REGION              TOTAL
        NUMBER   DESCRIPTION         SALES        CONTRIBUTION

        XX     XXXXXXXXXXXXXX    ZZ,ZZZ,ZZZ.99-      ZZZ.99-
        XX     XXXXXXXXXXXXXX    ZZ,ZZZ,ZZZ.99-      ZZZ.99-
        XX     XXXXXXXXXXXXXX    ZZ,ZZZ,ZZZ.99-      ZZZ.99-
        XX     XXXXXXXXXXXXXX    ZZ,ZZZ,ZZZ.99-      ZZZ.99-
        XX     XXXXXXXXXXXXXX    ZZ,ZZZ,ZZZ.99-      ZZZ.99-

               TOTAL            ZZZ,ZZZ,ZZZ.99-
```

Assignment

1. Perform the mapping process.
2. Develop the program structure chart.
3. Develop the flowchart or pseudo code for the entire program.

Part IV

Advanced Program Design

14

Processing Two Input Files

OBJECTIVES

- Understanding the concept of matching two files.
- Understanding the concept of key fields.
- Understanding the impact to the program organization.

INTRODUCTION

Until this chapter, all programs we have reviewed and designed have been limited to processing one sequential input file, with the exception of the array file in Chapter 13. In this chapter, we will review and discuss the concepts and logic required to process two sequential input files with each file containing data necessary to create the required output.

UNDERSTANDING THE CONCEPT OF MATCHING TWO FILES

It is important to comprehend three basic concepts that apply to matching two sequential input files:

1. Both files must share a common field, or key, and be presorted by that key.
2. One file will be designated at the master file; the other file will be designated as the transaction.
3. The master file will contain only one record with a given key, while the transaction file may contain multiple occurrences of any key.

What Is a Key?

Before we proceed any further, let's make sure we understand the definition of a *key*. The key field of a record uniquely identifies that record from other records in the file. For example, in a customer master file the key field would be the customer number. Because no two customers can have the same number, the customer number identifies each unique customer. Many companies today use the employee's social security number as the key to the employee file.

Both Files Must Share a Common Field, or Key, and Be Presorted by that Key

In previous chapters, we used a product sales file in our examples. In this chapter, we will build that product sales file. The process will use two input files. One file will be the item master; the other will be a file containing detail records from a sales order file. (Exhibit 14–1 contains the program specifications.) In order to properly combine the two input files and build the desired output file, we must determine what data element serves as the key field. The key to the item master file is the item number, since no two items will have the same number. Therefore, the assigned key to the order detail file will be the item number. Before this program can be executed, both files must be sorted in item number sequence.

One File Will Be Designated as the Master File; the Other File Will Be Designated as the Transaction File

The *master file* will be defined as the file that has the unique key and should contain a complete set of objects for which the file represents. For example, an employee master file will contain all employees for a company; a customer master file will contain all customers. In the program we will be designing in this chapter, we will use the item master file, which should contain all valid products sold by the company. The *transaction file* for this program wil be the order detail file, which contains sales order information.

The Master File Will Contain Only One Record with a Given Key, while the Transaction File May Contain Multiple Occurrences of Any Key

The item master file will contain one record per item. The transaction file, sales order detail, will contain multiple records for each item sold because many customers will purchase the same product.

Exhibit 14–1
PROGRAM SPECIFICATION FOR MATCHING THE ITEM MASTER FILE WITH THE ORDER DETAIL FILE AND CREATING THE SALES FILE

Objective

This program will create the sales file by matching the order detail file and the item master file. Both files will be sorted in item number sequence prior to program execution.

Processing Requirements

1. All records on the order detail file will be written to the sales file.
2. Match the records between the two files using the item number as the key.
3. When the items match, obtain the relevant item master data from the item master record for the output sales record. If no item master

record exists for the item on the order detail record, use default data for the sales data whose source is the item master record.

4. There can be multiple order records for any item. There will be only one item master record for any item.

ITEM MASTER FILE (INPUT)

01-05	ITEM NUMBER		IM-ITEM
06-20	DESCRIPTION		IM-DESC
21-22	SPORT CODE		IM-SPRTCD
23-24	EQUIPMENT TYPE		IM-ETYP
25-27	COMMISSION PERCENT	(3.3)	IM-PCT
28-34	PURCHASE COST	(7.2)	IM-COST
35-41	RETAIL PRICE	(7.2)	IM-PRICE
42-50	Unused		

ORDER DETAIL FILE (INPUT)

01-05	ORDER NUMBER		OD-ORD-NO
06-13	ORDER DATE (YYYYMMDD)		OD-DATE
14-18	CUSTOMER NUMBER		OD-CUST
19-23	ITEM NUMBER		OD-ITEM
24-28	QUANTITY	(5.0)	OD-QTY
29-37	SALES AMOUNT	(9.2)	OD-SLSAMT
38-40	Unused		

SALES FILE (OUTPUT)

01-02	SPORT CODE		SPRTCD
03-04	EQUIPMENT TYPE		ETYP
05-09	ITEM NUMBER		ITEM
10-24	ITEM DESCRIPTION		DESC
25-29	QUANTITY SOLD		QTY
30-38	SALES AMOUNT	(9.2)	SLSAMT
39-41	COMMISSION PERCENT	(3.3)	CMPCT
42-48	PURCHASE COST	(7.2)	PRCHCST
49-60	Unused		

PROCESSING FUNDAMENTALS

Until now, we have had a relatively standard PROCESS procedure. When designing programs that must match two sequential files, we will find it necessary to alter this procedure. In previous programs we read only one input file. In this program, we must develop the logic that allows us to process two input files concurrently. Logic to match key fields must be included. We must also consider the processing steps necessary to handle each possible condition resulting from the matching logic. Let's take a look at each of the main sections of the two file-matching programs, and see how they differ from the programs with a single input file.

INITIALIZATION

As we have already learned, all programs perform the first read of the input file as the last step of INITIALIZATION. This concept remains unchanged.

In programs that are matching two input files, INITIALIZATION will be required to read the first record from the master file as well as the transaction file. Figure 14–1a shows the new structure chart for INITIALIZATION, while Figure 14–1b depicts the flowchart for the revised INITIALIZATION process.

Reading the Files

Before proceeding, let's take a quick look at how the READ procedures for these files will differ from the normal READ. In our earlier programs, we set END-FLAG ON when we encountered the end-of-file at the time of our read. We must alter this logic to accommodate the fact that we have two files, both of which may not reach the end at the same time. When one file reaches the end, we will check to see if the other file has already been exhausted. If both files have reached the end, we will set END-FLAG ON. If one file has been exhausted, but the other file has not, we will set the end flag associated with the file that has reached the end ON, and force the key for that file to the highest possible value it can be. This will become clearer shortly. Figure 14–2 illustrates the READ procedures for both files.

PROCESS

Matching

In this program, we are matching two files so that we can build the output sales file. Without considering *how* to accomplish our objective, let's take a look at *what* we must do.

Our first step of PROCESS will be to match the keys in the two input records to determine if both files are processing the same item. Depending on the outcome of the comparison, we have three courses of action. How this is accomplished will be discussed later. Right now, let's concentrate on

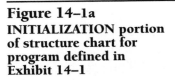

Figure 14–1a
INITIALIZATION portion of structure chart for program defined in Exhibit 14–1

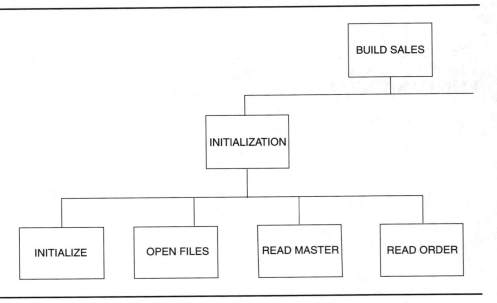

Figure 14–1b
INITIALIZATION for
example program

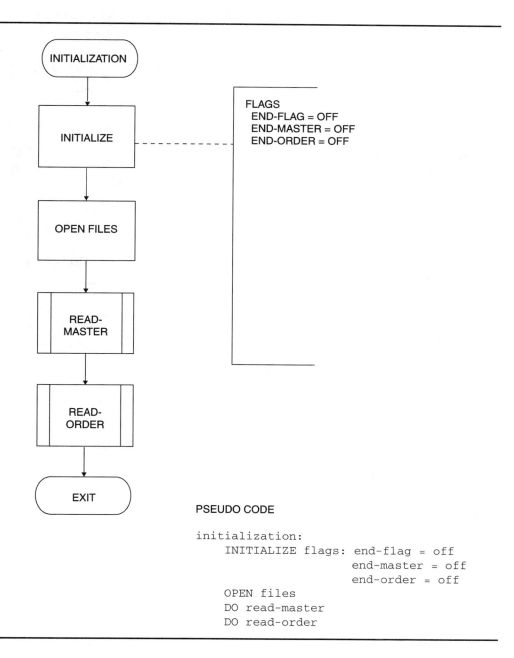

the three possible results of the comparison and what actions we take in each of the three conditions.

When we match the key fields from the master record and the transaction record, we will have one of three results:

1. Transaction key = Master key.

2. Transaction key > Master key.

3. Transaction key < Master key.

Let's take a look at the actions we need to perform in each of these three situations.

Figure 14–2
Revised read procedures as required by matching programs

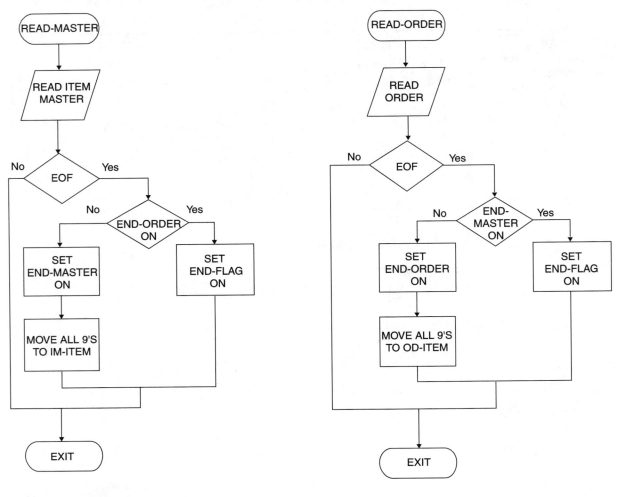

PSEUDO CODE

```
read-master:
        READ item master file
                IF end-of-file THEN
                        IF end-order = on THEN
                                LET end-flag = on
                        ELSE
                                LET end-master = on
                                LET im-item = all 9's
                        END-IF
                END-IF
        END-READ


read-order:
        READ order detail file
                IF end-of-file THEN
                        IF end-master = on THEN
                                LET end-flag = on
                        ELSE
                                LET end-order = on
                                LET im-master = all 9's
                        END-IF
                END-IF
        END-READ
```

Transaction Key = Master Key

Keeping in mind our objective of building the output sales file with data from the two input files, what are the basic steps we must accomplish when the keys of both records are equal? We must do the following:

1. Move the appropriate data from the order detail record to the sales record.
2. Move the appropriate data from the item master record to the sales record.
3. Write the output sales record.
4. Read the next record on the order detail file.

The first three points seem obvious. Since the records matched, we will move the appropriate data from both the order detail record and the master record to the output record before writing the sales record to the output. But why are we reading the order detail file only? Why not read just the master? Or better yet, why not read both files?

Remember how these files are constructed. The master file will contain only one record per item. The transaction file (in this case the order detail) may contain multiple records per item. It is possible that the next record on the order detail file (transaction) may be for the same item. If it is for the same item, we need to have the same master record available for processing. If we read the next master, but the order detail is for the same item, we will not have a match, and thus we will be unable to build the correct output record (since we will not have the appropriate master record data available). For this reason, we will read only the transaction file.

Transaction Key > Master Key

As we learned above, after we have a situation where the master key is equal to the transaction key, we read another transaction record. What if the next transaction record is for the next item? Because we have not read another master record, we will have the condition where the transaction key is greater than the master key. What do we do in this case? We do not want to write a record out just yet, because we do not have the correct master record for this item. Whenever the transaction key is greater than the master key, we need to read the master file until we either get a key that matches the transaction key, or is greater than the transaction key. Therefore, when this condition occurs, the only step taken is to read the master file.

Transaction Key < Master Key

This will occur only when we have an item on the transaction file (order detail) but there is no corresponding item on the master file. Although this condition should not happen, we must allow for this possibility, and address this occurrence appropriately. In this case we will still want to write the sales record, but we must be aware that we do not have any data from the master file to put into the output record. The tasks to be performed are as follows:

1. Move the appropriate data from the order detail record to the sales record.
2. Move default item master data to the sales record.

3. Write the output sales record.

4. Read the next record on the order detail file.

Default item master data might include things such as:

- Moving NOT ON MASTER to output item description.
- Set commission percent and purchase cost to zero.
- Set sport code and equipment type to zero.

Structure Chart

Figure 14–3 contains the structure chart for the PROCESS procedure. Remember that the structure chart is intended to provide the designer with an outline of what has to be done. Refer back to the steps required and see

Figure 14–3
PROCESS portion of structure chart for example program

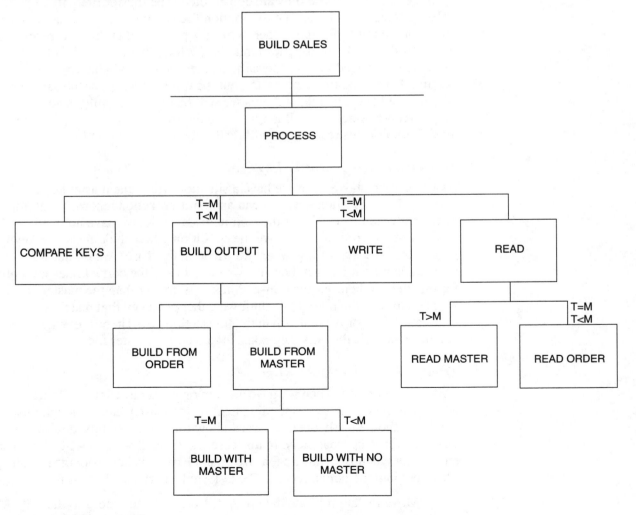

Legend: T = Transaction file
M = Master file

how they have been identified in the structure chart. Notice that when building the output record with data from the item master record, we have shown that there are two possible approaches. One approach is to build the output record from an existing master; the other is to build the output from default data when the master does not exist (i.e., Transaction key < Master key). Both procedures are depicted on the structure chart. In order to add clarity and indicate optional processes, we indicate the condition in which the procedure is executed. Other than this slight addition, the structure chart still concentrates on *what* is to be accomplished, and not *how* it is to be done. Likewise, we may elect to use this same method to show when the two read procedures are to be executed.

DEVELOPING THE FLOWCHART

Now that we have completed the structure chart for the PROCESS section of the program, let's take a look at the transition of the structure chart to the flowchart.

Comparing the Keys

The first step to be taken in the PROCESS section is to compare the key fields to determine which of the three possible conditions exist. Figure 14–4 contains this flowchart. To better understand this flowchart, remember that the order detail file is the transaction file and the item master file is the master file. Notice that we first check for the equal condition. We will check for this condition first because it is considered the normal condition of the data from a logical perspective. Secondly, we check for the Transaction key < Master key. Because our program is intended to build output data, we want to continue with decisions where a positive result will lead us to building the output data. Finally, you will notice that have no decision for Transaction key > Master key. This is assumed. If the first two decisions fail, then the third condition must be true.

Figure 14–4
Example of match logic that compares key fields

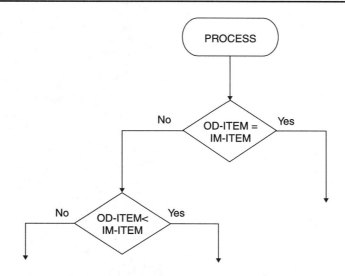

Completing the Process

Let's take a look at each matching condition, and build the flowchart that will perform the tasks outlined in the structure chart.

Transaction Key = Master Key

Figure 14–5 shows this leg of the flowchart. When referring to the structure chart, we include the processes indicated by the Transaction key = Master key (T=M).

Figure 14–5
Expanded logic when Transaction key = Master key

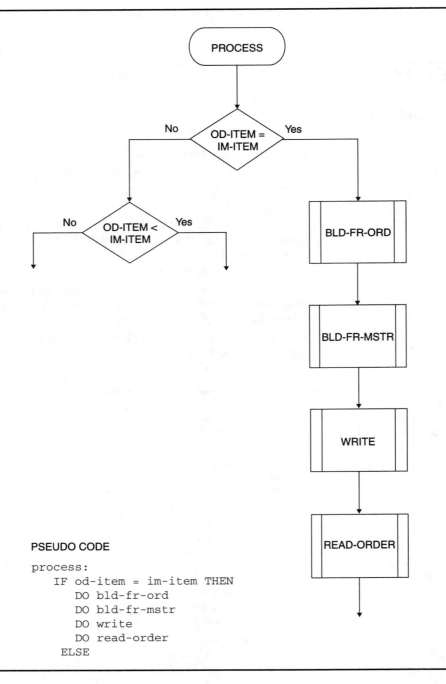

```
PSEUDO CODE

process:
    IF od-item = im-item THEN
        DO bld-fr-ord
        DO bld-fr-mstr
        DO write
        DO read-order
    ELSE
```

Transaction Key < Master Key

Figure 14–6 shows this leg of the flowchart. When referring to the structure chart, we include the processes indicated by the Transaction key < Master key (T<M).

**Figure 14–6
Expanded logic when
Transaction key < Master
key**

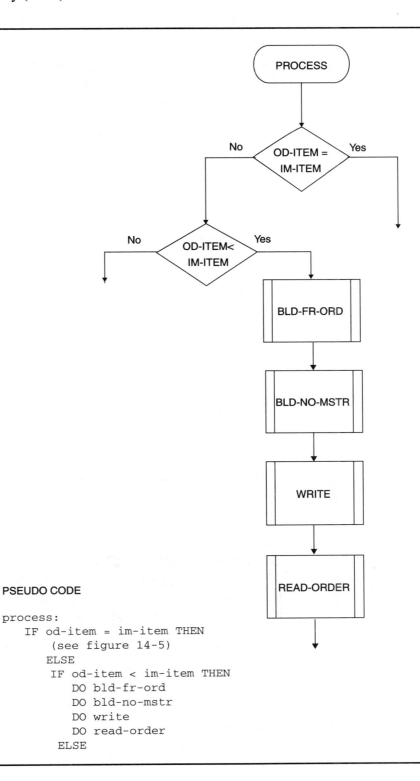

```
PSEUDO CODE

process:
    IF od-item = im-item THEN
        (see figure 14-5)
        ELSE
        IF od-item < im-item THEN
            DO bld-fr-ord
            DO bld-no-mstr
            DO write
            DO read-order
        ELSE
```

Transaction Key > Master Key

Figure 14–7 shows this leg of the flowchart. When referring to the structure chart, we include the processes indicated by the Transaction key > Master key (T>M).

**Figure 14–7
Expanded logic where
Transaction key > Master
key**

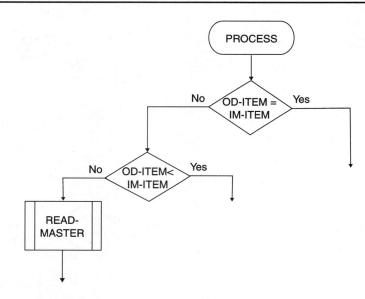

```
PSEUDO CODE

process:
   IF od-item = im-item THEN
      (see figure 14-5)
   ELSE
      IF od-item < im-item THEN
         (see figure 14-6)
         ELSE
           DO read-master
      END-IF
END-IF
```

Bringing It All Together

Figure 14–8 contains the entire flowchart for PROCESS. Let's use the flowchart, or pseudo code, and walk through the program with sample data in order to solidify our understanding.

**Figure 14–8
Complete PROCESS
procedure for example
program**

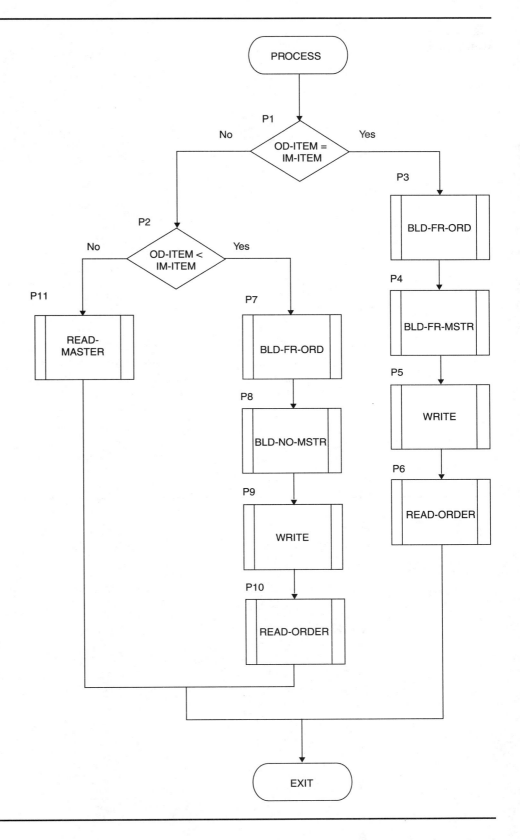

(continued on the next page)

Figure 14–8
(continued)

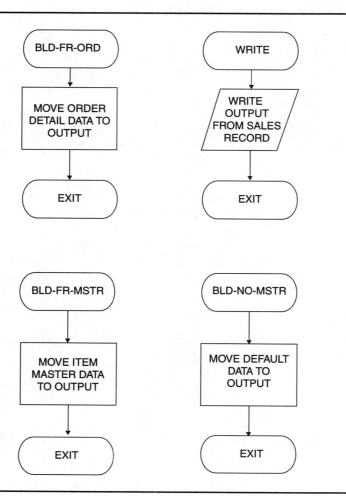

Figure 14–8
(continued)

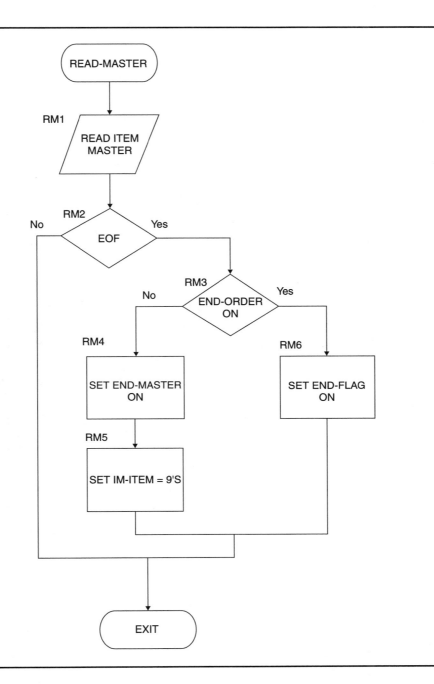

(continued on the next page)

Figure 14–8
(*continued*)

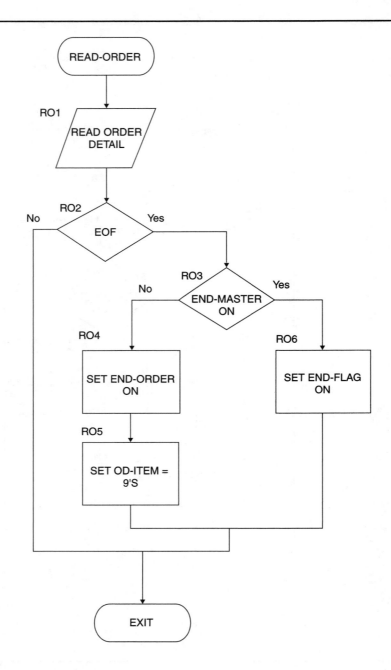

```
PSEUDO CODE

process:
        IF od-item = im-item THEN
                DO bld-fr-ord
                DO bld-fr-mstr
                DO write
                DO read-order
            ELSE
                IF od-item < im-item THEN
```

**Figure 14–8
(continued)**

```
                                        DO bld-fr-ord
                                        DO bld-no-mstr
                                        DO write
                                        DO read-order
                                ELSE
                                        DO read-master
                                END-IF
                        END-IF

bld-fr-ord:
        MOVE order detail data to output

bld-fr-mstr:
        MOVE item master data to output

bld-no-mstr:
        MOVE default data to output

write:
        WRITE output sales record

read-master:
        READ item master file
            IF end-of-file THEN
                IF end-order = on THEN
                    LET end-flag = on
                ELSE
                    LET end-master = on
                    LET im-item = all 9's
                END-IF
            END-IF
        END-READ

read-order:
        READ order detail file
            IF end-of-file THEN
                IF end-master = on THEN
                    LET end-flag = on
                ELSE
                    LET end-order = on
                    LET im-master = all 9's
                END-IF
            END-IF
        END-READ
```

PROGRAM WALK-THROUGH

Exhibit 14–2 contains sample data from the two input files. Let's walk through the program, step by step, to reinforce to program design principles we have just discussed. Exhibit 14–3 contains the output from this processing. *All sample records have spaces inserted between the fields to allow for easier reading during this exercise.* These spaces will not appear in the actual data. (Also, the item number is highlighted in all records.)

Exhibit 14–2
SAMPLE DATA FOR
PROGRAM LOGIC
WALK-THROUGH

Sample Data from Item Master File

		Item	Desc	Sport Code	Equip Type	Comm Pct	Cost	Price
Record	1	00001	SPORTS TOWEL	01	01	015	0000400	0000750
Record	2	00002	LOGO TOWEL	01	01	020	0000534	0001350
Record	3	00004	WRIST BANDS	01	02	041	0000095	0000250
Record	4	00006	HEAD BANDS	01	02	041	0000165	0000375
Record	5	00007	LOG HEAD BANDS	01	02	055	0000200	0000475
	EOF							

Sample Data from Order Detail File

		Order Number	Date	Cust	Item	Qty	Sales Amount
Record	1	4I013	940902	04387	00001	00100	000075000
Record	2	4I054	940913	00471	00002	00060	000081000
Record	3	4I065	940914	01988	00002	00015	000020250
Record	4	4I013	940902	04387	00005	00050	000017500
Record	5	4I005	940901	85901	00006	00010	000003750
	EOF						

First, Figure 14–1b shows the INITIALIZATION for this program. As you can see, the first record of both files will be read. As we enter PROCESS for the first time, the following records are available for processing:

```
Master Rcd 1 00001 SPORTS TOWEL    01 01 015 0000400 0000750
Order Rcd  1 4I013 940902 04387 00001 00100 000075000
```

The first step of PROCESS is to compare the key fields of both records (shown in Figure 14–8 as step P1). The key to the master record is 00001 and the key to the order detail record is 00001. Since the master record key (IM-ITEM) equals the order key (OD-ITEM), we follow the YES path of this decision. At this time we perform procedure BLD-FR-ORD (step P3). In the final program we would move the appropriate fields from the order record to the output. In this example, that would move the item number (00001), quantity sold (100), and sales amount ($750.00) to the output area. Next (step P4), we perform BLD-FR-MSTR to move the appropriate master data to the output record. This would move the description (SPORTS TOWEL), sport code (01), equipment type (01), percent commission (.015), and the purchase cost ($4.00) to the output. Our next step (P5) is to write the record. See record 1 in Exhibit 14–3 to see the record produced by this process.

Finally, we perform READ-ORDER (step P6) to obtain the next order detail record. We have not reached EOF for the detail file, so we follow the NO decision path from the EOF decision, and exit the procedure. Since we did not read another master record, we still have the original master record in memory. The records available to us now are as follows:

```
Master Rcd 1 00001 SPORTS TOWEL    01 01 015 0000400 0000750
Order Rcd  2 4I054 940913 00471 00002 00060 000081000
```

Since END-FLAG has not been turned on, MAINLINE returns us to PROCESS. Here again, our first step is to compare the item numbers from the two files. This time, however, the keys are not equal. The master key

(00001) is less than the order key (00002), so we take the NO path from step P1. Our next decision is to determine if OD-ITEM is less than IM-ITEM. Since the item on the order detail file is not less than the item on the item master, we again take the NO path. At this time we perform READ-MASTER. Notice that no output records are produced. In READ-MASTER we will read the second record. Because we have not reached the end of the master file, we follow the NO path and exit the procedure. The records available to us now are as follows:

```
Master Rcd 2 00002  LOGO TOWEL     01 01 020 0000534 0001350
Order Rcd  2 4I054 940913 00471 00002 00060 000081000
```

The keys to these two records are equal, so we again follow the YES path at the first decision of PROCESS. We build part of the output record from the order detail and the remainder of the output record from the master, and then write the output record. After writing the output, we read the next order detail. The records available to us now are as follows:

```
Master Rcd 2 00002 LOGO TOWEL      01 01 020 0000534 0001350
Order Rcd  3 4I065 940914 01988 00002 00015 000020250
```

Notice that this is the second record for the same item. Processing will follow the same path as before. After writing the third output record, we will read the next order detail record. The records available to us now are as follows:

```
Master Rcd 2 00002 LOGO TOWEL      01 01 020 0000534 0001350
Order Rcd  4 4I013 940902 04387 00005 00050 000017500
```

This time, the master key is less than the order key. As before when the same situation occurred, we will read only the master file. The records available to us now are as follows:

```
Master Rcd 3 00004 WRIST BANDS     01 02 041 0000095 0000250
Order Rcd  4 4I013 940902 04387 00005 00050 000017500
```

As with the previous set of records, the master key is again less than the order key. Once again, we will read only the master file. The records available to us now are as follows:

```
Master Rcd 4 00006 HEAD BANDS      01 02 041 0000165 0000375
Order Rcd  4 4I013 940902 04387 00005 00050 000017500
```

This time notice that the order detail is less than the item master. The answer to our first decision in PROCESS is NO since IM-ITEM is not equal to OD-ITEM. Next, check to see if OD-ITEM (00005) is less than IM-ITEM (00006). Since it is, we will follow the YES path. Our first step is to perform BLD-FR-ORD (step P7). Next, we perform BLD-NO-MSTR. BLD-NO-MSTR will move default data to the output record since no master record exists for the item on the order detail file. Next we write the record out (see record 4 in the output file). Finally we perform READ-ORDER and exit PROCESS. The records available to us now are as follows:

```
Master Rcd 5 00006 HEAD BANDS      01 02 041 0000165 0000375
Order Rcd  4 4I005 940901 85901 00006 00010 000003750
```

As we have encountered several times before, these two keys are equal. As a result, we will build and write the output record, and read the next order detail.

This time, however, things will be a little different. When we attempt to read the next order detail, we receive the EOF indication. Therefore, we will follow the YES path after the EOF test in step RO2. At this time we will check to see if the master file is at end. Since it is not, we will set the END-ORDER flag ON, and set the OD-ITEM field to 99999. We then exit the READ-ORDER procedure. The records available to us now are as follows:

```
Master Rcd 5 00006 HEAD BANDS        01 02 041 0000165 0000375
Order Rcd  4 99999
```

Because we had no order detail record, the only field with data is the item number, which we forced to nines. At this point, all subsequent masters will be less than the order item. We will continue to read the item master file until we have reached the EOF indicator. Let's take a look at READ-MASTER to see what happens when we reach the end. After reading the master record (step RM1), we test for EOF. When we reach the end of the master file, we will take the YES branch. Our next decision (step RM3) is to see if the order master is at end (END-ORDER = ON). Since it was, we proceed down the YES leg and set END-FLAG ON (step RM6). We then exit the READ-MASTER procedure, return control back to P11 (where we would have performed READ-MASTER), and exit the PROCESS procedure. Back in MAINLINE, we test END-FLAG. Since END-FLAG is now ON, we perform END-OF-JOB and stop the program.

Exhibit 14–3 **SAMPLE DATA FROM OUTPUT FILE**	**SALES FILE**

```
Record  1 01 01 00001 SPORTS TOWEL   00100 000075000 015 0000400
Record  2 01 01 00002 LOGO TOWEL     00060 000081000 020 0000534
Record  3 01 01 00002 LOGO TOWEL     00015 000020250 020 0000534
Record  4 00 00 00005 NOT ON MASTER  00050 000017500 000 0000000
Record  5 01 02 00006 HEAD BANDS     00010 000003750 041 0000165
```

SUMMARY

Matching programs are used to develop output files or reports where the required information is stored in two files. To perform the matching process, the two files involved must have identical key fields. Key fields are fields that identify individual records. Of the two files involved, one is considered the master, and the other is the transaction. Both files must be presorted on the key field before the program can be executed.

The PROCESS procedure is altered to accommodate the possible conditions that will result from the matching logic. These conditions include the transaction key = master key; transaction key < master key; and the transaction key > master key. Each scenario may require different logic depending on the program requirements.

REVIEW QUESTIONS

1. What is a transaction file?
2. What is a master file?
3. What is a key field?

4. When comparing the key fields on the transaction and master, what are the three possible results of the comparison? Which of these results will cause you to read the transaction? Which results will cause you to read the master?

5. In this chapter, we built an output record for each record on the transaction. Suppose, instead, that we wished to write only one record per item, with that record containing the total quantity of that item sold. How might the program design differ?

EXERCISE

This exercise will reinforce the concepts of matching two files. We will be designing a simple payroll program. One of our files will be the employee master file. The other file will be the timesheet file, containing the hours worked for each employee. You will be producing a report showing what the total payroll will be for the company.

Consider the following rules for the program:

1. No employee will be paid unless they have a record on the timesheet file.

2. Both files (timesheets and the employee master) will be sorted in employee number sequence.

3. There are no special rates for overtime hours. All hours worked are at the employee's standard hourly rate.

4. Gross pay is computed as hours worked multiplied by the employee's hourly rate.

5. Taxes are a flat 15% of gross pay.

6. Net pay is computed as gross pay – taxes.

7. Create a second report, an error report, if you encounter a timesheet for an employee who is not on the employee master file.

Required fields on the employee master include the following:

EMP-NBR	(Employee number)
EMP-NAME	(Employee name)
EMP-RATE	(Employee's hourly rate)

Fields on the timesheet file include the following:

TS-EMP-NBR	(Employee number)
TS-HRS-WRK	(Hours worked)

Flowchart PROCESS and the components of PROCESS.

PROJECT

Objective

This program will build the customer sales file used throughout this book. The program will have two input files. One input file will be a summarized version of the monthly sales file. The other file will be a customer sales file from the previous month. The output will be an updated customer sales file.

Processing Requirements

Match the files on the customer number.

Rules for processing the files are as follows:

1. Since the monthly sales file has already been summarized by customer, only one record for each customer will appear on this file. Likewise, there will be only one record for each customer on the incoming sales file.

2. Whenever the customer numbers on the two input files are equal, update the sales for the proper month and output the new sales record.

3. Whenever there is a customer on the monthly sales file who is not on the customer sales file, build a customer sales record and write it out.

4. Whenever there is a customer sales record with no monthly sales record, write the customer sales record as is.

MONTHLY SUMMARIZED CUSTOMER SALES RECORD

01-05	CUSTOMER NUMBER		MO-CUST
06-30	CUSTOMER NAME		MO-NAME
31-32	REGION NUMBER		MO-RGN
33-36	SALES YEAR		MO-YEAR
37-38	SALES MONTH		MO-MONTH
39-47	SALES AMOUNT	(9.2)	MO-SALES
48-50	Unused		

CUSTOMER SALES RECORD

01-05	CUSTOMER NUMBER	CS-CUST
06-30	CUSTOMER NAME	CS-NAME
31-138	CURRENT YEAR SALES	CS-CYSLS
	OCCURS 12 TIMES (9.2)	
138-245	PRIOR YEAR SALES	CS-PYSLS
	OCCURS 12 TIMES (9.2)	

UPDATED CUSTOMER SALES RECORD

01-05	CUSTOMER NUMBER	UCS-CUST
06-30	CUSTOMER NAME	UCS-NAME
31-138	CURRENT YEAR SALES	UCS-CYSLS
	OCCURS 12 TIMES (9.2)	
138-245	PRIOR YEAR SALES	UCS-PYSLS
	OCCURS 12 TIMES (9.2)	

15
Database Processing

OBJECTIVES

- Understanding the concepts of database file processing.
- Understanding the impact of a database management systems on program design.

INTRODUCTION

In the early years of computers, sequential files were used for all application processing. Initially, files were kept on punched cards. Eventually, files were moved to magnetic tape, where thousands of records, which may have required several boxes of cards, could be stored on one single magnetic tape. All magnetic tape processing was, and still is, sequential. As computers progressed over the years, magnetic disk became the standard for storing files that required frequent access.

As technology advanced, so did disk utilization. *Index Sequential Access Method (ISAM)* was one of the first popular disk file managers. The ISAM storage method allows files to be read sequentially, or directly through the use of a key field. With direct access, the desired record could be read directly, without having to read all the records that precede it in the file.

Today, we have several *database management systems (DBMS)* that provide direct access to data. The most popular databases used today are relational data structures such DB2, Oracle, and SQLServer. There are also several popular DBMS that are not relational. While each database management system requires unique design considerations and different program coding, the concepts are the same. This chapter will present the concepts that apply across all database management systems.

How Does a DBMS Work?

When a database is defined to a DBMS, the *database administrator (DBA)* will identify the key field of the record. A *key field* is the field than uniquely describes a record. Examples of key fields are the item number in an item master file or an employee number in the employee master. When accessing a DBMS directly, we specify the exact record we want to read by indicating the value of the key field. The DBMS locates the record we want and returns the data to the program. If the DBMS cannot locate the record we are looking for, the program will receive a message from the DBMS indicating that the key we are seeking is invalid (i.e., not found).

When reading an indexed file directly using the key field, the DBMS will never return an EOF condition. Because we are seeking only one specific record, the DBMS does not know that we have reached the end of the database; it only knows that the record we are looking for does not exist. On the other hand, if we are reading a database sequentially, as we have other files throughout this book, the DBMS will return an EOF after we have read the final record.

PROGRAM DESIGN CONSIDERATIONS: READING THE DATABASE

For purposes of illustration, we will design a program to perform the same function as the program we designed in Chapter 14. The difference will be that we will use direct access to read the item master on a DBMS, instead of matching two sequential files.

In order to read an indexed file directly, we must first specify the value of the key we are searching. In most cases, the value we are searching is obtained from a field of another file. In this instance, we will try to obtain the item master record with the same item number as we have in the order detail record. Figure 15–1 shows how we might read the item master.

Figure 15–1
Example of the READ procedure for direct read to a DBMS

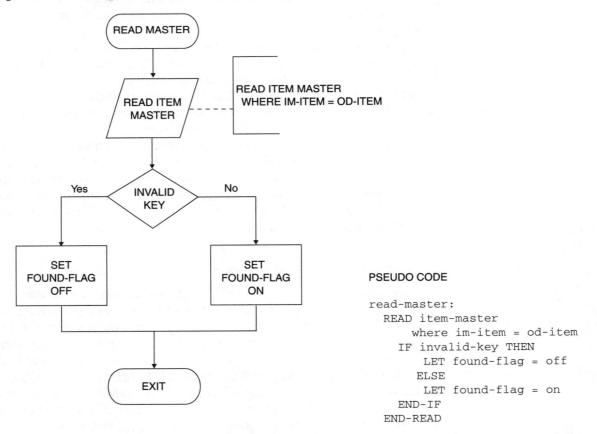

```
PSEUDO CODE

read-master:
   READ item-master
      where im-item = od-item
   IF invalid-key THEN
      LET found-flag = off
      ELSE
      LET found-flag = on
   END-IF
END-READ
```

Notice the decision following the read statement. Instead of checking for EOF, we now check to see if the DBMS had returned an *invalid key*. If the invalid key condition is true, we know that the record does not exist on the file. If the invalid key condition is false, then we know that the record was successfully retrieved. Following the decision, we have employed another flag, FOUND-FLAG, which will signal to PROCESS the results of the read. If FOUND-FLAG is on, then we know that the key was valid, and we have a record. If FOUND-FLAG is off, then we know we had the invalid key condition and we have no record.

STRUCTURE CHART CONSIDERATIONS

In Chapter 14, we had to read both files, and compare the key fields from them. When reading indexed files, we will not be required to match records from two files. Once we have read the transaction (order detail) and determined which item master record we want, we can read it directly. If the record exists, the record will be returned to the program. If the record does not exist, we will get an invalid key condition. The revised structure chart is shown in Figure 15–2.

Figure 15–2
Structure chart for example program

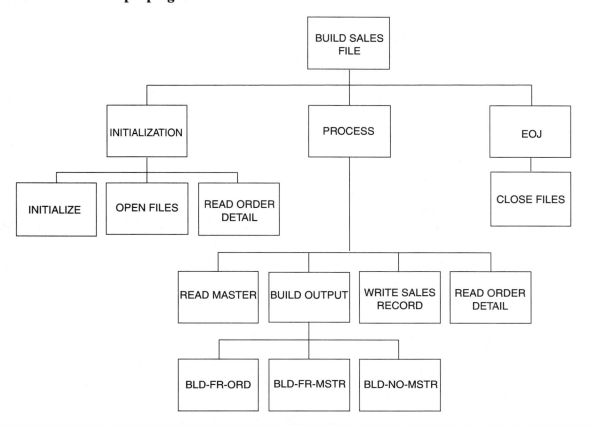

Notice that the INITIALIZATION section of the program no longer reads the master file, and PROCESS no longer compares the fields. The comparison in PROCESS has been replaced with the step to READ MASTER.

Flowchart Considerations

Figure 15–3 illustrates the flowchart for INITIALIZATION. Notice that this looks no different from those prior to Chapter 14.

Figure 15–4 shows the translation of PROCESS from the structure chart to the flowchart. Notice how FOUND-FLAG has been incorporated into the logic and how the logic varies depending on whether a master record or the invalid key message was returned from the DBMS.

Figure 15–5 contains the entire flowchart for this program.

**Figure 15–3
INITIALIZATION
procedure for example
program**

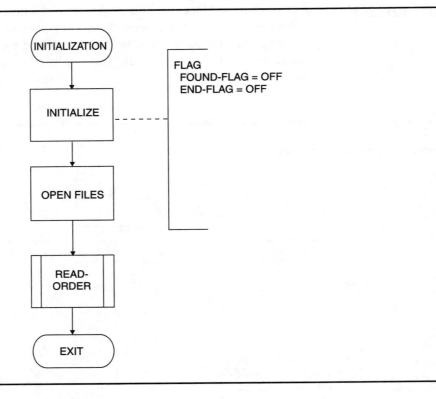

**Figure 15–4
PROCESS procedure for
example program**

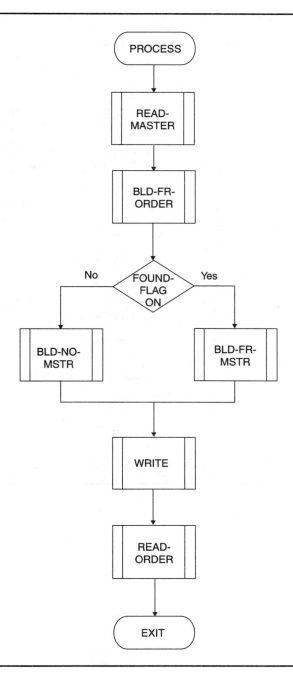

Figure 15–5
Complete program

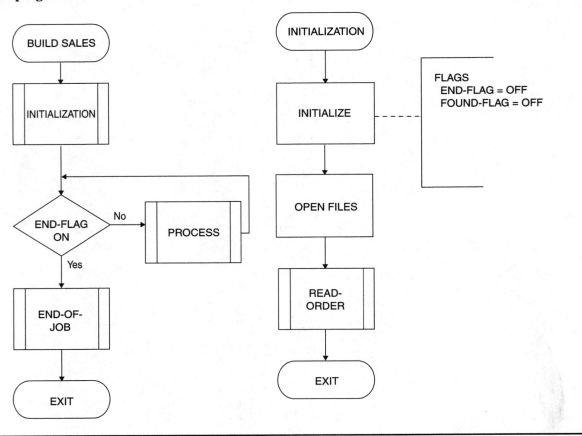

Figure 15–5
(*continued*)

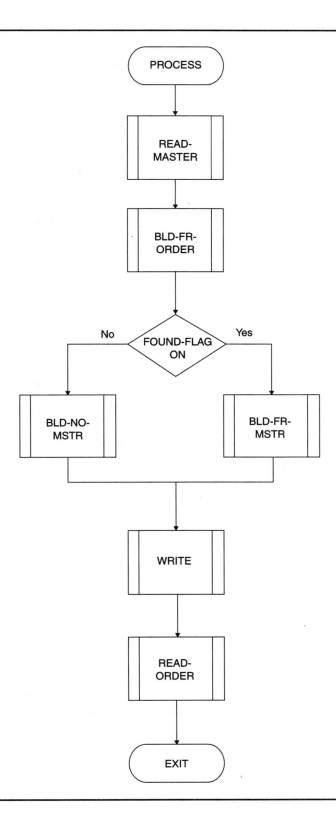

(*continued on the next page*)

Figure 15–5
(*continued*)

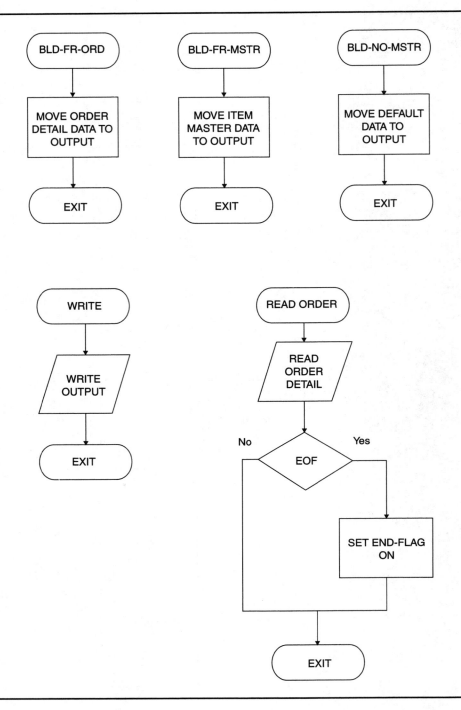

Figure 15–5
(continued)

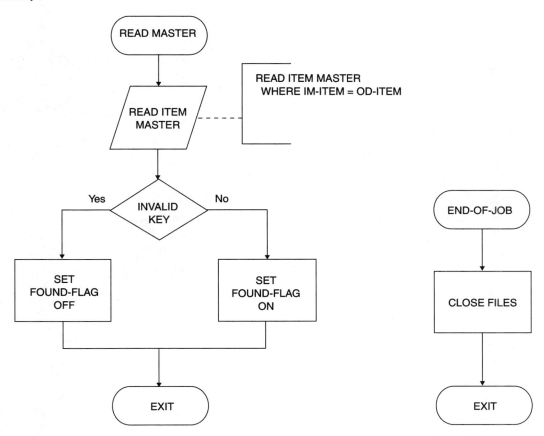

PSEUDO CODE

```
mainline:
        DO initialization
        DOWHILE end-flag off
            DO process
        END-DOWHILE
        DO end-of-job
        STOP


initialization:
        INITIALIZE   flags: end-flag = off
                            found-flag = off

process:
        DO read-master
        DO bld-fr-order
```

(continued on the next page)

Figure 15–5
(continued)

```
          IF found-flag on
               DO bld-fr-mstr
            ELSE
               DO bld-no-mstr
          END-IF
          DO write
          DO read-order

read-master:
          READ item master where im-item = od-item
               IF invalid-key THEN
                    LET found-flag = off
                  ELSE
                    LET found-flag = on
               END-IF
          END-READ

bld-fr-ord:
          MOVE order detail data to ouptut

bld-fr-mstr:
          MOVE item master data to output

bld-no-mstr:
          MOVE default data to output

write:
          WRITE output sales record

read-order:
          READ order detail
               IF end-of-file THEN
                    LET end-flag = on
               END-IF
          END-READ

end-of-job:
          CLOSE files
```

SUMMARY

Database management systems allow us to directly access data. We identify the value of the key field we want, and the DBMS will attempt to read that record. If the DBMS is successful, the record is returned to the program. If the read is not successful, the DBMS will return a message indicating that the desired key is invalid. Databases may be accessed directly or they may be processed sequentially.

REVIEW QUESTIONS

1. What is the difference between direct access and sequential access?
2. When reading a file using the direct access technique, how does the DBMS let the program know that the desired record could not be found?

3. Why is there no EOF check on a file that is being read using the direct access technique?

EXERCISE

This exercise will reinforce the concept of direct access to a DBMS file. You will find this exercise similar to the exercise in Chapter 14. Two files will be input to the program. The first file is the timesheet file. The second will be an employee master file maintained on a DBMS. As in Chapter 14, you will be producing a report showing what the total payroll will be for the company.

Consider the following rules for the program:

1. No employee will be paid unless they have a record in the timesheet file.

2. The key to the employee file is the employee number.

3. There are no special rates for overtime hours. All hours worked are paid at the employee's standard hourly rate.

4. Gross pay is computed as hours multiplied by the employee's hourly rate.

5. Taxes are a flat 15% of gross pay.

6. Net pay is computed as gross pay minus tax.

7. If a timesheet record is processed for an employee not on the employee master file, indicate that this is an invalid employee on the report. You may do this however you see fit.

Required fields on the employee master include the following:

EMP-NBR	(Employee number)
EMP-NAME	(Employee name)
EMP-RATE	(Employee's hourly rate)

Fields on the timesheet file include the following:

TS-EMP-NBR	(Employee number)
TS-HRS-WRK	(Hours worked)

With these criteria in mind, please flowchart PROCESS and the components of PROCESS.

PROJECT

Objective

This program will build the monthly summarized customer sales file. Inputs to the program will be the order detail file and the customer master file. The output file will contain sales data summarized by customer number.

Processing Requirements

Rules for processing the files are as follows:

1. Read and process all records on the order detail file. Files will be sorted in customer number sequence.

2. Summarize the sales by customer, and write only one output record for each customer who purchased during the month (OD-DATE).

3. Access the customer master file using the customer number as the key. If the customer is not found, move UNKNOWN CUSTOMER to customer name and set the region to 00.

4. The sales detail file will contain sales for only one month.

MONTHLY SALES DETAIL RECORD

01-05	ORDER NUMBER		OD-ORD-NO
06-11	ORDER DATE (YYYYMM)		OD-DATE
12-16	CUSTOMER NUMBER		OD-CUST
17-21	ITEM NUMBER		OD-ITEM
22-26	QUANTITY	(5.0)	OD-QTY
27-35	SALES AMOUNT	(9.2)	OD-SLSAMT
36-40	Unused		

CUSTOMER MASTER RECORD

01-05	CUSTOMER NUMBER	CM-CUST
06-30	CUSTOMER NAME	CM-NAME
31-32	REGION	CM-RGN
33-100	Unused	

MONTHLY SUMMARIZED CUSTOMER SALES RECORD

01-05	CUSTOMER NUMBER		MO-CUST
06-30	CUSTOMER NAME		MO-NAME
31-32	REGION NUMBER		MO-RGN
33-38	SALES DATE (YYYYMM)		MO-DATE
39-47	SALES AMOUNT	(9.2)	MO-SALES
48-50	Unused		

Assignment

1. Perform mapping process.

2. Develop the program structure chart.

3. Develop the flowchart or pseudo code for the entire program.

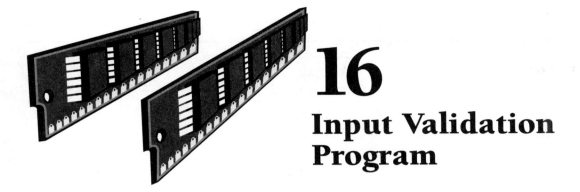

16
Input Validation Program

OBJECTIVES

- Understanding the master file update process.
- Understanding the role of the input validation program in the update process.
- Using the different types of validity tests.

INTRODUCTION

In Chapter 14, we briefly discussed the master file, but spent little time defining it. In simple terms, a *master file* contains relatively permanent data. In Chapters 14 and 15, we read the item master file. This file contains the data that defines each item, and the data rarely changes. While you may change a few prices or add new items, the data doesn't undergo significant change from one day to the next, or from one month to the next. Although the data is relatively permanent, there are occasions when it must be changed.

In this chapter and the next chapter, we will investigate the programs used to update master files. In this chapter, we will study the process behind testing the input data to guard against putting invalid data in our master file. In Chapter 17, we will concentrate on the program that updates the master file.

UNDERSTANDING THE CONCEPTS OF THE UPDATE PROCESS

Before proceeding any further, let's be sure we have a solid understanding of the update process. Data for the master file update normally begins from manual input. That is, somebody decides a change to the data is necessary and completes a form (either paper or electronic) that describes the changes required. If the changes were written on paper, the data would be manually keyed into the computer system. Exhibit 16–1 contains an example master item file change form, one that might be used to record changes to the item master file. Normally, *add transactions* will require that all fields are filled in. *Change transactions* will normally have only the item number and the field(s) being changed (such as an updated price). *Delete transactions* will

Figure 16–1
System flowchart of the
update process

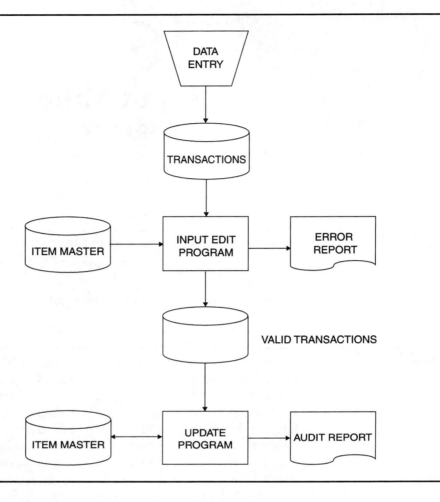

normally have only the item number being deleted. At this point, the new data will be kept in a *sequential file,* which we will call the *transaction file.* A transaction file contains records that will be used to update a master file in *batch mode.* This chapter will deal only with the batch update process.

The update process is normally accomplished in two steps. Figure 16–1 illustrates the update process. Notice that the first step is the *input valida-tion* program, which validates the transactions. Because the transaction data began from a manual source, it is not uncommon to have errors. We perform this validation process to avoid updating the master file with known data errors. This validation step cannot guarantee the accuracy of the data, but it can identify known errors and eliminate them from the up-date process. This first step creates two types of output. The first is an error report containing all errors encountered. The second is a file containing the transactions that passed all validation tests. Exhibit 16–2 contains the record layout of the input transaction record.

After the data has been validated, the error-free records will be for-warded to the second step of the process, the update program. Here, the master file data will be updated to reflect any changes. An audit report will be generated and given back to the user. This audit report contains all updates to the master file.

Chapter 17 will address the process of updating the master file.

Exhibit 16–1
ITEM MASTER
CHANGE FORM

_____ADD

_____CHANGE

_____DELETE

Item Number_____

Description_____

Sport Code_____

Equip Type:_____

Comm. Pct._____

Purchase Cost_____

Retail Price_____

Exhibit 16–2
TRANSACTION FILE

01-01	CHANGE CODE	TR-CD
02-06	ITEM NUMBER	TR-ITEM
07-21	DESCRIPTION	TR-DESC
22-23	SPORT CODE	TR-SPRTCD
24-25	EQUIPMENT TYPE	TR-ETYP
29-35	PURCHASE COST (7.2)	TR-COST
26-42	RETAIL PRICE (7.2)	TR-PRICE
43-45	COMMISSION PCT (3.3)	TR-COMMPCT
46-50	Unused	

DATA VALIDATION: FIRST STEP OF THE UPDATE PROCESS

Overview of the Validation Process

Notice the first field in the record layout, shown in Exhibit 16–2, is the change code. This change code will contain one of three valid values. If the item is to be added to the item master file, this code will have an A. If data for the item is to be changed, this field will have a C, and if the item is to be deleted, the value will be a D.

Before proceeding, let's take a look at some obvious rules with regard to add, change, and delete transactions. First, ADD indicates that this is a new item that is to be added to the file. Therefore, if the item already exists on the master, we must consider this an error. Likewise, CHANGE and DELETE can be performed only on a record that exists. If the item does not exist on the master file, we must consider this transaction an error.

The organization of this chapter will differ from previous chapters. Normally we have examined the implications to the program structure before reviewing flowcharting techniques. In this chapter, we will look first at the different types of validation tests and how these tests are performed. Later in this chapter, we will review the impact to the structure chart. And, as usual, we will follow the transition from the structure chart to the flowchart.

Program Outputs

If you look at Figure 16–1, you will notice that the input validation program has two outputs. One of these is the valid transaction file; the other is an error report.

Valid Transactions

Each input transaction processed will undergo a series of validation tests. Validations for add transactions may differ from those for change and delete transactions. We will cover this in greater detail later. If the program determines that the transaction is free from errors, the transaction will be written to the valid transaction file.

Error Report

If any errors are detected on a transaction, the appropriate error message is printed on the error report. In most cases, all errors encountered in each transaction are written to the error report. We will cover the error report in greater detail later in this chapter.

Validation Tests

The data validation step interrogates each field of the transaction record to determine if the data contained in the field is correct. We have six types of validations to consider. While only one validation type is normally relevant to a field, it is possible that a field may undergo multiple tests, using more than one validation type. It is important to understand that these validation tests cannot verify correctness or accuracy of the data. We can only test to ensure that the data content conforms to the rules of the field. The validation types are as follows:

1. Presence test.
2. Numeric test.
3. Existence test.
4. Relationship test.
5. Valid value test.
6. Range/reasonableness test.

Error Handling

Each of the flowchart segments that will be presented has two very important features that must be understood. First, you will notice that each time an error is detected, ERROR-FLAG is turned ON. This will be discussed in greater detail when we review the flow of PROCESS. The second item of interest is how the error report is generated. Each time an error is encountered, the flowchart indicates an error message and that data is to be moved to output. Following this, the procedure WRITE-ERROR is performed. The report being created is shown in Exhibit 16–3.

Presence Test

The presence test checks to see if there is any data in the field. It does not perform any additional validation. The assumption is that if any data is there, it is correct. We cannot determine the correctness of the item description nor can we check for accurate spelling. We can only test to see if any data is in the field. Figure 16–2 illustrates the presence test.

Figure 16–2
Flowchart for presence test

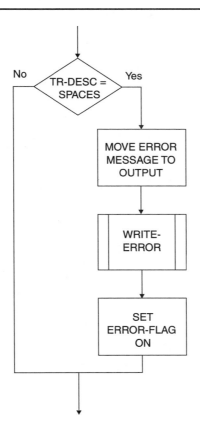

PSEUDO CODE

```
IF tr-desc = spaces
    MOVE error message to output
    DO write-error
    LET error-flag = on
END-IF
```

Numeric Test

The numeric test determines if the data within the field is a valid numeric value. Numeric values are 0 through 9, and do not includes commas (,). Depending on the programming language used to write the program, you may be able to accept decimal points (.) as numeric data in the input field. We will be performing numeric tests on all three numeric fields. If the field does not contain numeric data, it would generate an error message. Figure 16–3 illustrates a numeric test.

Existence Test

The existence test validates the value of the data by checking to see if the value exists on another file. For example, if we are performing an ADD transaction, the item should not exist on the item master file. If we are performing CHANGE or DELETE, the item must exist on the item

**Figure 16–3
Flowchart for numeric test**

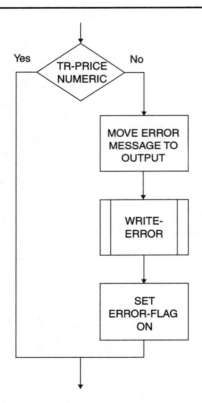

PSEUDO CODE

```
If tr-price not numeric
     MOVE error-message to output
     DO write-error
     LET error-flag = on
END-IF
```

Figure 16–4
**Flowchart for existence
test for change and delete
transactions**

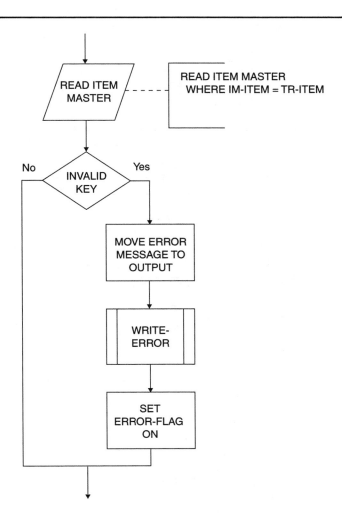

PSEUDO CODE

```
READ item-master where im-item = tr-item
    IF invalid key
        MOVE error-message to output
        DO write-error
        LET error-flag = on
    END-IF
END-READ
```

master file. Figure 16–4 illustrates an existence test for the CHANGE and DELETE transactions by reading the item master file for the item in question.

Relationship Test

While two fields may pass the appropriate validation tests independently, there is a possibility that together, two fields may be invalid. For example,

**Figure 16–5
Flowchart for
relationship test**

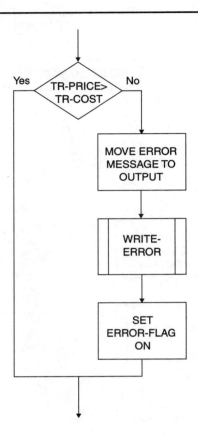

PSEUDO CODE

```
IF tr-price not > tr-cost THEN
    MOVE error message to output
    DO write-error
    LET error-flag = on
END-IF
```

purchase cost and retail price may both pass their independent numeric test. However, it would be invalid to have a retail price less than the purchase cost. Therefore, while each field is valid, they would fail the relationship test. Another example is date validation. We will need to ensure that the month is valid, and that the day is valid. Valid months are 01–12. Valid days are 01–31. However, a month of 02 and a day of 30 would fail the relationship test because there is no February 30th. Figure 16–5 illustrates the price/cost relationship test, by comparing the values of the selling prices and the purchasing cost.

Valid Value Test

The valid value test interrogates the field for specific values. For example, the transaction code field must contain an A, C, or D. If the field does not

Figure 16–6
Flowchart for valid value test

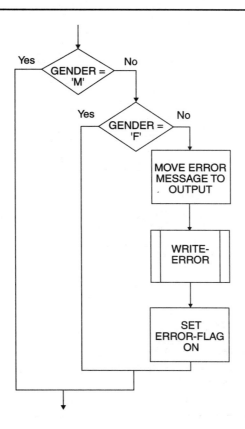

```
PSEUDO CODE

IF gender not = "M" THEN
    IF gender not = "F" THEN
        MOVE error-message to output
        DO write-error
        LET error-flag = off
    END-IF
END-IF
```

contain one of these values, it will generate an error. Another example might be found when updating an employee master file. The field that designates the employee's gender can contain only one of two values. The employee must either be a male (M) or a female (F). The appropriate validity test would be to ensure that the gender code equals an M or an F. If the employee's gender were neither, we would handle this as an error. Figure 16–6 illustrates this test.

Range/Reasonableness Test

The range/reasonableness test cannot check for absolute validity; rather it determines if the data is within a normal range. For example, Acme Distributors does not sell products that have a retail price exceeding $1000.

Figure 16–7
Flowchart for range/
reasonableness test

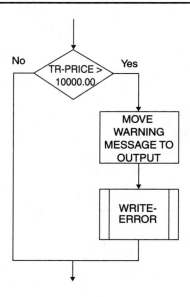

PSEUDO CODE

```
IF tr-price > 1000 THEN
    MOVE warning-message to output
    DO write-error
END-IF
```

Therefore, we may want to make sure that no item is entered with a price greater than $1000. However, there is no business rule that says we cannot sell an item for more than a $1000, but to do so would not be expected. Therefore, since it might be valid (however unlikely) we will not treat this as an error. Instead, we will indicate this occurrence on the error report as a warning. Figure 16–7 illustrates the reasonableness test. Notice that in this example, the error flag is not turned on, and a warning message is issued in lieu of an error message.

Exhibit 16–3
ERROR REPORT EXAMPLE

```
RUN MM/DD/YY  HH:MM                          ACME DISTRIBUTORS                           PAGE ZZZZ9
                                          ITEM MASTER ERROR REPORT
```

ITEM NUMBER	TRANSACTION CODE	FIELD	VALUE	MESSAGE
1B550	D			ITEM DOES NOT EXIST - CANNOT DELETE
26C3B	A	PRICE	100.4A	FIELD NOT NUMERIC
54MM9	C	PRICE	1400.00	WARNING - EXCEEDS $1000

DESIGNING THE INPUT VALIDATION PROGRAM

In this section, we will begin to put some order to the types of validation tests discussed earlier. As usual, let's begin with the development of the program's structure chart.

Building the Structure Chart

We begin building the structure chart by establishing the requirements of the program. The requirements for our program are as follows:

1. Validate the input data. We will apply the following rules:
   - Transaction Code must be an A, C, or D.
   - We cannot add a record that already exists, nor can we delete or change a record that does not exist.
   - All fields must be present on an ADD record.
   - For a CHANGE transaction, validate only the fields that are present on the transaction record.
   - Sport Code and Equipment Type must exist on the appropriate description files.
   - Commission Percent, Purchase Cost, and Retail Price must be numeric. Commission Percent cannot exceed 35% (0.35).
   - Purchase Cost cannot exceed Retail Price.
   - Retail Price should not exceed $1000. If it does, this should be noted as a warning, but allow the update to continue.
   - Provide for multiple errors for each record.

2. Produce the error report for all errors and warnings. Place the appropriate error message in the MESSAGE field.

3. If the transaction passes the validation phase, write the transaction to the output valid transaction file.

Based on the requirements, let's take a look at organizing the INITIAL-IZATION section of the program. In order to prepare the program for execution, the follow tasks must be performed:

1. Initialize.
2. Open files.
3. Load Sport Code description array.

   (This array will be used to validate the Sport Code.)
4. Load Equipment Type description array.

   (This array will be used to validate the Equipment Type.)
5. Read first record from Transaction File.

The PROCESS section of the program will be somewhat different than previous programs. Let's first consider the steps necessary to validate the transactions. The structure chart must include the following tasks:

1. Validation.
   a. Validate transaction code.
   b. Perform add validations.
      - Validate Item.
      - Validate Description.

- Validate Equipment Type.
- Validate Sport Code.
- Validate Commission Percent.
- Validate Cost.
- Validate Price.
- Validate Price/Cost Relationship.

c. Perform change validations.
- Validate Item.
- Validate Description.
- Validate Equipment Type.
- Validate Sport Code.
- Validate Commission Percent.
- Validate Cost.
- Validate Price.
- Validate Price/Cost Relationship.

d. Perform delete validation.
- Validate Item.

2. Read next transaction record.

The structure chart is shown in Figure 16–8.

Figure 16–8
Structure chart for validation program

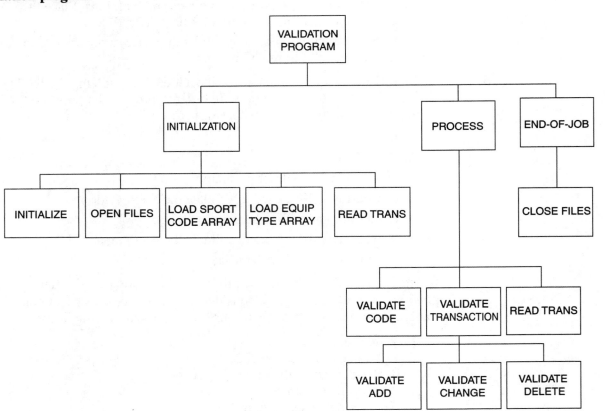

TRANSITION TO FLOWCHART

Let's take a look at the transition of this structure to the flowchart, and determine how the logic is constructed for this input validation program. You may find some significant differences in this program compared to previous programs, but while the program appears to be different, notice also the similarities. Figure 16–9 contains the flowchart for this entire program.

Figure 16–9
Complete flowchart and pseudo code for validation program

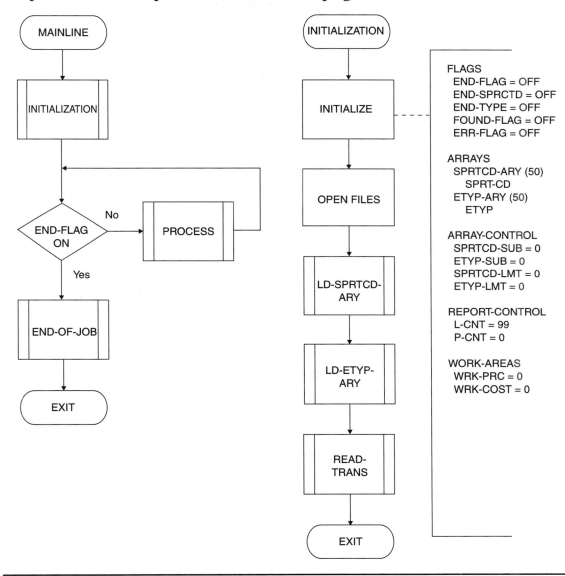

(continued on the next page)

Figure 16–9
(continued)

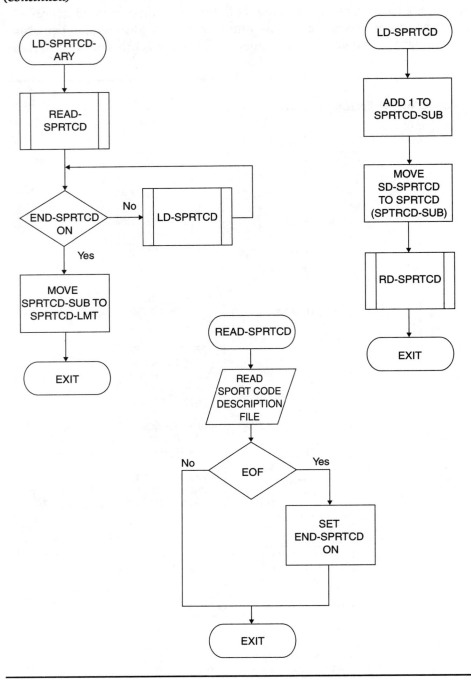

Figure 16–9
(continued)

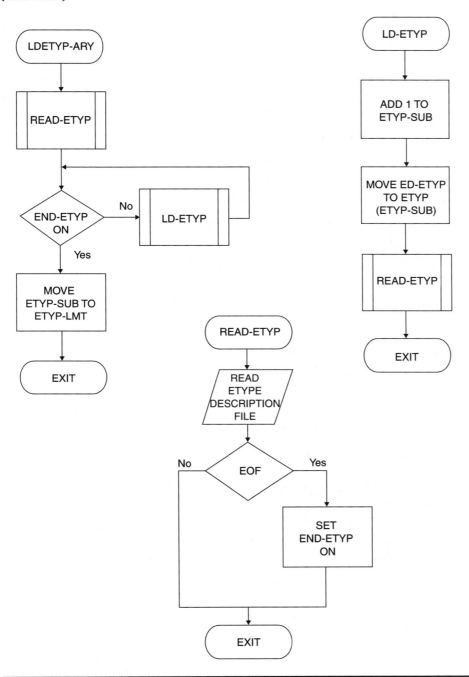

(continued on the next page)

Figure 16–9
(continued)

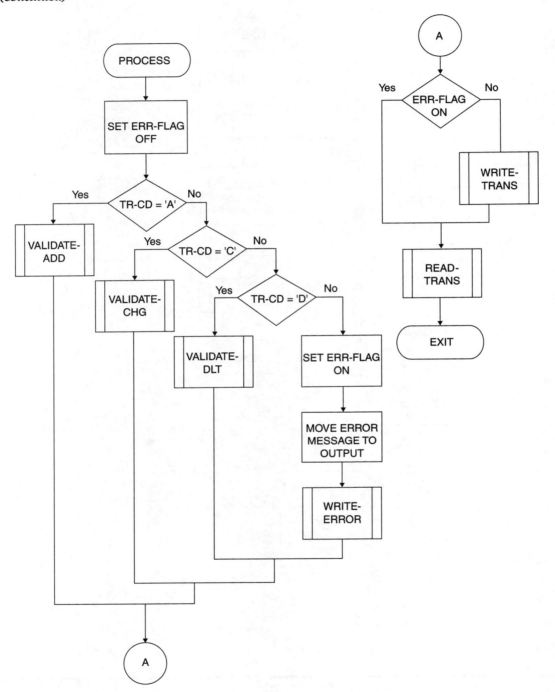

Figure 16–9
(continued)

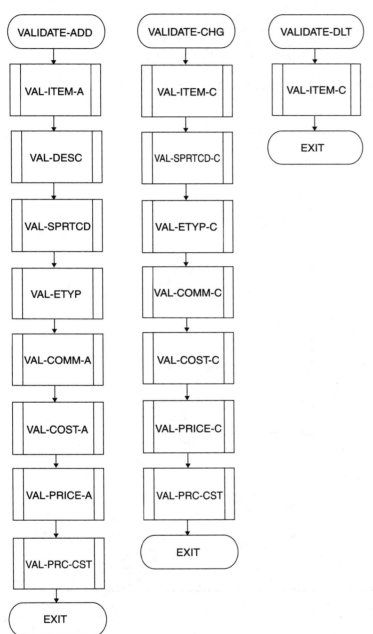

(continued on the next page)

Figure 16–9
(*continued*)

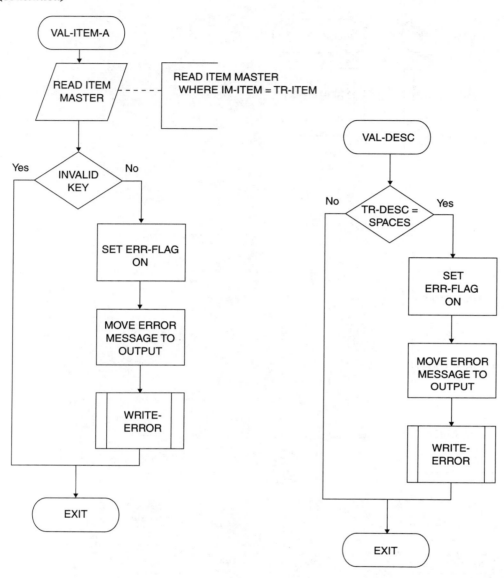

Figure 16–9
(continued)

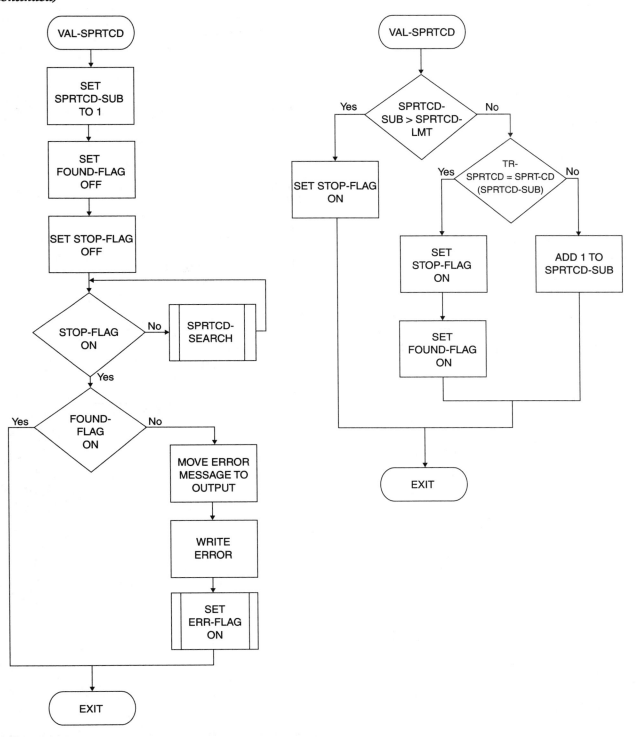

(continued on the next page)

Figure 16–9
(continued)

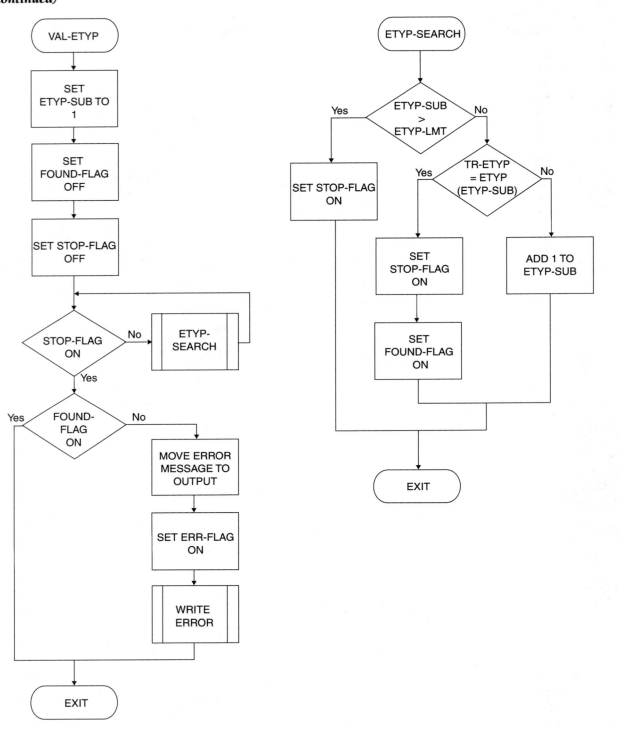

Figure 16–9
(continued)

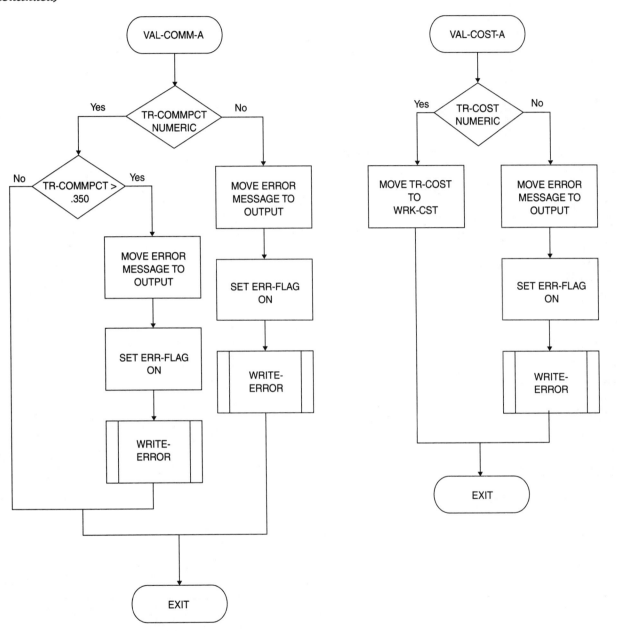

(continued on the next page)

Figure 16–9
(*continued*)

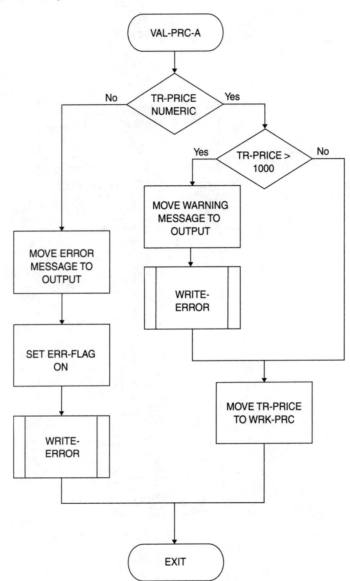

Figure 16–9
(continued)

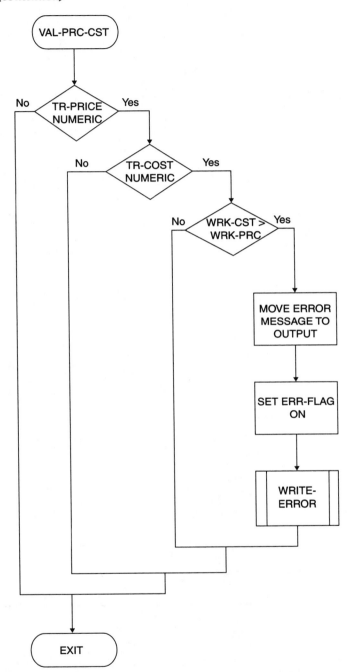

(continued on the next page)

Figure 16–9
(*continued*)

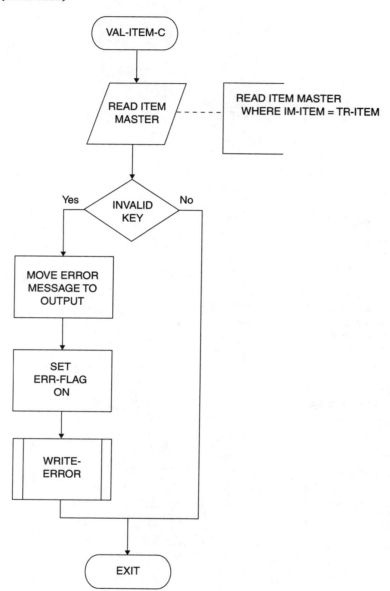

Figure 16–9
(continued)

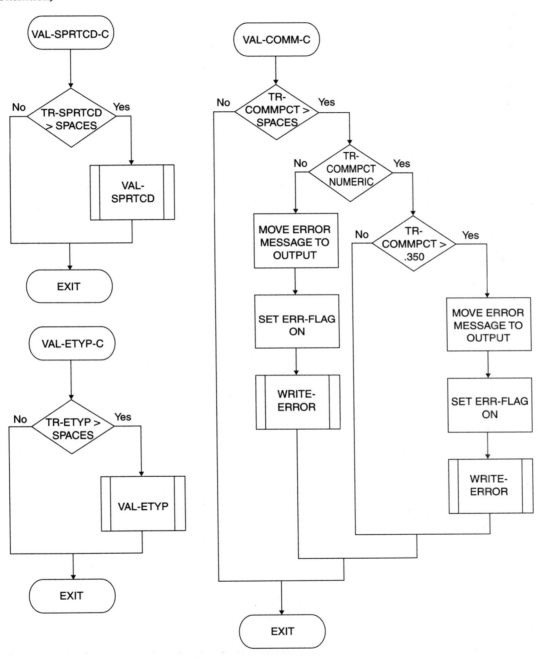

(continued on the next page)

Figure 16–9
(continued)

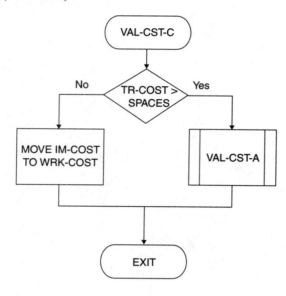

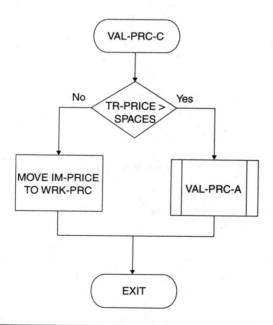

Figure 16–9
(*continued*)

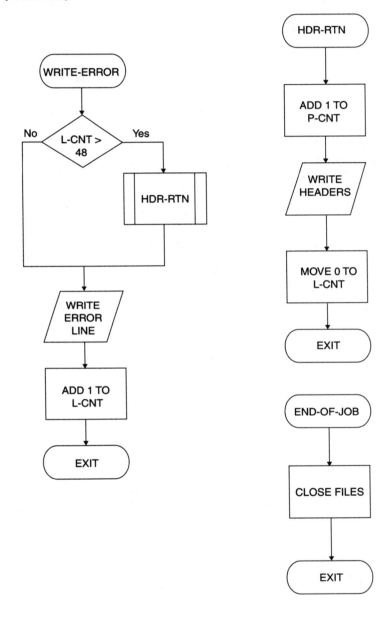

PSEUDO CODE

```
mainline:
        DO initialization
        DOWHILE end-flag off
            DO process
        END-DOWHILE
        DO end-of-job
        STOP
```

(*continued on the next page*)

Figure 16–9
(continued)

```
initialization:
        INITIALIZE     flags:                end-flag = off
                                             end-sprtcd = off
                                             end-etyp = off
                                             found-flag = off
                                             err-flag = off

                       sprt-cd-ary occurs 50 times
                                             sprt-cd = spaces

                       etyp-ary occurs 50 times
                                             etyp = spaces

                       array-control: sprtcd-sub  = 0
                                      etyp-sub = 0
                                      sprtcd-lmt = 0
                                      etyp-lmt = 0

                       report-control: l-cnt =99
                                       p-cnt = 0

                       work-areas: wrk-prc = 0
                                   wrk-cost = 0
        OPEN files
        DO ld-sprtcd-ary
        DO ld-etyp-ary
        DO read-trans

  ld-sprtcd-ary:
        DO read-sprtcd
            DOWHILE end-sprtcd off
                        DO ld-sprtcd
            END-DOWHILE
        LET sprtcd-lmt = sprtcd-sub

  ld-sprtcd:
        ADD 1 to sprtcd-sub
        MOVE sd-sprtcd to sprtcd (sprtcd-sub)
        DO rd-sprtcd

  rd-sprtcd:
        READ sprtcd file
            IF end-of-file THEN
                LET end-sprtcd = on
            END-IF
        END-READ

  ld-etyp-ary:
        DO read-etyp
        DOWHILE end-etyp off
            DO ld-etyp
        END-DOWHILE
        LET etyp-lmt = etyp-sub
```

Figure 16–9
(continued)

```
ld-etyp:
        ADD 1 to etyp-sub
        MOVE ed-etyp to etyp (etyp-sub)
        DO rd-etyp

rd-etyp:
        READ etyp file
            IF end-of-file THEN
                    LET end-etyp = on
            END-IF
        END-READ

process:
        LET err-flag = off
        IF tr-cd = "A" THEN
            DO validate-add
          ELSE
            IF tr-cd = "C" THEN
                    DO validate-chg
                ELSE
                    IF tr-chg-cd = "D" THEN
                            DO validate-dlt
                      ELSE
                            LET err-flag = on
                            MOVE error-message to output
                            DO write-error
                    END-IF
                END-IF
        END-IF
        IF err-flag not on
            WRITE output transaction record
        END-IF
        DO read-trans

validate-add:
        DO val-item-a
        DO val-desc
        DO val-sprtcd
        DO val-etyp
        DO val-comm-a
        DO val-cost-a
        DO val-price-a
        DO val-prc-cst

validate-chg
        DO val-item-c
        DO val-desc-c
        DO val-sprtcd-c
        DO val-etyp-c
        DO val-comm-c
        DO val-cost-c
        DO val-price-c
        DO val-prc-cst
```

(continued on the next page)

Figure 16–9
(continued)

```
validate-dlt:
        DO val-itm-c

val-item-a:
        READ item master  where im-item = tr-item
            IF not invalid-key THEN
                    LET err-flag = on
                    MOVE error-message to output
                    DO write-error
            END-IF
        END-READ

val-desc:
        IF tr-desc = spaces THEN
            LET error-flag = on
            MOVE error-message to output
            DO write-error
        END-IF

val-sprtcd:
        LET sprtcd-sub = 1
        LET found-flag = off
        LET stop-flag = off
        DOWHILE stop-flag off
            DO sprtcd-search
        END-DOWHILE
        IF found-flag off THEN
            LET error-flag = on
            MOVE error-message to output
            DO write-error
        END-IF

sprtcd-search:
        IF sprtcd-sub > sprtcd-lmt THEN
            LET stop-flag = on
          ELSE
            IF tr-sprtcd = sprt-cd(sprtcd-sub) THEN
                    LET found-flag = on
                    LET stop-flag = on
              ELSE
                    ADD 1 to sprtcd-sub
            END-IF
        END-IF

val-etyp:
        LET etyp-sub = 1
        LET found-flag = off
        LET stop-flag = off
        DOWHILE stop-flag off
            DO etyp-search
        END-DOWHILE
        IF found-flag off THEN
            LET error-flag = on
            MOVE error-message to output
            DO write-error
        END-IF
```

Figure 16–9
(continued)

```
etyp-search:
        IF etyp-sub > etyp-lmt THEN
            LET stop-flag = on
          ELSE
            IF tr-etyp = etyp(etyp-sub) THEN
                LET found-flag = on
                LET stop-flag = on
              ELSE
                ADD 1 to etyp-sub
            END-IF
        END-IF

val-comm-a:
        IF tr-comm not numeric THEN
            LET error-flag = on
            MOVE error-message to output
            DO write-error
          ELSE
            IF tr-comm > .350
                LET error-flag = on
                MOVE error-message to output
                DO write-error
            END-IF
        END-IF

val-cst-a:
        IF tr-cost not numeric THEN
            LET error-flag = on
            MOVE error-message to output
            DO write-error
          ELSE
            LET wrk-cst = tr-cost
        END-IF

val-price-a:
        IF tr-price not numeric THEN
            LET error-flag = on
            LMOVE error-message to output
            LDO write-error
          ELSE
            LIF tr-price > 1000
                MOVE warning-message to output
                DO write-error
            LEND-IF
            LLET wrk-prc = tr-price
        END-IF

val-prc-cst:
        IF tr-price numeric THEN
            IF tr-cost numeric THEN
                IF wrk-prc not > wrk-cst THEN
                    LET error-flag = on
                    MOVE error-message to output
                    DO write-error
```

(continued on the next page)

Figure 16–9
(*continued*)

```
                        END-IF
                END-IF
        END-IF


  val-item-c:
                READ item master where im-item = tr-item
                        IF invalid key THEN
                                LET error-flag = on
                                MOVE error-message to output
                                DO write-error
                        END-IF
                END-READ


  val-sprtcd-c:
                IF tr-sprtcd > spaces THEN
                        DO val-sprtcd
                END-IF


  val-etyp-c:
                IF tr-etyp > spaces THEN
                        DO val-etyp
                END-IF


  val-comm-c:
                IF tr-commpct > spaces THEN
                        IF tr-commpct numeric THEN
                                IF tr-commpct > .350 THEN
                                        LET error-flag = on
                                        MOVE error-message to output
                                        DO write-error
                                END-IF
                          ELSE
                                LET error-flag = on
                                MOVE error-message to output
                                DO write-error
                        END-IF
                END-IF


  val-cst-c:
                IF tr-cost > spaces THEN
                        IF tr-cost numeric THEN
                                DO val-cst-a
                        END-IF
                END-IF


  val-prc-c:
                IF tr-price > spaces THEN
                        IF tr-cost numeric THEN
                                DO val-prc-a
                        END-IF
                END-IF
```

Figure 16–9
(continued)

```
write-error:
        IF l-cnt > 48 THEN
                DO hdr-rtn
        END-If
        WRITE error-line
        ADD 1 to l-cnt

hdr-rtn:
        ADD 1 to p-cnt
        WRITE headers
        LET l-cnt = 0

end-of-job:
        CLOSE files
```

INITIALIZATION

For the most part, INITIALIZATION is no different than the programs we have studied earlier. We have added the load procedures for the sport code, and the equipment type arrays that support the validation process. According to the requirements, if the sport code or equipment type on the transaction record are not on the appropriate arrays, then the transaction is in error. After we have finished loading these arrays, we will keep track of the number of elements loaded using the appropriate limit field (SPRTCD-LMT and ETYP-LMT).

PROCESS

Let's review the PROCESS section of this program carefully. In order to focus on the different aspects of this program, key components of the input validation process have been highlighted. Refer to the PROCESS procedure shown in Figure 16–9.

Turning the ERR-FLAG Off

Our requirements indicate that we must identify all possible errors. To do this, we cannot simply identify one error and move on to the next transaction. If the transaction passes all validation tests, we will write the transaction record to the output file destined for the update program. If an error has been uncovered during the validation process, we will turn an error flag on. We can then interrogate this error flag prior to writing the transaction to the output file. If the error flag is on, then we know that the program discovered at least one error with this transaction. If the error flag is off, we know that no error was found. As we enter PROCESS with each new transaction, we will turn the error flag off. It will be turned on only when an error has been discovered.

Determine Type of Update

The first series of decisions is used to determine which type of transaction we are processing. ADD, CHANGE, and DELETE transactions all require different validation logic. Notice that if the transaction code is not an A, C, or D, the transaction is considered to be in error, and all subsequent validation steps are bypassed.

Validating the ADD Transaction

Validate the Item

The first step in validating the ADD transaction is to ensure the item does not already exist. An item being added to the master file cannot already exist on the master file. If the read for the item master returns an invalid key condition, then we know that the item does not exist. If the read to the item master is successful, then we know that the item is already there, and thus this add transaction is invalid.

Validate the Description

We cannot validate the description in terms of correctness. All we can do is determine if the description field has any content. At this time, we perform a presence test on the description field. If the field is equal to spaces, then we know that there is no data, and we must treat this field as an error.

Validate Sport Code

This validation step determines if the sport code of the item being added exists in the sport code array. We will execute a search of the sport code array to find the sport code. If we do not find the sport code of the item being added, this will be considered an error.

Validate Equipment Type

Like the sport code, the equipment type validation determines if the equipment type of the item being added exists in the equipment type array. We will execute a search of the equipment type array to find the equipment type. If we do not find the equipment type of the item being added, this will be considered an error.

Validate Commission Percent

This will ensure that the commission percentage field is numeric and does not exceed 35%.

Validate Cost and Price

First, both fields will be validated using the numeric test to make sure they are numeric. These tests will be performed in separate procedures. If the price field is numeric, it will also be tested to see if the price is greater than $1000. If the price exceeds $1000, a warning message is printed, but notice that the error flag is not turned on. A price greater than $1000 is not necessarily an error, but rather it fails the reasonableness test because it is not normal for a price to exceed $1000.

If both fields pass the numeric test, then the product cost is compared to the price. If the cost exceeds the price then an error results. This is a relationship test between cost and price, which is performed in a separate procedure.

Check to See If an Error Has Occurred

After all of the validation checks for the add transaction are complete, we will test ERR-FLAG to see if has been turned on. If no errors were found in the transaction record, we will write the record to the output transaction file. As you saw earlier in Figure 16–1, this file is passed to the update program for processing. If any validation steps uncovered an error, the write step is bypassed.

Finally, as with all programs, we read the next record for processing, and return to MAINLINE, where PROCESS is again invoked.

Validating the CHANGE Transaction

Validate the Item

The first step in validating the CHANGE transaction is to ensure the item exists on the item master file. We cannot change an item that does not currently exist. If the read for the item master returns an invalid key condition, we know that the item does not exist and we have an error condition. If the read to the item master is successful, we know that the item exists and we can proceed with the transaction.

Validate the Description

We can perform no validation on the description. Remember that only fields present in the transaction record are fields that will be updated on the item master. If the description is not present, it simply means that no change to the description will be made. If anything is there, then the update program will change the description. Because the only validation we can perform on this field is presence, it would be a useless test. Therefore, we will not validate the description.

Validate Sport Code

If data is present in the sport code field, we must determine if the sport code exists in the sport code table. We will execute a table search to find the sport code. If we do not find the sport code specified in the change transaction, we will treat this as an error. The table search will be executed only if a sport code is present in the transaction record.

Validate Equipment Type

Like the sport code, the equipment type validation determines if the equipment type on the transaction record exists in the equipment type table. We will execute a table search to find the equipment type. If we do not find the equipment type specified in the change transaction, we will treat this as an error. The table search will be executed only if a new equipment type is present in the transaction record.

Validate Commission Percent

If the transaction record contains a commission percent, this step will ensure that the percentage field is numeric and does not exceed 35%.

Validate Cost

Cost and price are validated separately in the change transaction. First, we will validate the cost fields. If the field is present, we will check to see if the field is numeric. If the cost field passes the validity check, it will be placed in a work area for later comparison to the price. If the cost was not changed, the cost from the item master record is loaded to the work area for comparison to the new price.

Validate Price

If there is data in the price field, we check to ensure the data is numeric. If the new price is numeric, we will check to see if the price exceeds $1000. If so, we will issue the warning message. If the new price passes the presence and numeric test, the new price will be loaded to a work area for comparison to the cost. If the price was not changed, the price field in the item master record is moved to the work area for the comparison.

Determine If Cost Exceeds Price

We now have the cost and price of the item stored in the appropriate work areas. We next need to check if the cost exceeds the price. Again, like with the add transaction validation, this is the relationship test between the cost and price fields.

Check to See If an Error Has Occurred

After all of the validation is complete, we will test ERR-FLAG to see it has been turned on. If no errors were found in the transaction record, we will write the record to the output transaction file. If any validation steps uncovered an error, the write step is bypassed.

Finally, we read the next record for processing and exit PROCESS.

Validating the DELETE Transaction

Validate the Item

The only validation necessary for the delete transaction is to ensure that the item being deleted exists. If a read to the item master results in an invalid key, we know we cannot delete this item and it will be treated as an error. If the item exists, we will write this record to the output transaction file and proceed with reading the next transaction.

SUMMARY

The process of updating master files is normally accomplished in two steps. The first step is to validate the transactions using one of six types of validation checks on each field. Types of validation testing include presence, numeric, existence, relationship, valid value, and range/reasonableness testing. Transactions found to be in error are written to the error report while transactions that are free from errors are sent to the update program. When an error is found, the appropriate error message is written to the error report and the error flag is turned on. After all validation steps have been performed, the error flag is checked. If the error flag is on, then this transaction is not written to the valid transaction file. If the error flag is off, then we know the transaction is clean, and it is to be written to the output transaction file that is passed to the update program.

The second step of the update process is the program that actually updates the master file. This will be addressed in Chapter 17.

REVIEW QUESTIONS

1. What are the two steps of the update process?
2. What are the six types of validations we can perform, and what exactly are we validating for in each of the six?
3. Why does data validation not guarantee data correctness?
4. What is the purpose of the error flag?

PROJECT

Objective

This program will be the first step of the two-step update process. The purpose of this program will be to validate the data that will be used to update the customer master file.

Processing Requirements

1. Validate all data based on the following types of validation:
   - Customer Number must be present.
   - Customer Name, Street Address, City, and State must all be present.
   - Zip Code must be numeric.
   - Customer Type must exist on the Customer Type Description file.
   - Region must exist on the Region Description file.
   - Area must exist on the Area Description file.
   - Headquarters ID will not be validated.
   - Last Purchase Date will not be on the input transaction record.
2. Follow these standard rules for data validation:
   - A customer that already exists cannot be added.
   - A customer that does not exist cannot be changed or deleted.
   - On change transactions, only fields being changed are required on the transaction record.
   - Transaction code must be A, C, or D.
3. The customer master file is a database file and can be read directly using the Customer Number as the key.

CUSTOMER MASTER RECORD

01-05	Customer Number	CUST-NO
06-30	Customer Name	NAME
31-50	Street Address	ADDR
51-65	City	CITY
66-67	State	ST
68-72	Zip Code	ZIP
73-74	Customer Type	CTYPE
75-76	Region	REG
77-78	Area	AREA
79-83	Headquarters ID	HQ
84-91	Last Purchase Date (YYYYMMDD)	LSTPRCH
92-100	Unused	

TRANSACTION RECORD

01-01	Transaction Code	TR-CD
02-06	Customer Number	TR-CUST-NO
07-31	Customer Name	TR-NAME
32-51	Street Address	TR-ADDR
52-66	City	TR-CITY
67-68	State	TR-ST
69-73	Zip Code	TR-ZIP
74-75	Customer Type	TR-CTYPE
76-77	Region	TR-REG
78-79	Area	TR-AREA
80-84	Headquarters ID	TR-HQ

CUSTOMER TYPE DESCRIPTION

01-02	Customer Type	CTD-CTYPE
02-26	Customer Type Description	CTD-DESC

REGION DESCRIPTION

01-02	Region	RD-REG
03-26	Region Description	RD-DESC

AREA DESCRIPTION

01-02	Area	AD-AREA
03-37	Area Description	AD-DESC

Printer Spacing Chart

```
RUN  MM/DD/YY  HH:MM                    ACME DISTRIBUTORS                    PAGE ZZZZ9
                                  CUSTOMER MASTER ERROR REPORT

       CUST    TRANSACTION
      NUMBER      CODE      FIELD        VALUE                    MESSAGE

      XXXXX        X                                             XXXXXXXXXXXXXXXXXXXXXXXXXXXXXXXXXXXX

      XXXXX        X      XXXXXXXXXX   XXXXXXXXXXXXXXXXXXXXXXXXX   XXXXXXXXXXXXXXXXXXXXXXXXXXXXXXXXXXXX

      XXXXX        X      XXXXXXXXXX   XXXXXXXXXXXXXXXXXXXXXXXXX   XXXXXXXXXXXXXXXXXXXXXXXXXXXXXXXXXXXX
```

Assignment

1. Develop a complete structure chart for this program.

2. Develop the flowchart or pseudo code for the entire program.

17

Updating Master Files

OBJECTIVES

- Understanding how master files are updated.
- Understanding the importance of the audit report and how it is created.

INTRODUCTION

In Chapter 16, we reviewed the concept of updating master files. The first step, detailed in Chapter 16, is to validate the data by identifying and eliminating known errors before the transactions are applied to the master file. The second step, which we will study in this chapter, is the process of updating the master file with the changes contained in the transaction file.

UNDERSTANDING THE CONCEPTS OF THE UPDATE PROCESS

First, remember that we have three types of transactions. We can add a new item, change an existing item, or delete an item from the file. Each of these updates will require unique logic to address the fundamental differences between them. For this reason, you will notice a slight departure from the normal structure we have followed in our earlier programs.

Before proceeding, remember the concept of a record key as discussed in Chapter 15. Each transaction must contain the item number to which the transaction applies. The key field, which in this case is the item number, cannot be changed.

Because we have already validated the data, we will not concern ourselves with any further validation. We know, for example, that the input validation program ensured that any item to be added did not already exist on the file. Therefore, we will offer no provision in the program for adding a record that already exists. Likewise, the input validation program in Chapter 16 excluded from the output any changes or deletes for items that do not exist on the master.

As you will see in this chapter, adding records and deleting records is a straightforward process. Changes to existing records, however, are more complex. Remember how the input validation program handled change transactions. If a field did not contain any data, it was not validated. This is because only fields to be changed will have data entered. Therefore, our program must interrogate each field of each record to determine what updates are to be applied to the master. If a field does not contain any data, it is not updated. If data exists, we update the master record accordingly.

The Audit Report

Each update program must provide a comprehensive audit report showing all changes made to the master file. Records added must be shown, with all appropriate data fields. Records being changed will show each field changed, with the old and the new values. A record being deleted must be shown. People responsible for the update will review these audit reports. It is important to remember that the input validation program can validate only certain aspects of the data. For example, if an item is added with the wrong item number, as long as the item didn't already exist, the validation program does not recognize the error. Also, the program cannot validate the spelling of the item description. As long as the field contains data, it passes the presence test. No quality test to the data can be made. Likewise, as long as the price is numeric, under $1000, and greater than the purchase cost, it passes the validity test, even though it may be oncorrect data.

For these reasons, the program will print the audit report, which is carefully reviewed by the responsible employees to better ensure the accuracy of the update. Exhibit 17–1 contains a sample audit report.

Exhibit 17–1
SAMPLE AUDIT REPORT

```
RUN  MM/DD/YY                        ITEM MASTER UPDATE AUDIT TRAIL                          PAGE ZZZZZ9

  ITEM        TRANSACTION
 NUMBER         TYPE            FIELD      NEW VALUE                     OLD VALUE

 13B22           ADD            DESC       TENNIS RACKET
                                SPORT CD   21
                                EQUIP TYPE 15
                                COMM PCT   .100
                                PRICE      00039.95
                                COST       00013.50

  2366B         CHANGE          PRICE      00014.75                      00011.50

  276E4         CHANGE          COST       00010.00                      00009.40

  34C2S         DELETE


     NUMBER OF TRANSACTIONS READ    4
     NUMBER OF ADDS.................1
     NUMBER OF CHANGES..............2
     NUMBER OF DELETES..............1
```

The Update Process

Let's take a look at the tasks to be completed in the update program. First, let's review our tasks within INITIALIZATION. As expected, we find nothing new here. Our tasks are as follows:

- Initialize.
- Get date and time.
- Open files.
- Read the first transaction record.

Our program will take a different direction once we enter the PROCESS section. Gone are the control-breaks, calculates, and writes as we knew them. The PROCESS section of an update program must now perform the following tasks:

- Update the record:

  Transaction process for the ADD transaction:

    Update master file.
    Write audit log.

  Transaction process for the CHANGE transaction:

    Read master file.
    Interrogate each field for update and write the audit report.
    Update the master file.

  Transaction process for the DELETE transaction:

    Read master file.
    Delete record from master.
    Write audit log.

- Read next transaction.

Before proceeding, let's take a close look at each of these processes. First, review the audit trail in Exhibit 17–1. Notice how the report reflects the three types of transactions. In order to ensure that our program will handle all data correctly, let's take some time to really understand the processing we will be doing based on our task list.

ADD Transaction

Update Master File We will build an item master record based on the data provided in the transaction record. After this, we will issue an ADD statement for the master file to write the new item to the file.

Write Audit Log The required fields from the add transaction will be written to the audit report as shown in Exhibit 17–1. Because each transaction type has different reporting requirements, we will need to build the audit report for each separately. However, to keep our program modular, we will still use a single WRITE process. In this case, WRITE will no longer move data to output, it will simply check line counts, perform the header routine, and write the reports.

CHANGE Transaction

Read Master File

Before we can change any values of the item being maintained, we must read the master record to which the transaction relates. Each database management system has a unique approach to preparing data for update, and as before, we will discuss this in a generic manner. If you intend to update an existing record, some database management systems require that you perform a "read for update" for the record that you want. This informs the database management system that you intend to update this record, and thus it will prevent any other program running in the computer from reading that same record until you are finished with the update.

Interrogate Each Field for Update

Here, we will examine each field of the transaction record, which could contain new data for the master record. If the field contains data other than spaces, we will assume the data is valid and that the corresponding field in the master record will be changed to the new value. During the evaluation, it will be appropriate to move the new data values to the master record. It is also very important at this point to save the original value of each being changed. Referring to Exhibit 17–1 you will notice that for the change transaction, each field changed is shown with the original and new value. As we determine which fields are being updated, we will also write the audit report.

Update the Master File

At this time we will issue an UPDATE statement to the database management system (DBMS). The UPDATE tells the DBMS to write the new record contents over the existing record and release the record for another program to read.

DELETE Transaction

Read Master File

As with the change transaction, we must read the master record that we are going to delete with the "read for update."

Delete Record from Master

We need to issue a DELETE statement to the DBMS. This will remove the record from the file.

Write Audit Log

We will need to write the fact that this item was deleted from the file.

Figure 17–1
Structure chart for update program

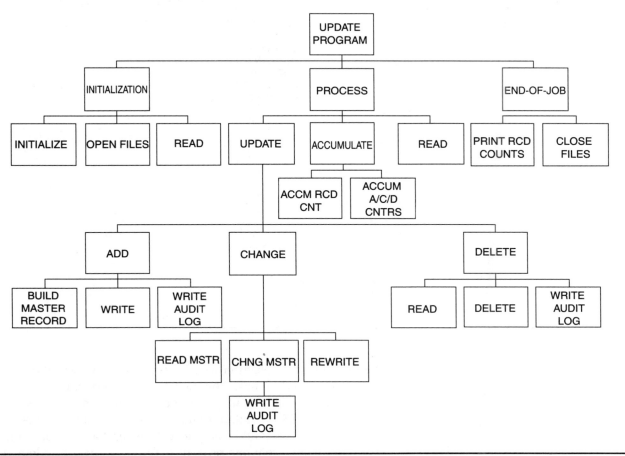

Record Counts

Finally, we will notice that at the end of the report, we need to print the number of transactions read, and the number of items added, changed, or deleted. So we must remember to address these record counts in our structure chart. The final structure chart is shown in Figure 17–1.

TRANSLATION TO THE FLOWCHART

INITIALIZATION

The basics of this section of the program have not changed. Figure 17–2 contains INITIALIZATION.

PROCESS

Remember to keep PROCESS free from clutter to avoid making it overwhelming. For this reason, PROCESS will contain only a high-level flow of the program. Figure 17–3 illustrates the PROCESS flowchart. We will

**Figure 17–2
INITIALIZATION**

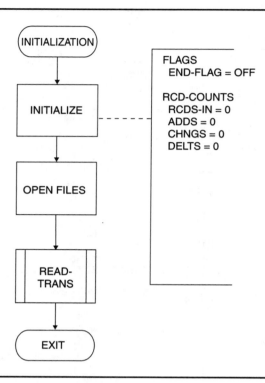

first determine the type of transaction we are processing. We will then perform the appropriate procedure based on the transaction code. Remember, when designing a program, it is of utmost importance to remain focused. If we expanded the PROCESS procedure to include the components of ADD, CHANGE, and DELETE, we could easily lose focus on the real reason for PROCESS. We will create a separate procedure for each type of update and refer to it using the predefined process symbol. After performing the appropriate update step, we will accumulate the record counts. Finally, we will read the next transaction and exit the procedure.

Again, it is important to keep PROCESS simple, readable, and understandable. This approach does exactly that.

ADD-RECORD

Looking at the structure chart for the add transaction, we see that only three tasks are required: building the master record, writing the master record, and writing the audit log. Figure 17–4 contains the flowchart for this procedure.

CHANGE-RECORD

Figure 17–5 contains a sample flowchart and pseudo code for the change procedure and one field. Procedures similar to CHNG-DESC would be required for each field on the transaction record. Because each piece of the change process can be somewhat complex, it may be wise to break it into separate procedures. Again, a key to success is to remain focused. By breaking down the change procedure into smaller procedures, we can

**Figure 17–3
PROCESS procedure for
the example update
program**

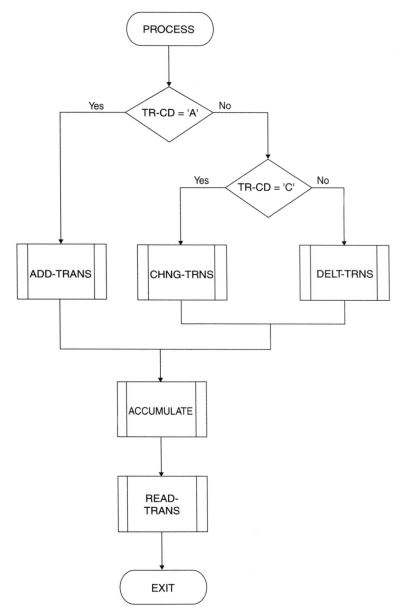

PSEUDO CODE

```
process:
   IF tr-cd = "A" THEN
      DO add-trns
    ELSE
      IF tr-cd = "C" THEN
         DO chng-trns
       ELSE
         DO delt-trns
      END-IF
   END-IF
   DO accumulate
   DO read-trans
```

Figure 17–4
Flowchart required for adding records to master file

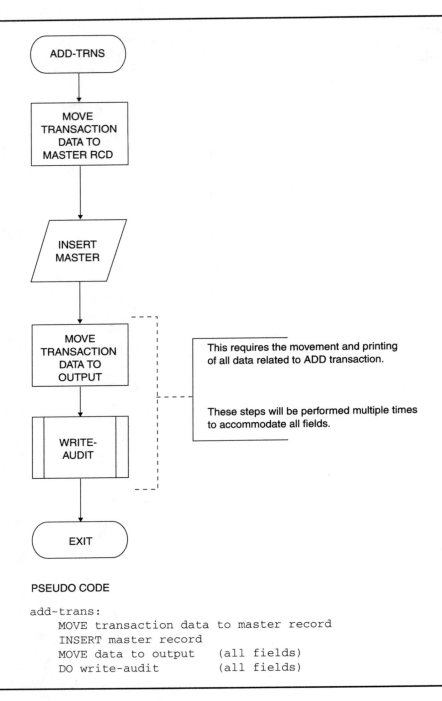

```
PSEUDO CODE

add-trans:
    MOVE transaction data to master record
    INSERT master record
    MOVE data to output     (all fields)
    DO write-audit          (all fields)
```

remain focused on a smaller section of the program. Notice first, that we read the master file for update. This was explained earlier. Next, we examine each field for update. For each field to be changed, we move the original value and the new value to the audit report. We then write the audit report. We next move the new value of the field from the transaction record to the master record. The sample flowchart illustrates the logic required to change

Figure 17–5
Flowchart of changing
data on master record
(only changes to the
description are
illustrated)

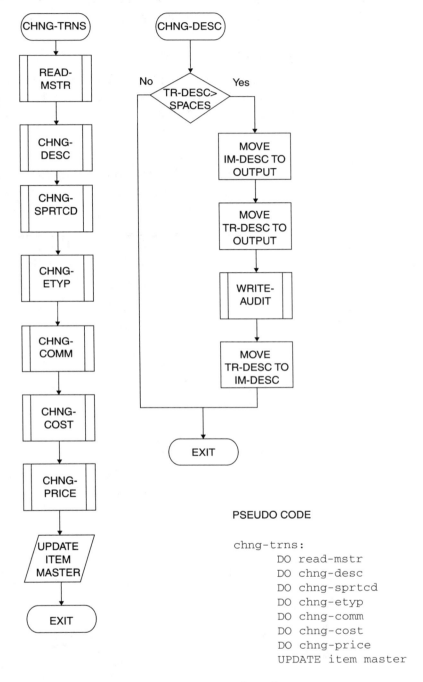

PSEUDO CODE

```
chng-trns:
      DO read-mstr
      DO chng-desc
      DO chng-sprtcd
      DO chng-etyp
      DO chng-comm
      DO chng-cost
      DO chng-price
      UPDATE item master

chng-desc:
      IF tr-desc > spaces THEN
            MOVE im-desc to output
            MOVE tr-desc to output
            DO write-audit
            MOVE tr-desc to im-desc
      END-IF
```

one field. All other fields would be addressed in the same fashion. After all fields have been properly processed, we will update the master record.

DELETE-RECORD

Figure 17–6 contains the flowchart for the delete procedure. As defined by the structure chart, we first read the record and then issue the delete statement. Next, we write the appropriate line to the audit log.

ACCUMULATE

After we have completed the update process, we want to add to the appropriate record count fields. Figure 17–7 illustrates this procedure.

Figure 17–6
Flowchart for deleting records from a master file

PSEUDO CODE

```
delt-trns:
    DO read-mstr
    DELETE master
    MOVE delete-message to output
    DO write-audit
```

Figure 17–7
Flowchart for counting the number of adds, changes, and deletes to master file

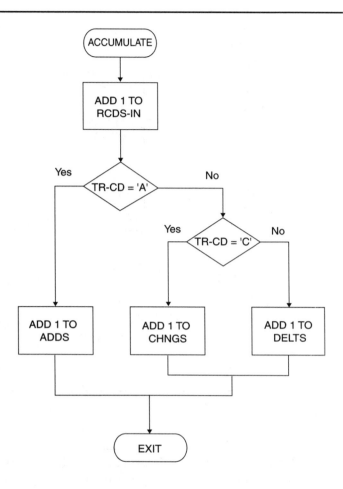

PSEUDO CODE

```
accumulate:
   ADD 1 to rcds-in
   IF tr-cd = "A" THEN
      ADD 1 to adds
    ELSE
      IF tr-cd = "C" THEN
         ADD 1 to chngs
       ELSE
         ADD 1 to delts
      END-IF
```

END-OF-JOB

Update programs do not contain a complex END-OF-JOB procedure. The only important item to remember is to print the record counts we have accumulated along the way. After the counts are written, we can close the files and exit. Figure 17–8 contains the flowchart for the END-OF-JOB procedure.

Figure 17–8
Flowchart for END-OF-JOB procedure

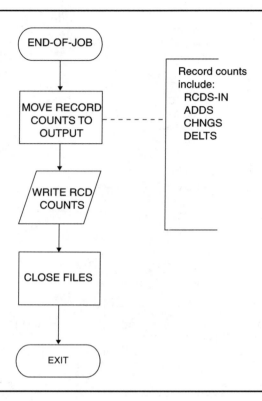

SUMMARY

Update programs will perform no validation of input data because this was completed in the input validation program that precedes the update. It is assumed that by this point, all invalid data has been removed from the transaction file. Update programs require different logic for each of the three types of transactions. Before you can update or delete a record in a database management system, you must first issue a "read for update" command. Finally, the audit trail report is generated to provide before and after images of the data being updated.

REVIEW QUESTIONS

1. Different logic is required for each of the three transaction types. What is some of the unique logic required for each type of transaction that makes separate logic paths necessary?

2. Why does the update program perform no data validation prior to updating the master file?

3. What is the purpose of the "read for update" command when updating a DBMS?

4. What is the purpose of the audit trail report?

PROJECT

In Chapter 16, you completed the project that validated transactions that will be used to update the customer master file. You will complete the updating process with this assignment. In this project, you are required to design the update program for those transactions that successfully passed the validations defined in Chapter 16.

Objective

This program will update the customer master file from transactions validated in a prior program. Based on the transaction code, the program will add a new customer, update data for an existing customer, or delete an existing customer record. An audit trail is also required to log all updates that occur.

Processing Requirements

1. For ADD transactions, move all input data to the new customer record and insert into the database. Last Purchase Date should be set to zeroes because this customer has yet to purchase a product.
2. For CHANGE transactions, update only the fields that contain data in the transaction record.
3. DELETE the customer if the transaction code is a D.
4. Print the appropriate record counts when the program completes.

CUSTOMER MASTER RECORD

01-05	Customer Number	CUST-NO
06-30	Customer Name	NAME
31-50	Street Address	ADDR
51-65	City	CITY
66-67	State	ST
68-72	Zip Code	ZIP
73-74	Customer Type	CTYPE
75-76	Region	REG
77-78	Area	AREA
79-83	Headquarters ID	HQ
84-91	Last Purchase Date (YYYYMMDD)	LSTPRCH
92-100	Unused	

TRANSACTION RECORD

01-01	Transaction Code	TR-CD
02-06	Customer Number	TR-CUST-NO
07-31	Customer Name	TR-NAME
32-51	Street Address	TR-ADDR
52-66	City	TR-CITY
67-68	State	TR-ST
69-73	Zip Code	TR-ZIP
74-75	Customer Type	TR-CTYPE
76-77	Region	TR-REG
78-79	Area	TR-AREA
80-84	Headquarters ID	TR-HQ

Printer Spacing Chart

```
                                                               11111111111
        11111111112222222222233333333334444444444555555555566666666667777777777888888888899999999990000000000 1
123456789012345678901234567890123456789012345678901234567890123456789012345678901234567890
```

```
RUN  MM/DD/YY                    ITEM MASTER UPDATE AUDIT TRAIL                    PAGE ZZZZZ9


     CUSTOMER      TRANSACTION
     NUMBER          TYPE        FIELD      NEW VALUE                      OLD VALUE

     XXXXX          ADD          XXXXXXXXXX  XXXXXXXXXXXXXXXXXXXXXXXXX      XXXXXXXXXXXXXXXXXXXXXXXXX
                                 XXXXXXXXXX  XXXXXXXXXXXXXXXXXXXXXXXXX      XXXXXXXXXXXXXXXXXXXXXXXXX
                                 XXXXXXXXXX  XXXXXXXXXXXXXXXXXXXXXXXXX      XXXXXXXXXXXXXXXXXXXXXXXXX

     XXXXX          CHANGE       XXXXXXXXXX  XXXXXXXXXXXXXXXXXXXXXXXXX      XXXXXXXXXXXXXXXXXXXXXXXXX
                                 XXXXXXXXXX  XXXXXXXXXXXXXXXXXXXXXXXXX      XXXXXXXXXXXXXXXXXXXXXXXXX


     XXXXX          DELETE



        NUMBER OF TRANSACTIONS READ      Z,ZZZ
        NUMBER OF ADDS.................Z,ZZZ
        NUMBER OF CHANGES..............Z,ZZZ
        NUMBER OF DELETES..............Z,ZZZ
```

18
Transitioning to a Programming Language

OBJECTIVES

- Understanding the transition from the program design to a programming language.
- Understanding what parts of the program design are expanded when converting to a programming language.

INTRODUCTION

Previous chapters of this book have dealt with the design of a business application program. The development of a business application program is accomplished in four main steps. The first step is to understand what output the program will produce and where the data for the output is obtained. This is accomplished in the data mapping process explained in Chapter 3. The next step is to determine what functionality the program must perform in order to achieve the objectives. This is done using the structure chart. Step three of the process is determining how to accomplish the functionality defined in the structure chart. Program designers may use either flowcharts or pseudo code to complete this step. The final step to program development is to write the program in the language used by your company. This chapter will address the transition from the design to program code.

PROGRAMMING LANGUAGES

The most common language for programs written for mainframe and midrange computers is Cobol. Desktop applications designed to work on a personal computer may be written in C, C++, Cobol, Visual Basic, or one of many other languages. Internet based applications may use a variety of languages including Visual Basic, JAVA, and Active Server Pages (ASP).

With most programming languages, you will start by writing *source code*. Source code will vary between languages, but is generally a text file that contains the step-by-step instructions that the computer will follow when executing the program. Once written, the source code is input into a language compiler. The compiler checks for syntax and format of the language. Any errors encountered during the compilation are reported to the programmer, who then must correct the source code and recompile.

When the program compiles successfully, the compiler will generate an executable program that can be read only by the computer. EXE files on the PC are an example of such programs. These executable files contain machine level instructions for the computer.

Transition to Source Code

To illustrate the final step in the program development process, we will use the program designed in Chapter 8 and translate the design into a Cobol program. Cobol will be used because of the close relationship with the English language and the relative ease of understanding the program code.

First, let's get reacquainted with this program. Exhibit 18–1 contains the program specification. Figure 18–1 contains the structure chart. Figure 18–2 contains the flowchart and Figure 18–3 contains the pseudo code for this program.

Figure 18–1
Structure chart for example reporting program

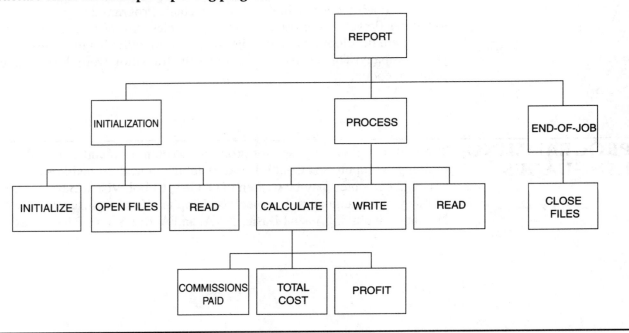

Figure 18–2
Flowchart for example program

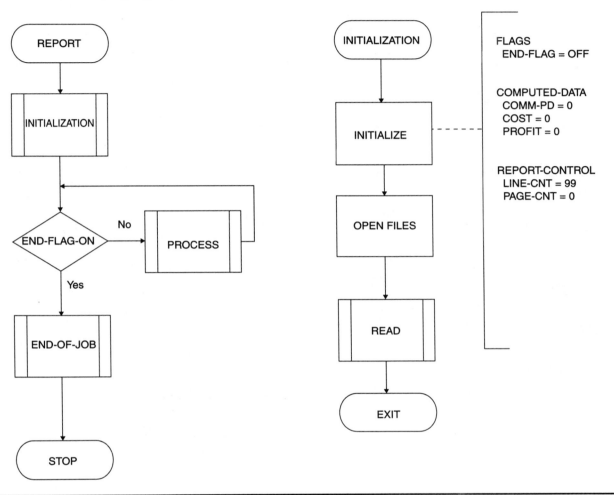

(continued on the next page)

Figure 18–2
(*continued*)

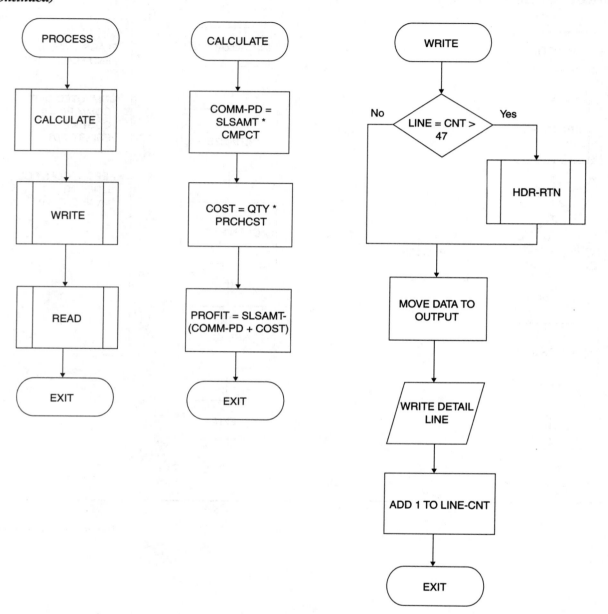

Figure 18–2
(continued)

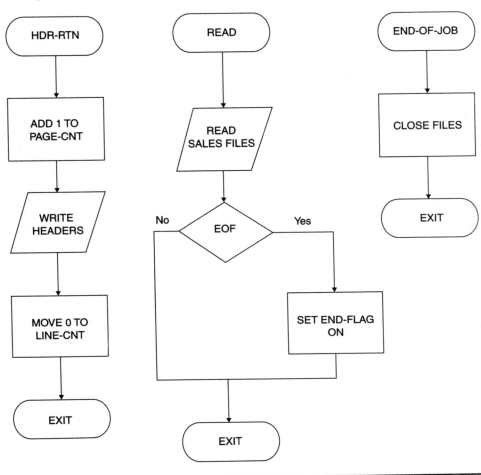

Figure 18–3
Pseudo code for example program

```
mainline:
        DO initialization
        DOWHILE end-flag off
            DO process
        END-DOWHILE
        DO end-of-job
        STOP

initialization:
        INITIALIZE
            flags:            end-flag = off
            computed-data: comm-pd = 0
                              cost = 0
                              profit = 0
            report control l-cnt = 99
                              p-cnt = 0
        OPEN files
        DO read

process:
        DO calculate
        DO write
        DO read

calculate:
        LET comm-pd = slsamt * cmpct
        LET cost = qty * prchcst
        LET profit = slsamt - (comm-pd + cost)

write:
        IF line-cnt > 47 THEN
            DO hdr-rtn
        END-IF
        MOVE data to output
        WRITE detail line
        ADD 1 to line-cnt

hdr-rtn:
        ADD 1 to page-cnt
        WRITE headers
        LET line-cnt = 0

read:
        READ item file
            IF end-of-file THEN
                    LET end-flag = on
            END-IF
        END-READ

end-of-job:
        CLOSE files
```

Exhibit 18–1
PROGRAM
DESCRIPTION

Objective
Produce a report that will list, for each item, the quantity sold and the profit earned on the sales.

Processing Requirements

1. Process all records on the file.
2. For each record read, calculate the following:
   - Commissions Paid = Sales Amount * Commissions Percent.
   - Total Cost = Quantity Sold * Purchase Cost.
   - Profit = Sales Amount - (Commissions Paid + Total Cost).
3. Write the report showing all of the information on the printer spacing chart.
4. Single-space the report.

SALES RECORD

01-02	SPORT CODE		SPRTCD
03-04	EQUIPMENT TYPE		ETYP
05-09	ITEM NUMBER		ITEM
10-24	ITEM DESCRIPTION		DESC
25-29	QUANTITY SOLD	(5.0)	QTY
30-38	SALES AMOUNT	(9.2)	SLSAMT
39-41	COMMISSION PERCENT	(3.3)	CMPCT
42-48	PURCHASE COST	(7.2)	PRCHCST
49-60	Unused		

Printer Spacing Chart

```
                                                                    1111111111111111111111111111111111
          11111111112222222222333333333344444444445555555555666666666677777777778888888888999999999900000000001111111111222222222 3
123456789012345678901234567890123456789012345678901234567890123456789012345678901234567890123456789012345678901234567890123 4567890

RUN  MM/DD/YY   HH:MM                              ACME DISTRIBUTORS                                                PAGE ZZZZ9
                                                    SALES REPORT

     SPORT      EQUIP    ITEM                       QUANTITY     SALES        COMMISSIONS      TOTAL
     CODE       TYPE     NMBR    ITEM DESCRIPTION     SOLD       AMOUNT          PAID           COST          PROFIT

      XX         XX     XXXXX   XXXXXXXXXXXXXXX     ZZ,ZZZ-   Z,ZZZ,ZZZ.99-   ZZZ,ZZZ.99-   ZZZ,ZZZ.99-   ZZZ,ZZZ.99-
      XX         XX     XXXXX   XXXXXXXXXXXXXXX     ZZ,ZZZ-   Z,ZZZ,ZZZ.99-   ZZZ,ZZZ.99-   ZZZ,ZZZ.99-   ZZZ,ZZZ.99-
      XX         XX     XXXXX   XXXXXXXXXXXXXXX     ZZ,ZZZ-   Z,ZZZ,ZZZ.99-   ZZZ,ZZZ.99-   ZZZ,ZZZ.99-   ZZZ,ZZZ.99-
```

Translating the Program Design into Program Code

Cobol programs have four divisions: Identification, Environment, Data, and Procedure. The Identification Division contains information related to program name, description of the program, who wrote the program, and when it was written. While the example program will contain this data, it will not be discussed in this chapter. The Environment Division is used to identify to the program what files are being read and where the files can be found. Contents of the Environment Division can change across platforms (mainframe, midrange, and PC). Like the Identification

Division, the Environment Division will be included in the example, but will not be discussed.

Data Division

The transition first begins with the data division, which is used to define all data used by the program. The Data Division has two sections, file section and working-storage section. The file section contains file definitions and record format. The working-storage sections contains the report layouts, derived data, and logical data. Exhibit 18–3 contains the example program for this chapter. Data Division begins on line 11 of the program. The input file for the program, SALES-FILE, has been defined to conform exactly to the file layout in the program specification. The output file, REPORT-FILE, contains a single 132-character record definition.

The working-storage section of the program begins on line 27. Within the working-storage section we defined the report layout, along with all derived and logical data. Notice that the derived data fields on lines 28 through 34 of the working-storage section have names that match the names of the derived data fields on the flowchart and pseudo code. Also, notice that these derived data fields have all been given a starting value that matches the values indicated in the INITIALIZATION section of the flowchart and pseudo code.

You will also find the report format entries in working-storage. These are TITLE-LINE-1, TITLE-LINE-2, HEAD-LINE-1, HEAD-LINE-2, and DETAIL-LINE. It is not important at this time to fully understand the coding, but nevertheless, take a look at the field names associated with the DETAIL-LINE. Notice that the fields for sport code, item, description, and the rest are the same as the input file description, but prefixed with a DL, which indicates DETAIL-LINE. Using simple, meaningful prefixes when programming can greatly assist others who will need to understand your programs at some later date.

Procedure Division

The program logic is contained in the Procedure Division, beginning on line 103. The logic proceeds through the following steps:

MAINLINE (LINE 104)

Cobol uses a DO UNTIL loop rather than a DO WHILE. Other languages will use the DO WHILE. Cobol's PERFORM UNTIL will function the same as a DO WHILE. You will also notice that the Cobol equivalent to a predefined process is the PERFORM statement. With this understanding, you will notice that the MAINLINE procedure in the program directly reflects both the flowchart and pseudo code.

INITIALIZATION (LINE 110)

The initialize step of INITIALIZATION is not needed in Cobol because the fields were defined in working-storage. However, with other languages, you will declare new variables, such as derived data, to the program. In

this example, INITIALIZATION will open files and perform the READ
procedure, exactly as indicated in the design.

PROCESS (LINE 120)

The flowchart illustrates PROCESS as a series of predefined processes.
Likewise, the pseudo code indicates that PROCESS will DO calculate,
write, and read. A study of the PROCESS procedure in the program
shows that this procedure was translated directly from the design to the
Cobol code.

CALCULATE (LINE 125)

As with the other sections, you will see that the Cobol code for the
CALCULATE procedure is a series of compute statements that will
calculate the derived data. The formulas in the Cobol code are identical to the formulas in the flowchart and pseudo code. The results of
the calculations are stored in the derived data fields specified in the
formula.

WRITE (LINE 130)

As with the flowchart and pseudo code, the first step of WRITE is to determine if we need to print the headers. You will notice that the design
statement "Move data to output" has been replaced by a series of MOVE
statements. When writing the program, it will become necessary to
specify each field being moved by the field's source and destination. In
Cobol, this is written as MOVE <source field> TO <destination field>.
After the data has been moved to the output fields, the detail line is
moved to the output record as defined in the FILE SECTION (see program line 25). After the detail line has been moved, the program writes
the line to the printer.

HEADER ROUTINE (LINE 147)

As in the program design, the header routine first adds one to the page
counter. This is followed by the instructions to move the page counter to
the title line, and printing the titles and headers. Notice that the program
code expands the single WRITE HEADERS process in the program design into multiple write statements, one write statement for each line of
title and header.

READ (LINE 166)

The AT END phase in the READ statement is equivalent to the if end-of-
file in the program design. When the AT END condition is true, the program will move ON to end-flag.

END-OF-JOB (LINE 162)

As defined by the program design, END-OF-JOB will close files.

Exhibit 18–3
COBOL PROGRAM

```
1. IDENTIFICATION DIVISION
2. PROGRAM-ID.   SAMPLE.
3. AUTHOR.          PROGRAMMER-NAME.
4.
5. ENVIRONMENT DIVISION.
6. INPUT-OUTPUT SECTION.
7. FILE-CONTROL.
8.     SELECT SALES-FILE    ASSIGN "C:\DATA\SALESFYL.DAT".
9.     SELECT REPORT-FILE   ASSIGN LPT1.
10.
11. DATA DIVISION.
12. FILE SECTION.
13. FD   SALES-FILE.
14. 01   SALES-RECORD.
15.      03   SPRTCD            PIC X(02).
16.      03   ETYP              PIC X(02).
17.      03   ITEM              PIC X(05).
18.      03   DESC              PIC X(15).
19.      03   QTY               PIC S9(05).
20.      03   SLSAMT            PIC S9(07)V9(02).
21.      03   CMPCT             PIC V9(03).
22.      03   PRCHCST           PIC 9(07)V9(02).
23.      03   FILLER            PIC X(12).
24. FD   REPORT-FILE.
25. 01   REPORT-RECORD         PIC X(130).
26.
27. WORKING-STORAGE SECTION.
28. 01   FLAGS.
29.      03   END-FLAG          PIC X(03)       VALUE "OFF".
30.
31. 01   COMPUTED-DATA.
32.      03   COMM-PD           PIC S9(07)V9(02)  VALUE 0.
33.      03   COST              PIC S9(07)V9(02)  VALUE 0.
34.      03   PROFIT            PIC S9(07)V9(02)  VALUE 0.
35.
36. 01   DATE-TIME-FIELDS.
37.      03   DTF-DATE          PIC 9(06).
38.      03   DTF-TIME.
39.          05   DTF-HOUR      PIC X(02).
40.          05   DTF-MIN       PIC X(02).
41.          05   DTF-SEC       PIC X(02).
42.
43. 01   REPORT-CONTROL.
44.      03   LINE-CNT          PIC 9(02)       VALUE 99.
45.      03   PAGE-CNT          PIC 9(05)       VALUE 0.
46.
47. 01   TITLE-LINE-1.
48.      03   FILLER            PIC X(05)       VALUE "RUN".
49.      03   TL1-DATE          PIC 99/99/99.
50.      03   FILLER            PIC X(03)       VALUE SPACES.
51.      03   TL1-HOUR          PIC X(02).
52.      03   FILLER            PIC X(01)       VALUE ":".
53.      03   TL1-MIN           PIC X(02).
54.      03   FILLER            PIC X(35)       VALUE SPACES.
55.      03   FILLER            PIC X(64)       VALUE
56.          "ACME DISTRIBUTORS".
57.      03   FILLER            PIC X(05)       VALUE "PAGE ".
```

```
58.      03  TL1-PAGE          PIC ZZZZ9.
59.
60. 01  TITLE-LINE-2.
61.      03  FILLER            PIC X(59)        VALUE SPACES.
62.      03  FILLER            PIC X(73)        VALUE
63.          "SALES REPORT".
64.
65.
66. 01  BLANK-LINE            PIC X(132)        VALUE SPACES.
67.
68. 01  HEAD-LINE-1.
69.      03  FILLER            PIC X(55)        VALUE
70.          "      SPORT    EQUIP    ITEM"
71.      03  FILLER            PIC X(77)        VALUE
72.          "QUANTITY    SALES       COMMISSIONS      TOTAL".
73.
74. 01  HEAD-LINE-2.
75.      03  FILLER            PIC X(57)        VALUE
76.          "      CODE    TYPE    ITEM DESCRIPTION".
77.      03  FILLER            PIC X(44)        VALUE
78.          "SOLD       AMOUNT         PAID".
79.      03  FILLER            PIC X(31)        VALUE
80.          "COST       PROFIT".
81.
82. 01  DETAIL-LINE.
83.      03  FILLER            PIC X(08)        VALUE SPACES.
84.      03  DL-SPRTCD         PIC X(02).
85.      03  FILLER            PIC X(06)        VALUE SPACES.
86.      03  DL-ETYP           PIC X(02).
87.      03  FILLER            PIC X(06)        VALUE SPACES.
88.      03  DL-ITEM           PIC X(05).
89.      03  FILLER            PIC X(04)        VALUE SPACES.
90.      03  DL-DESC           PIC X(15).
91.      03  FILLER            PIC X(06)        VALUE SPACES.
92.      03  DL-QTY            PIC ZZ,ZZZ-.
93.      03  FILLER            PIC X(04)        VALUE SPACES.
94.      03  DL-SLSAMT         PIC Z,ZZZ,ZZZ.99-.
95.      03  FILLER            PIC X(04)        VALUE SPACES.
96.      03  DL-COMM-PD        PIC ZZZ,ZZZ.99-.
97.      03  FILLER            PIC X(04)        VALUE SPACES.
98.      03  DL-COST           PIC ZZZ,ZZZ.99-.
99.      03  FILLER            PIC X(04)        VALUE SPACES.
100.     03  DL-PROFIT         PIC ZZZ,ZZZ.99-.
101.     03  FILLER            PIC X(06)        VALUE SPACES.
102.
103. PROCEDURE DIVISION.
104. 0000-MAINLINE.
105.     PERFORM 1000-INITIALIZATION.
106.     PERFORM 2000-PROCESS UNTIL END-FLAG = "ON".
107.     PERFORM 3000-END-OF-JOB.
108.     STOP RUN.
109.
110. 1000-INITIALIZATION.
111.     ACCEPT DTF-DATE FROM CURRENT-DATE.
112.     ACCEPT DTF-TIME FROM TIME-OF-DAY.
113.     MOVE DTF-DATE    TO TL1-DATE.
114.     MOVE DTF-HOUR    TO TL1-HOUR.
115.     MOVE DTF-MIN     TO TL1-MIN.
```

```
116.        OPEN INPUT  SALES-FILE
117.             OUTPUT REPORT-FILE.
118.        PERFORM 9000-READ.
119.
120. 2000-PROCESS.
121.        PERFORM 2100-CALCULATE.
122.        PERFORM 2200-WRITE.
123.        PERFORM 9000-READ.
124.
125. 2100-CALCULATE.
126.        COMPUTE COMM-PD = SLSAMT * CMPCT.
127.        COMPUTE COST = QTY * PRCHCST.
128.        COMPUTE PROFIT = SLSAMT - (COMM-PD + COST).
129.
130. 2200-WRITE.
131.        IF LINE-CNT > 47
132.             PERFORM 2250-HDR-RTN
133.        END-IF.
134.        MOVE SPRTCD          TO DL-SPRTCD.
135.        MOVE ETYP            TO DL-ETYP.
136.        MOVE ITEM            TO DL-ITEM.
137.        MOVE DESC            TO DL-DESC.
138.        MOVE QTY             TO DL-QTY.
139.        MOVE SLSAMT          TO DL-SLSAMT.
140.        MOVE COMM-PD         TO DL-COMM-PD.
141.        MOVE COST            TO DL-COST.
142.        MOVE PROFIT          TO DL-PROFIT.
143.        MOVE DETAIL-LINE     TO REPORT-RECORD.
144.        WRITE REPORT-RECORD AFTER ADVANCING 1 LINE.
145.        ADD 1                TO LINE-CNT.
146.
147. 2250-HDR-RTN.
148.        ADD 1 TO PAGE-CNT.
149.        MOVE PAGE-CNT        TO TL1-PAGE.
150.        MOVE TITLE-LINE-1    TO REPORT-RECORD.
151.        WRITE REPORT-RECORD AFTER ADVANCING PAGE.
152.        MOVE TITLE-LINE-2    TO REPORT-RECORD.
153.        WRITE REPORT-RECORD AFTER ADVANCING 1 LINE.
154.        MOVE HEAD-LINE-1     TO REPORT-RECORD.
155.        WRITE REPORT-RECORD AFTER ADVANCING 2 LINES.
156.        MOVE HEAD-LINE-2     TO REPORT-RECORD.
157.        WRITE REPORT-RECORD AFTER ADVANCING 1 LINE.
158.        MOVE BLANK-LINE      TO REPORT-RECORD.
159.        WRITE REPORT-RECORD AFTER ADVANCING 1 LINE.
160.        MOVE 0               TO LINE-CNT.
161.
162. 3000-END-OF-JOB.
163.        CLOSE SALES-FILE
164.              REPORT-FILE.
165.
166. 9000-READ.
167.        READ SALES-FILE AT END MOVE "ON" TO END-FLAG.
```

SUMMARY

The program design process, whether you use flowcharting or pseudo coding, is a crucial step in the program development process. The translation of the design to the programming language's source code should closely follow the program design. A good design will use consistent field names throughout the design and these names will translate directly to the program code. The compilation process that the computer used to translate the source code into a machine level executable file can fail if the compiler cannot interpret a data name. Maintaining consistency in your naming conventions will minimize these compilation errors.

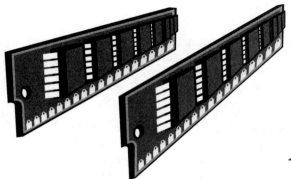

Appendix

FILES

CUSTOMER MASTER FILE

This file defines the customers who purchase products.

Field:	Customer (key field)	Name: CUST-NO
	Class:	Numeric
	Size:	5
	Description:	This is the unique identifier for each customer doing business with Acme Distributors.

Field:	Customer Name	Name: NAME
	Class:	Alphanumeric
	Size:	25
	Description:	This is the customer's name.

Field:	Street Address	Name: ADDR
	Class:	Alphanumeric
	Size:	25
	Description:	This is the customer's street location.

Field:	City	Name: CITY
	Class:	Alphanumeric
	Size:	15
	Description:	This is the customer's city location.

Field:	State	Name: ST
	Class:	Alphanumeric
	Size:	2
	Description:	State where customer is located. This is the U.S. Postal Service's approved abbreviation.

Field:	Zip Code	Name: ZIP
	Class:	Numeric
	Size:	5
	Description:	Customer's zip code as defined by the U.S. Postal Service.

Field:	Customer Type	Name: CTYPE
	Class:	Alphanumeric
	Size:	2

	Description:	Code defining type of customer. Examples include DS (Department Store), SG (Sporting Goods store), SD (Sporting Discount), etc.
Field:	Region	Name: RGN
	Class:	Numeric
	Size:	2
	Description:	Code defining the geographical area of the customer within the United States. Regions may be composed of up to five areas. Example: the southeast U.S. would be one region.
Field:	Area	Name: AREA
	Class:	Numeric
	Size:	2
	Description:	Code defining a subsection of the region. There may be up to five areas within a region. Within the southeast U.S. region, areas might include Atlanta, Miami, Orlando, and Greenville.
Field:	Headquarter ID	Name: HQ
	Class:	Numeric
	Size:	6
	Description:	This contains the customer HQ number. The HQ number must be defined as an active customer on the customer master file.
Field:	Last Purchase	Name: LSTPRCH
	Class:	Numeric – YYYYMMDD format
	Size:	8
	Description:	Contains the date on which the customer placed the most recent order.

ITEM MASTER

The item master file defines all attributes of the items sold by Acme Distributors.

Field:	Item Number (key field)	Name: IM-ITEM
	Class:	Alphanumeric
	Size:	5
	Description:	This is the item number of the product. Each item will have a unique item number.
Field:	Description	Name: IM-DESC
	Class:	Alphanumeric
	Size:	15
	Description:	This is the item's description.
Field:	Sport Code	Name: IM-SPRTCD
	Class:	Numeric
	Size:	2

Description: This is the item's sport code. Valid values are 1 thru 99. The sport code is used to define the type of sport for which this item is most often used.

Field: Equipment Type   Name: IM-ETYP
        Class: Numeric
        Size: 2
        Description: This is the item's equipment type. Valid values are 1 through 99. The equipment type is used to group similar products, such as shoes, rackets, and jackets.

Field: Commission Percent   Name: IM-PCT
        Class: Numeric
        Size: 3.3
        Description: The percentage of commissions paid to the salesperson when this product is sold.

Field: Vendor   Name: IM-VNDR
        Class: Numeric
        Size: 6
        Description: This is the vendor number from which the item is purchased.

Field: Purchase Cost   Name: IM-COST
        Class: Numeric
        Size: 7.2
        Description: The cost of purchasing this item from the vendor.

Field: Retail Price   Name: IM-PRICE
        Class: Numeric
        Size: 7.2
        Description: The selling price of the item.

Field: Quantity on Hand   Name: IM-QOH
        Class: Numeric
        Size: 5.0
        Description: Inventory level currently available for sale.

Field: Order Point   Name: IM-ORDPT
        Class: Numeric
        Size: 5.0
        Description: Minimal acceptable inventory level before item must be reordered. When the inventory level drops below this order point, the product should be reordered.

Field: Order Quantity   Name: IM-ORD-QTY
        Class: Numeric
        Size: 5.0
        Description: The quantity of product ordered from the vendor when the quantity on hand drops below the order point.

SALES FILE

This file contains total year-to-date sales data by item.

Field: Sport Code   Name: SPRTCD
       Class: Numeric
       Size: 2
       Description: This field defines the item's sport code. Valid
                           values are defined in the item master de-
                           scription.

Field: Equipment Type   Name: ETYP
       Class: Numeric
       Size: 2
       Description: This field defines the item's equipment type.
                           Valid values are defined in the item master
                           description.

Field: Item Number   Name: ITEM
       Class: Alphanumeric
       Size: 5
       Description: This field contains the item number of the
                           product sold.

Field: Item Description   Name: DESC
       Class: Alphanumeric
       Size: 15
       Description: This field contains the description of the
                           item.

Field: Quantity Sold   Name: QTY
       Class: Numeric
       Size: 5.0
       Description: Total units of the item sold for the year. This
                           quantity may be negative if returns were
                           greater than sales.

Field: Sales Amount   Name: SLSAMT
       Class: Numeric
       Size: 9.2
       Description: Total sales dollars for the year. This amount
                           could be negative if the returns for the year
                           were greater than the sales.

Field: Commission Percent Name: CMPCT
       Class: Numeric
       Size: 3.3
       Description: The percentage of commissions paid to the
                           salesperson when this product is sold.

Field: Purchase Cost   Name: PRCHCST
       Class: Numeric
       Size: 7.2
       Description: The cost of purchasing this item from the
                           vendor.

Index

A

Accumulate, 111
   as a type of processing, 6
Annotation
   symbol, 37
Arrays, 179
   accumulating into, 200–204
   array limit, 191, 194
   direct access, 210
   loading
      in-process load, 208–210
      pre-process load, 188
   dumping/printing, 204, 213
   searching, 194–199
   stop flag, 191, 196
   subscripts, 181
Assumed decimal, 22
Attribute, 4
Audit report, 294

B

Business applications systems, 19
   as a category of programs, 14

C

Calculate
   as a type of process, 6
   final totals, 119–121
   procedure, 79–80
   relationship to derived data,
      9–11
Connector, 37
   Offpage, 37
   Onpage, 37
Control-break, 131
   as a type of process, 7
   break-routine process, 134,
      137–138, 141, 156
   calculation of subtotals, 169
   hold fields, 134, 136
   identifying occurrence, 136–137,
      155

multiple-level, 153
single-level, 131
summary reporting, 172–174
Control fields, 134
Computer
   assumptions made by a, 15
   limitations, 13
   programs, types of, 6

D

Data
   classes
      alphanumeric, 5
      numeric, 5
   definition, 3–4, 11
   dictionary, 30
   hierarchy of, 4, 11, 21
   how the computer manages, 8–11
   relationship to processing, 7
   storage within a program, 8
   types of
      derived, 7, 11
      external, 7, 11
      logical, 7, 11, 45
      validation—as a type or process,
         7, 257. *See also* Input valida-
         tion
Database, 243
Decision
   AND logic, 95
   OR logic, 96
   structure, 38
   symbol, 34
Destructive read, 10, 134
Destructive write, 10
Documentation
   description of, 19
   program specifications, 19–22

E

End-Flag, 42–43
End-of-job procedure, 43
Entity, 4, 11

relationship to records, 4, 11
Error flag, 287, 289

F

Fields, 5, 11
   names, 21–22
   relationship to attributes, 5
   relationship to hierarchy, 5
File, 5, 11
   relationship to hierarchy, 5
   creation—as a type of program, 6
   formats, 21–22
   sequence, 132, 155
   sorting, 132
Flags. *See* Status flags
First Record Flag, 137
Flowchart
   definition, 33
   how to read, 46–51
   structures, 37–39
   symbols, 35–37
   transition from structure chart,
      60–64
Flowlines, 35

H

Headers. *See* Report headers
Hold fields, 134, 136

I

Information
   definition, 3–4, 11
   processing, 4, 11
Initialization procedure, 42
Inquiry
   as a type of program, 6
Input operation, 34
Input validation, 256
   error handling, 258
   error report, 258
   tests, 258–263
   valid transactions, 258